Nile Valley Contributions to Civilization

By

Anthony T. Browder

Exploding The Myths
Volume 1

NILE VALLEY CONTRIBUTIONS TO CIVILIZATION
Exploding The Myths - Volume 1

by
Anthony t. Browder

Published by
The Institute of Karmic Guidance
P.O. Box 73025
Washington, D.C. 20056
(301) 853-6027
www.ikg-info.,com

Cover Illustration: Michael Brown
Publication Design: Tony Browder

Library of Congress Catalog Card Number: 92-73925

ISBN 0-924944-03-X
Paperback - $20.00

ISBN 0-924944-0408
Hardcover - $39.95

10th Printing

January 2007

Printing: International Graphics, Beltsville, Maryland

Dedication

To my elders who have guided me and given my life purpose.

John G. Jackson
John Henrik Clarke
Yosef ben-Jochannan

John Henrik Clarke, John G. Jackson and Yosef ben-Jochannan

Acknowledgements

Acknowledgement must be given to the *Creator* and the *ancestors* for giving this book life and allowing me to be the conduit through which it was brought into existence. Special thanks to *Akh-Me-Ra* for his editorial assistance, *Russ Davis* for the layout, and to *Sharon Steele, Sabrina Johnson* and *Robin Rhodes* for reviewing the text. I am eternally grateful to my mother *Anne Browder* for overseeing the production of this product. The artist within me sincerely thanks *Malcolm Aaron, Michael Brown* and *Cheiko Hall* for their creative input. A token of gratitude is extended to *Clyde McElvene, Greg Thomas, Mosi Chamberlain, Wayne Chandler, Joslin Morgan* and *Barbara Thomas* for their invaluable contributions. Last, but not least, I must thank my daughter *Atlantis* for helping me understand that everything I do is for her and those yet to be born.

About The Cover

"The events which transpired 5,000 years ago; five years ago or five minutes ago, have determined what will happen five minutes from now; five years from now or 5,000 years from now. All history is a current event."

John Henrik Clarke

"All History is a Current Event"

The cover illustration embodies the spirit of Dr. Clarke's statement that all history is a current event. It symbolizes the timelessness which is expressed in the African concept that all time (the past, present and future) exists simultaneously in what has been referred to as the "eternal now."

The illustration portrays the statue of Her-em-akhet as it originally appeared thousands of years ago. Above its head are seven contemporary architectural structures which are held aloft on the wings of a falcon. The falcon is the spiritual/symbolic representation of Heru and serves as a bridge between the past and the present. The pyramid-shaped building at the top of the illustration represents the future which is built on the foundation that was established in the present, which in turn originated in the past. All history *is* a current event. This reality can be better understood by studying the Nile Valley contributions to civilization.

Illustrator: Michael Brown, Cultural Circles
Concept: Tony Browder & Michael Brown
Cover Design: Tony Browder
Layout: Cheiko Hall, Graphic Dimensions

Know Thy Self*

A person who knows not
And knows not that they know not
Is foolish - disregard them

A person who knows not
And knows that they know not
Is simple - teach them

A person who knows not
And believes that they know
Is dangerous - avoid them

A person who knows
And knows not that they know
Is asleep - awaken them

A person who knows
and knows that they know
Is wise - follow them

All of these persons reside in you
Know Thy Self
And to Maat be true

A modern adaptation of an ancient proverb

Contents

Dedication..3

Acknowledgements..4

About the Cover...5

Know Thy Self..6

Introduction by John Henrik Clarke...9

Author's Introduction...13

Commentary..25

Part One - Nile Valley Civilization

Chapter One: The Nile Valley...45

Chapter Two: The Peopling of Kemet and Egypt..53

Chapter Three: The Historical Accomplishments of Kemet............................71

Part Two - The Stolen Legacy

Chapter Four: The Europeanization of Kemet...137

Chapter Five: The Rape of Egypt..173

Chapter Six: The Nile Valley Presence in Europe...189

Chapter Seven: The Nile Valley Presence in America....................................197

Part Three - The African Renaissance

Chapter Eight: The World's Best-Kept Secret..221

Chapter Nine: How To Free Your African Mind..235

Chapter Ten: Questions and Answers..257

Glossary..268

Bibilography...280

Index...285

About The Author..292

Introduction

By Dr. John Henrik Clarke

The civilization of Egypt, and of Africa in general, is the most written about and the least understood of all known subjects. This is not an accident or an error in misunderstanding the available information. Except for Egypt, African people have been programmed out of the respectable commentary of history. Europeans have claimed the non-African creation of Egypt in order to downgrade the position of African people in world history. They have laid the foundation of what they call Western Civilization on a structure that the Western mind did not create. In doing so, they have used no logic.

Egypt, a Nile Valley civilization, was already old before Europe was born. Nile Valley civilization also existed before the Western Asian civilization of the Tigris and the Euphrates rivers. This fact was acknowledged for years by the European academic hypocrites who thought they had gotten away with claiming Egypt as a European, or at least Asian, creation. The archaeological research of Europeans disproved their claim. They could not find a single artifact in Western Asia, or in mainland Asia, that was older than the artifacts of Nile Valley civilization, or Africa in general. This revelation created a new dilemma for the European claimers of Egypt. They were saying, in effect, figuratively speaking, a child gave birth to himself, then he created his own mother.

Tony Browder's book, *Nile Valley Contributions to Civilization*, is about correcting some of these misconceptions so the reader, in fact, can be introduced to a Nile Valley civilization in order to understand its role as the parent of future civilizations. When we speak of Nile Valley civilization and its contributions, it must be considered that we are not talking about Egypt alone. We are referring to a strip of geography that extends over 4,000 miles into the body of Africa and that touches on a multiplicity of civilizations in Africa. It was, indeed, the last great civilization in Africa.

The country the Greeks called Egypt was never referred to as such by Africans during its formative period. What became Egypt was a composite of a number of nations using the Nile River as the world's first cultural highway. The rehearsal for what would become Egypt occurred in the south, in the nations known on present maps as Ethiopia, the Sudan and adjacent territories.

John Henrik Clarke

The African world lost one of its favorite sons with the passing of Dr. John Henrik Clarke on July 16, 1998. He was 83 years old when he made his transition.

Dr. Clarke will long be remembered as one of America's foremost autodidacts and educators. His thoughts and writings have influenced students and leaders worldwide. He helped draft the charter of the Organization of Afro-American Unity, and was the founding president of the African Heritage Studies Association.

Dr. Clarke was an advisor and confidant of many notables, including Kwame Nkrumah, Zora Neale Hurston, Malcolm X, Martin Luther King, Jr., James Baldwin, Betty Shabazz, William and Camille Cosby.

Dr. Clarke's accomplishments are depicted in *"A Great and Mighty Walk,"* an award-winning documentary which was produced by actor Wesley Snipes.

He will be missed by all who loved him and his spirit will never be forgotten.

Tributaries of rivers in these nations fed into the Nile and made it the great historical river of the world. In technology, Nile Valley civilization gave the world an achievement in building and in spirituality over and above anything any nation or people have achieved before or since. Out of Nile Valley civilization came the world's first organized spiritual literature. This literature was so profound, some of it inspired the writing of the Bible. The three major Western religions, Hebrewism, Christianity and Islam, were extracted from the spirituality created by the priests and wise men in the Nile Valley.

Early in its history and its development, Nile Valley civilization created a basic way of life that attracted teachers, technocrats and priests from other parts of Africa, always enriching the original composite composition of the Nile Valley. Organized farming and the domestication of animal life gave the population a more than adequate food supply.

Therefore, Egypt could attract workers from other parts of Africa. Some of these workers were farmers for part of the year, and builders another part of the year. At the time the Nile was overflowing its banks and depositing rich soil on adjacent farmland, the workers and craftsmen were building on the high ground away from the river. The assumption that this great period of building required a massive use of slaves is an assumption and nothing more.

When you look at the pyramids, the Sphinx and the great temples in Egypt and the Nile Valley, you have to consider the fact that no slaves would have built with such skill and exactness. Many of these structures have been standing 6,000 years or more and they are still sound. The word "slave" and the image of the slave as worker is a recurring image in the mind of Western man. It is hard for him to conceive of extended work of this nature without the use of forced labor. The factor that has not been taken into consideration is a great flowering of spiritual fervor and commitment before the formation of organized religions.

A factor in the matter, still not understood, is that the Africans tried to bring man in harmony with Nature. Western man tries to defy Nature and often forgets that man cannot start a hurricane or stop one; that before the force of Nature, man is small and puny. The European mind, with all its misconceptions, wants to rule everything, including the elements.

When you consider that Nile Valley civilization also includes the Sudan and Ethiopia, the contribution to civilization becomes more massive. The parent of what would later be called Egyptian Civilization came from the South. The first organized society was in the South. The evidence of an ancient mining complex that is older than the existence of Egypt has been found in the South. There are more than a dozen pyramids in the

Sudan, indicating that the rehearsal for pyramid building started in the South. Europeans have problems with this revelation because they assume black Africa presupposed a legitimate white Africa. What they forget is that everybody in Africa who cannot be referred to as an African is an invader or the descendant of an invader.

to suppose beforehand-

The Arab invasion of Africa started about 632 A.D. The fact that the Arabs have been in Africa over 1,000 years does not rule out the fact that they are invaders, and part of a massive occupying army. At the time Egypt was getting its great civilizing show on the road, the Arabs did not exist as a people. Like all invaders, they, too, have done Africa more harm than good.

Tony Browder is one of the latest of a number of messengers attempting to tell the story of the Nile Valley contribution to civilization. For 37 years in the classrooms of Howard University, William Leo Hansberry made an attempt to get this message across to nearly two generations of students, and he died before his massive four-volume work on the subject could be published. Willis N. Huggins in the Harlem History Club of the 30's made the same attempt, until his death in 1940.

The Jamaican-born J.A. Rogers devoted over 50 years of his life in the study of the role of African personalities, both men and women, in world history. Carter G. Woodson in his book, *African Background Outlined* and W.E.B. Du Bois in his work, *The World and Africa,* added a new dimension to the search for Nile Valley contributions to world civilization, and Africa in general. George G.M. James challenged the assumed originality of Greek philosophy, and indicated its Nile Valley origins.

In recent years, the greatest explanation of Nile Valley contributions to world civilization has been made by African historians themselves. In the work of Cheikh Anta Diop, I call your attention to his book, *African Origins of Civilization: Myth or Reality,* and the last book finished before his untimely death, *Civilization or Barbarism.* Cheikh Anta Diop's finest essay on this subject is included in the Nile Valley edition of *The Journal of African Civilization.* The essay is called "African Contribution to Civilization: The Exact Sciences."

backwardness barbarian

In his book, *Nile Valley Contributions to Civilization,* Tony Browder has associated himself with some top-level academic company. He is both a teacher and a learner. In both cases he has done well.

John Henrik Clarke
April, 1992

Author's Introduction

In November of 1989, at a small restaurant in downtown Cairo, I was having a farewell meal with an associate, Abou El Naga H. Gabrail. Mr. Naga is an Egyptologist and tour guide, whose services I have used for a number of my annual study tours to Egypt. During the course of our dinner, Naga asked me if I could explain to him why black Americans exude so much enthusiasm during the course of our study tours. Naga commented, "The Germans are some of the most well-read tourists traveling in Egypt, but I've found that the black Americans have a passion for the history that is lacking in most tourists who visit my country."

Abou El Naga H. Gabrail

I shared with my friend the fact that many African Americans travel to Africa, not as tourists, but as pilgrims, in search of the missing pages of their history. The history of Africa and African people is a story which has been denied, distorted and often presented as other peoples' history. When African Americans visit Egypt, it is not only the fulfillment of a dream, but for many, it is often a life-changing experience.

I asked Naga to imagine how different his world would be if his Egyptian ancestors had been enslaved by Americans 300 years ago, displaced from their homelands, given new names, denied the right to speak Arabic, practice their native customs and worship Allah. I asked him to also imagine his people now beginning to return to their homelands, in an attempt to reconstruct their history, culture, language and religion, only to discover that the Americans now controlled their land. To make matters worse, these same Americans have also written Egyptians out of their own history and replaced them with a history of Americans or "other" peoples.

Over the last decade, thousands of African Americans who have traveled to Africa have become acutely aware that the hypothetical scenario I outlined for my Egyptian friend is a reality for people of African descent. Any culturally orphaned people would delight at the prospect of uncovering the smallest fragment of their historical past. Passion, enthusiasm and anger are just some of the emotions felt when people begin to come face to face with formerly hidden truths.

For more than 350 years, tens of millions of Africans were torn away from their homeland, enslaved and systematically stripped of their name, culture and historical memory. Today, thousands of African Americans are awakening from a state of cultural amnesia and are discovering that Africans possessed a mighty history prior to their enslavement and colonization. Many people are also becoming aware of racist revisionists who have excluded Africans from their own history, while falsely attributing their story to people who were mere barbarians during the time of ancient African high civilization.

The role racism played, and continues to play, in shaping world history, is a tragedy which negatively influences all people. There are those who are correct in their belief that the race issue is irrelevant and is an impediment to human development. In reality there is only one race, "the human race," which has been proven to have originated in Africa. Yet, for years scientists have ignored and even fabricated data, to show that humanity developed in Europe or Asia, rather than acknowledge Africa as the site where the greatest evidence of early human development is to be found.

Regarding the issue of the African origins of humanity, Dr. Louis B. Leakey, one of the world's foremost paleontologists and author of *Progress and Evolution of Man in Africa* stated:

> In every country that one visits and where one is drawn into a conversation about Africa, the question is regularly asked by people who should know better 'But what has Africa contributed to world progress?' The critics of Africa forget that men of science today are, with few exceptions, satisfied that Africa was the birthplace of man himself and that for many hundreds of centuries thereafter, Africa was in the forefront of all world progress.

Dr. Leakey was quite correct in his assertion that Africa was the birthplace of man and civilization. It is generally an accepted fact that the primary implements necessary for the development of civilization —an alphabet, paper, pen and ink —all had their beginnings in Africa. Writing is an art form which we often take for granted, but its profound influence on the evolution of civilization was noted by James Breasted, famed Egyptologist and author of *Ancient Times*:

> The invention of writing and of a convenient system of records on paper has had a greater influence in the uplifting of the human race than any other intellectual achievement in the career of man. It was more important than all the battles ever fought and all the constitutions ever devised.

The advent of an alphabet, paper, pen and writing made it

possible for man to preserve for future generations the observations of personal events and natural phenomenon. These early writers were also the world's first scholars and scientists. The noted social anthropologist, Lord Raglan, believed that civilization only exists in societies that contain scholars and scientists. In his publication *How Came Civilization*, Raglan comments:

> The scholar consolidates and clarifies the knowledge which has already been acquired, and hands it on to the scientist, who, thus provided, proceeds to experiment, and thus to the increase of knowledge. Without the torch of learning, the scientist is reduced to groping in the dark, and without the scientist to use and test the results of his learning, the scholar sinks into a barren pedantry. Thus scholarship and science, in the widest sense of these terms, are the warp and woof of civilization. And the scientist, no less than the scholar, is dependent upon the written word; not only must he be able to use the learning of the scholar, but he must be able to record the results of his own investigations. Since, then, civilization depends upon scholarship and science, and these depend upon writing, civilization can only arise where the art of writing is known.

Raglan viewed writing as one of the major cornerstones in the development of civilization. Unfortunately, in recent years, racism has played a major role in determining how people of color would be portrayed in the writing of the history of the world. Scholars and scientists were sometimes employed by politicians and businessmen and paid to exaggerate the historical accomplishments of Europeans at the expense of most peoples of color.

The many biases which exist in the scientific and academic community have prompted the following remarks from attorney/historian Legrand Clegg:

> ...As long as the world is dominated by White people, as long as those White scientists—who now claim that there is no validity to the study of race—continue to practice racism socially and academically and, most important, as long as the Black race bears the universal badge of inferiority forced upon it by scientists who have distorted or suppressed Black history, we shall prominently focus on it whenever and wherever the truth can be told until sincere men of science return the Black race to its former position of respect and reverence on the earth.

The issue of race, as it pertains to the people of ancient Egypt, has become the subject of intense debate as more non-white scientists enter the fields of anthropology, Egyptology and other related disciplines. Many scholars are now challenging the previously uncontested theories that were introduced in the nineteenth century which claimed that the ancient Egyptians were "dark skinned whites." These biased views continued to be espoused despite the existence of scientific evidence to the contrary and "eye witness" accounts by men such as Herodotus, Homer, Plutarch and others who described the Egyptians as indigenous Africans.

Because of the racism which exists in many institutions of higher learning, there are many educators who not only question the role that Africans played in ancient Egypt, but also view Egypt as separate and apart from the African continent. References to the ethnicity of the ancient Egyptians ignited a storm of protests in 1989 when the "Rameses the Great" exhibit toured the United States. When the exhibit went to Dallas, Texas, members of the African American community openly expressed their outrage over the portrayal of Rameses and the Egyptians as "nonblack."

The ensuing debate over the exhibit, and the ethnicity of Rameses II, led to the stinging criticism of the African American community by Abdel-Latif Aboul-Ela, Egypt's cultural emissary to the United States. Mr Aboul-Ela disputed any African involvement in ancient Egypt and commented:

> Egypt, of course, is a country in Africa, but this doesn't mean it belongs to Africa at large...this is an Egyptian heritage, not an African heritage. We are not in any way related to the original black Africans of the deep south.

Spurred on by Mr. Aboul-Ela (who was later reprimanded by the Egyptian government for his comments) the African American community continued to press the issue. A threatened boycott of the exhibit eventually led to changes in the exposition and the convening of a conference entitled, *Rameses II and the African Origin of Civilization*. This three-day national conference featured 14 distinguished scholars who provided evidence to support the thesis of an African origin of civilization. The event was sponsored by The Third Eye, a local community-based organization, and the Dallas Institute of Humanities and Culture.

The Rameses II conference prompted the following remarks from Diane Ragsdale, the deputy mayor pro tem of Dallas:

> This conference, more than any other event held in Dallas, exemplifies direct positive action being taken by the Dallas African American community to research and interpret African history for the purpose of uplifting the national consciousness of the community.

While the Rameses II conference sensitized the citizens of Dallas and made them acutely aware of the many distortions relating to Africans and African history, the event was all but ignored by the media. At the outset, a great deal of media coverage was given to the initial controversy regarding the "blackness of Rameses," but the presentations which substantiated the African origins of Rameses and other pertinent aspects of Egyptian civilization were neither acknowledged by the media nor challenged by critics.

The lack of balanced coverage on this matter led many to speculate that there are those who wished to deny and cover up any information which conflicted with the myth that ancient Egyptian civilization was white at best, mixed at the very least and African only in the minds of people who have a "neurotic need to invent a pedigree."

For years historians have written scholarly papers disassociating "Negroes" from the development of civilization in Africa, while attributing those accomplishments to a race of people called "Hamites." This "Hamitic myth" was invented in the 1920's by C.G. Seliguman, a British anthropologist and author of *Races of Africa*. According to Seliguman, "Negroes" were too primitive to be capable of any advanced thought. Seliguman believed that civilizations in Africa were created by Hamites, whom he regarded as "Caucasians...(belonging) to the same branch of mankind as almost all Europeans..."

As recently as 1977, the World Book Encyclopedia described the Egyptians as black-haired, dark-skinned peoples who "belonged to the Mediterranean race of the Caucasoid (white) stock." The encyclopedia further states that as time went on "the Egyptians mixed with peoples from Asia, Negroes from other parts of Africa and peoples from lands around the Mediterranean Sea."

The following is a list of comments made by some of history's most renowned thinkers, and their views of African people.

Arnold Toynbee , historian:
When we classify mankind by color, the only one of the primary races...which has not made a creative contribution to any of our twenty-one civilizations is the black race.

David Hume, philosopher:
I am apt to suspect the Negroes...to be naturally inferior to the White. There never was a civilized nation of any other complexion than white, nor even any individual eminent either in action or speculation, no ingenious manufacturers amongst them, no arts, or sciences.

John Burgess, scholar:
A Black skin means membership in a race of men which has never created a civilization of any kind. There is something natural in the subordination of an inferior race even to the point of enslavement of the inferior race...

Richard Burton, explorer and writer:
The study of the Negro is the study of man's rudimentary mind. He would appear rather a degeneracy from the civilized man than a savage rising to the first step, were it not for his total incapacity for improvement...

Benjamin Franklin, scientist:
Why increase the sons of Africa, by planting them in America, where we have so fair an opportunity, by excluding all blacks and tawnys, or increasing the lovely white and red?

Thomas Jefferson, president:
I advanced it, therefore, as a suspicion only, that the blacks, whether originally a distinct race or made distinct by time or circumstance, are inferior to the whites in the endowments of both body and mind.

Abraham Lincoln, president:
There is a physical difference between the white and the black races which I believe will forever forbid the two races living together...while they do remain together there must be the position of superior and inferior, and I as much as any man am in favor of having the superior position assigned to the white race.

Henry Berry, Virginia House of Representatives:
We have, as far as possible, closed every avenue by which the light may enter the slave's mind. If we could extinguish the capacity to see the light, our work will be complete. They would then be on the level of the beast of the fields and we then should be safe.

Are black people inherently inferior to white people? Were the preceding comments made by racists, or by learned men? There are some behavioral scientists who believe that racism is a learned behavior. If that is a reality, then it is quite possible to trace this behavior to its source. In this particular instance a specific educational institution, and a single individual, has been identified as a primary source for the invention of the doctrine of racial inferiority.

The creation of this myth was fabricated in 1795 by Johann Friedrich Blumenbach, a professor at Gottingen University in Germany. Blumenbach produced the first scholarly work on human racial classification, and invented the term Caucasian. Martin Bernal, author of *Black Athena, The Afroasiac Roots of Greece*, discusses the impact of Blumenbach's research:

> Blumenbach was the first to publicize the term 'Caucasian', which he used for the first time in the third edition of his great work (*De Generis Humani Varietate Nativa*) in 1795. According to him the white or Caucasian was the first and most beautiful and talented race, from which all the others had degenerated to become Chinese, Negroes, etc. Blumenbach justified the curious name 'Caucasian' on 'scientific' and 'racial' grounds. Blumenbach was conventional for his period in that he included 'Semites' and 'Egyptians' among his Caucasians.

Between 1775 and 1800, Gottingen established the concept of the "science of antiquity" upon which future universities would build. The slanted and distorted research which emerged from this institution "established much of the intellectual framework within which later research and publication within the new professional disciplines was carried out," states Bernal.

The myths that were created at Gottingen have held sway in academe for more than 200 years. Very few scholars took seriously any theory that conflicted with the accepted belief that the ancient Egyptians could have been anything other than "Caucasian." But in the early 1970's these biases were scholarly, intellectually and scientifically challenged by two sons of Africa, the late Senegalese multidisciplinarian Dr. Cheikh Anta Diop and his associate from Gabon, Dr. Theophile Obenga.

Drs. Diop and Obenga both presented papers at the Cairo Symposium which unequivocally destroyed the myths of black racial inferiority. From January 28, through February 3, 1974, the United Nations Educational, Scientific and Cultural Organization (UNESCO) sponsored the symposium, which was held in the capital of Egypt. The symposium was attended by 20 of the most prominent Egyptologists in the world who assembled to debate, among other topics, the race of the ancient Egyptians.

Dr. Diop was a brilliant scientist who held degrees in Egyptology, physics, linguistics and anthropology. He was regarded by his contemporaries as the "pharaoh" of African studies. Dr. Diop presented a paper entitled *Origins of the Ancient Egyptians* and argued, irrefutably, that there were 11 categories of evidence to support the thesis that the ancient Egyptians were indigenous "black" Africans.

Dr. Obenga's paper was entitled *The Peopling of Ancient Egypt and the Deciphering of the Meroitic Script.* He provided data which confirmed the existence of substantial linguistic relationships between the ancient Egyptian language and traditional African languages. The papers presented by Diop and Obenga were virtually unchallenged by the other scholars present, which prompted the following comment by a reporter attending the symposium:

> Although the preparatory working paper sent out by UNESCO gave particulars of what was desired, not all participants had prepared communications comparable with the painstakingly researched contributions of Professor Cheikh Anta Diop and Obenga. There was consequently a real lack of balance in the discussions.

The general consensus reached at the Cairo Symposium was that there was no evidence that the ancient Egyptians were white, and that Egypt was not influenced by Mesopotamia, but by peoples from "the Great Lakes region in inner-equatorial Africa." The symposium also rejected the notion that Pharaonic Egyptian, which remained a stable language for more than 4,500 years, was influenced by Semitic language. The proceedings of the conference were published by UNESCO in 1978.

One of the most significant revelations presented at the Cairo Symposium was Diop's development of the "melanin dosage test." This one simple test provided the means by which one could determine the phenotype of the Egyptian royal mummies by examining the melanin content present in their skin.

The test involved the acquisition of specimens, consisting of a few square millimeters of mummified skin, which were then coated with ethyl benzoate and exposed to natural or ultraviolet light. This procedure rendered the melanin granules in the skin specimen fluorescent, thus enabling them to be counted by Diop who stated that the experiments:

> ...show a melanin level which is nonexistent in the white skinned races. Let us simply say that the evaluation of melanin level by microscopic examination is a laboratory method which enables us to classify the ancient Egyptians unquestionably among the black races.

Despite the research of Drs. Diop and Obenga, numerous issues concerning the ethnicity of the ancient Egyptians and the Egyptian contributions to civilization continue to be discussed and debated. Some scholars will never accept the fact that Africans (blacks) had anything to do with the development of Nile Valley civilizations and the culture that emerged in the northern most region of the Nile Valley, Egypt. The myths that were created at Gottingen are too powerful for many to overcome. Other scholars will only begin to modify their position when they are overwhelmed by the plethora of evidence, now coming forth, which supports the reality of the African origins of Nile Valley civilizations.

Since the beginning of time, myths have played a powerful role in the formation of institutions and shaping the beliefs, customs and religious rites of humans. Most myths are of unknown origin but may be traced to some historic event from times long gone. Many believe that myths have the power to liberate the mind and guide the soul along a spiritual path of human potentiality. Without myths, life has little meaning, but when fabricated for the benefit of a 'chosen few,' myths become a detriment to humanity by impeding mental growth and understanding.

The purpose of this and future volumes of the *Exploding the Myths* series, is to examine the potent force of myths and to understand how they influence the thinking of millions of people worldwide. This series will provide, in lay terms, a clear and concise analysis of data which supports the African presence in world history and its influence on various cultures throughout the ages.

The reasons for my focus are few. Over the years I have come to realize that many myths associated with *'Man, God and Civilization'* have evolved out of concepts which originated in Africa, the birthplace of humanity. And secondly, the story of African people is probably one of the most continually distorted stories of any people on the planet.

The term "Conceptual Incarceration" has been used by Dr. Asa G. Hilliard to describe the mental condition which affects the thinking processes of millions of peoples of African descent. Dr. Hilliard, an educational psychologist and historian, suggests that victims of fabricated histories are often confused, isolated and disoriented as a result of a loss of historical continuity. The remedy for such a malady lies in the victim making a "unilateral mental declaration of independence." Dr. Hilliard states that:

> Free and critical minds can emerge only by a return to the source - the primary sources. A free and critical mind takes nothing for granted and is not intimidated by "authorities" who frequently may be more confused than the general public. Free and critical minds seek truth without chauvinism or shame.

The first volume of the *Exploding the Myths* series is entitled: *Nile Valley Contributions to Civilization*. It is divided into three parts, each focusing on specific themes relative to Nile Valley history, the disintegration of Nile Valley culture and the reconstruction of the Nile Valley legacy. Part One is entitled "Nile Valley Civilization" and it consists of three chapters. The early chapters explore the physical geography of the Nile Valley, the origins of the two branches of the Nile River and the migratory patterns of the early Nilotic people. Subsequent chapters examine the 6,000-year history of ancient Kemet and the development of its educational, philosophical and social infrastructure.

Part Two is entitled "The Stolen Legacy" and consists of four chapters. The first chapter provides a survey of George G.M. James' masterful work, *Stolen Legacy*. The remaining chapters detail the Europeanization of Kemet after its conquest by the Greeks and subsequent invasions by the Roman, Arabic, French and British armies. The last chapters provide an account of the Kemetic/Egyptian presence in Europe, the United States and Mesoamerica.

Part Three is entitled "The African Renaissance" and comprises three chapters. The first chapter describes methods of symbolic interpretation through which the history of Kemet can be recognized, and identifies Kemetic art elements which have been infused into iconography, stone masonry, fashion and advertising. The following chapter focuses on the negative psychological effects of "mis-education" and how they can be overcome through the practical application of accurate historical information and imagery. Part Three continues with a discussion on African Centeredness, what it is, what it is not, and its relationship to multiculturalism and Eurocentrism. This chapter explores the significance of study groups and how they are formed and structured. It also includes information on networking with existing community organizations, national institutions and businesses.

The last chapter in *Nile Valley Contributions to Civilization* consists of a question and answer segment which explores significant issues pertaining to African history and their impact upon African people. If all history is indeed a current event, as stated by Professor John Henrik Clarke, then the truthful knowledge of African history and the application of that knowledge into a spiritually oriented value system, will serve as the first step toward the continued liberation of African people for generations to come.

Two additional volumes of *Exploding the Myths* are currently being researched for future publication. They include:

Volume 2. *An African-Centered View of Washington, D.C., Masonry and the United States*, an analysis of Kemetic architecture and symbolism and its influence on the design of architectural structures in Washington, D.C. This publication also will explore the African origins of masonry and the role of masonry in the development of the United States.

Volume 3. *The African Origins of Christianity*, a further study of Nile Valley philosophical traditions which have been modified and incorporated into the religious systems associated with Christianity.

Undeniably, Nile Valley civilization plays a central role in the development of this and future titles in the *Exploding the Myths* series. It is my sincere hope that these works will cause many to read and to study with a "free and critical mind," and that we come to understand the significance of the comments made by the late Cheikh Anta Diop when he stated:

> For us the return to Egypt [Nile Valley Civilization] in every domain is the necessary condition to reconcile African civilization with history....Egypt will play the same role in the rethinking and renewing of African culture that ancient Greece and Rome plays in the culture of the West.

Cheikh Anta Diop

Commentary

In my first book, *From The Browder File: 22 Essays on The African American Experience*, one essay stood out from the rest and elicited the greatest response from my readers. That essay was entitled, *The Creation of the Negro*. The question regarding the creation of the Negro, and his cultural significance, is one which has intrigued me all of my life.

As a young "Negro" child growing up in Chicago, I remember my grandfather's rejection of that designation and his refusal to check any box labeled "Negro" on applications, census forms or other documents. He always checked "other." My grandfather was a fiercely proud man who never accepted the negative stereotypes associated with the image of a Negro, and while he couldn't change how American society viewed him, he could and did determine how *h e* viewed himself.

I also recall conversations with my grandmother who would often refer to herself and other Negroes as "Colored." I'd frequently ask her to be more specific and would inquire, "What color was this 'Colored' person, red, green, black or white?" It was only after much feigned aggravation that my grandmother would force herself to utter that dreadful word "Black." Eventually, and with much prompting on my part, my grandmother stopped using the terms "Colored" and "Negro" and began to regularly use the word "Black" in her vocabulary as a more appropriate description for people of African descent. After all, this was the 60's and "Black" people were just beginning to develop a positive appreciation for themselves.

It wasn't until the 1970's that I was able to clearly understand my grandmother's reluctance to use the word "black," and my grandfather's rejection of the word "Negro." In their day, to call someone "black" was a most serious insult which could result in a physical confrontation, and a Negro was viewed as a person unworthy of respect in the white man's world. I began to understand how my grandparents had struggled with an issue that I had often taken for granted.

During the course of their lifetime, my grandparents and their contemporaries had to endure being called "negro, nigger, coon, colored, blackie," any name except a child of God. Now they were being asked to refer to themselves as "Black." To them it was just another name - a name only to be used for

a brief period of time, and then discarded along with all the others which preceded it.

As a child of the 60's, I was fortunate to live in an era where the racial epithets hurled in my direction were minimized because of the white response to our newfound identity with blackness and Africa. I was blessed to live in a time when I could wear my ethnicity like a badge of honor instead of rejecting it because of inbred feelings of inferiority. In December of 1988, blacks in America were asked to accept another name change, one which reflected an even stronger sense of racial and cultural identification. That new name was "African American."

The media responded to this latest development by interviewing "former Blacks and Negroes" and asking them their feelings regarding this *new* name. Of the responses given, most fell within three categories which are reflected in the following comments:

> The first group of respondents stated, "I think the name 'African American' is appropriate because it correctly describes us as people of African descent who currently reside in America."

> The second group remarked rather jokingly, "I just got used to calling myself 'Black' after all these years, and now I'm being told that I should call myself an *African American*."

> The comments made by the third group of people surveyed were quite disturbing because most stated emphatically, "I'm not an African anything, I didn't come from Africa and I don't have anything to do with African people."

The latter comments were made most frequently by older citizens who had acquiesced to the decision to call themselves "Black" two decades earlier, but were not willing to make the next step and see themselves as African, or in any way related to African people. This attitude was created by a socialization process which instilled within the minds of most Negroes an unnatural hatred for dark skin pigmentation. This attitude is reflected in a disturbing put-down of blackness that has been a part of the African community for years. It states:

> If you're white, you're alright
> If you're yellow, you're mellow
> If you're brown, stick around
> But, if you're black, get back.

If it were considered an insult to call someone "black" in the 1920's, then calling them "African" was certainly an invitation to physical abuse. And to dare refer to a Negro or Colored person as a "black African" was surely a justifiable reason to commit manslaughter. Throughout most of this century, Africans have been viewed by both blacks and whites as savage and ignorant subhuman beings. These degrading caricatures continue to exist in *The Phantom* comic strip and in the numerous remakes of Edgar Rice Burroughs' masterful novel of propaganda, *Tarzan, the Ape Man.*

The mere mention of the word Africa continues to evoke, in the minds of most people, images of Tarzan and Jane, jungles and half naked cannibals cooking "civilized" white people for dinner. Very few people realize that these stereotypes, and numerous others of a similar nature, were originally created by non-African writers, artists and movie producers. These images continue to negatively influence the thinking of millions of people worldwide.

Despite the "bum rap" Africa has received over the years, many of the old racist stereotypes are being challenged by Africans in the Diaspora who have accepted their African heritage, and now view themselves through culturally sensitive eyes. A new interpretation of some of those old images reveals some interesting findings:

- Tarzan, the reputed "King of the Jungle," would probably have died of skin cancer because he lacked sufficient amounts of melanin in his skin, which is necessary for survival in a tropical environment,

- The entire continent of Africa, relative to its overall size, has less jungle than all of Europe,

- Regarding the issue of cannibalism, a person of color would run a greater risk of being eaten in Milwaukee, Wisconsin, than in any country in Africa; and

- There have been more documented instances of whites eating humans than any other group of people.

It is important that African people look beyond the image of Africa which was created for them and the world by Europeans. It is also most important to remember that Africans were the only immigrants who came to America against their will. They were stripped of their history, and had no humanity that their slavemasters were willing to recognize. Their sole purpose for being was to provide free labor for the economic development of the country.

W.E.B. Du Bois reminded us that Africans were said to have been brought to America as "temporary immigrants" who would eventually be returned to Africa. The process for returning African Americans to Africa was indeed temporary. It began in 1822, with the creation of Liberia, which,

A New Eve Of Discovery!

So there really was an Eve in some kind of a Garden of Eden. She lived about 150,000 years ago in Kenya and she is the mother of us all.

That at least is the claim of the world's leading fossil hunter, anthropologist Richard Leakey in *In Search Of What Makes Us Human.....*

Leakey once believed that humankind evolved in independent groups scattered all over the Old World. But now he thinks that unlikely because geographically isolated groups would diverge and become reproductively isolated —in short different species unable to interbreed.

Africans have the deepest genetic roots. Though we are still a few fossils short of final proof, it is most likely humankind began there with a few thousand people and then spread all over the Old World.

Bible believers may take some comfort—but the Ku Klux Klan will be furious to think Eve was black.

(London) Daily Express,
November 5, 1992

coincidentally, is the oldest independent "black" nation in Africa.

The name "Liberia" was derived from the Latin word liber, which means free. This new African nation was founded by an American charitable society with the expressed intention of providing a home for freed black slaves from America. Liberia was not only created by Americans, but its governmental structure, of an elected President, Senate and House of Representatives, was also modeled after the United States' system of government. The capital of Liberia, "Monrovia," was named in honor of James Monroe, the fifth president of the United States.

The transformation of enslaved people from *African* to *Negro* to *Colored* to *Black* and currently, to *African American*, has been quite an evolution. In eighteenth century America, "free blacks" saw themselves as African and incorporated their ethnicity into the names of their newly created institutions. For example, in Philadelphia, Pennsylvania, in 1784, a Barbadian named Prince Hall, founded the first black Masonic Order, which he named African Lodge #459. Richard Allen, another resident of Philadelphia, founded the Free African Society in 1787 and the African Methodist Episcopal Church (AME) in 1794.

After emancipation in the mid nineteenth century, black Americans no longer identified with the term "African" and began to refer to themselves as "Colored" or "Negro" in order to distinguish themselves from Africans living in Africa and elsewhere. Some of the black institutions that were developed in the early twentieth century began to reflect this new orientation in name - such as the National Association for the Advancement of *Colored* People (NAACP), 1909; the Association for the Study of *Negro* Life and History, 1915; and the National Council of *Negro* Women, 1935.

The name *Black* came into prominence after the birth of the civil rights movement in 1955, and gained wider acceptance with the development of the Black Power and Black Studies Movements in the 1960's. The latest name, *African American*, was officially ushered into existence in April, 1989, at the African American Summit in New Orleans, and is currently used by politicians, newscasters and individuals nationwide.

However, a nationwide telephone survey of 759 African Americans, conducted by the Joint Center for Political Studies in the fall of 1990, disclosed the following:

> Despite the increasing use of the term African-American, most Black Americans still prefer to be called Black; 72 percent preferred Black; 15 percent preferred African-American and 2 percent Negro, with the rest giving no opinion or other responses.

Identification with one's past (history) is an important step towards mental liberation, but the process must begin with the identification and use of your correct name. Noted historian Dr. John Henrik Clarke provides us with a working definition of history:

> History is a clock that people use to tell their political and cultural time of day. It is also a compass that people use to find themselves on the map of human geography. The role of history is to tell a people what they have been, and where they have been, what they are and where they are. The most important role that history plays is that it has the function of telling a people where they still must go and what they still must be.

Minister Malcolm X

History should tell a people who they are, where they came from and what their potential is as a people. If it fails to do so, it is useless. The name that a people call themselves must provide them with an understanding of their history by connecting them to a land mass, a language, a culture, a religion, a philosophy and so on. If a people's name fails to accomplish these simple tasks, then their name is useless.

The name "Colored" means little because all people are colored, varying in shades of melaninated pigment that range from "crow to snow," as referenced by historian Alice Windom. The names "Negro" or "Black" mean little because they do not serve the primary function of a name, which is to culturally orient a people to a specific land mass.

When people are free to travel and immigrate to other lands, they usually bring their name, language and culture with them. The Europeans who immigrated to America would later insist upon their independence from England, but their cultural orientation remained European. The official language of America is English, and the northeastern coast of the United States is still referred to as "New England." The states of New Hampshire, New Jersey and New York all refer to provinces in "jolly ole" England.

In 1682, the French explorer Rene Robert Cavelier, Sieur de La Salle, claimed the entire Mississippi Valley for France. La Salle erected a cross and a column bearing the French coat of arms near the mouth of the river and named the region *Louisiana*, in honor of Louis XIV, the King of France. New Orleans, the former state capital of Louisiana, was named in memory of the city of Orleans in France. The city of St. Louis, Missouri, was named in honor of King Louis IX.

If a German Shepherd were born in Baltimore, Maryland, it would still be called a German Shepherd. If a French Poodle were born on the moon it would still be called a French Poodle. Malcolm X once stated that "if a cat had kittens in an oven, you wouldn't call them biscuits." What then would one call an African who had been enslaved, transported across the Atlantic Ocean and renamed "Negro?" This is the $64,000 question that the 35 million former Negroes, Coloreds and Blacks, currently living in the United States, are struggling to answer.

It is important to note that there is no such place as Negroland, Coloredland or Blackland. Africa is the point of origin for millions of people who now reside in the United States, the Caribbean Islands, and South America. Brazil has an estimated population of 60 million people of African descent, which is the largest population of African people living outside of the African continent. Worldwide, Africans and Chinese are the only people on earth whose numbers possibly exceed one billion.

In reference to the word "Negro," Dr. John Henrik Clarke states that the name means nothing and refers to nowhere. In the introduction to John Jackson's *Introduction to African*

Civilization, Dr. Clarke wrote:

> There is an urgent need to discard the term 'Negro Africa' and the word 'Negro' and all that it implies. This word grew out of the European slavery and colonial systems and it fails to relate the people of African descent to land, history and culture. There is no 'Negroland.' When one hears the word 'France' or 'French,' it is easy to visualize the land, history and culture of a people. The same thing is true of the words 'English' or 'Englishman.' When one hears or reads the word 'Negro,' the only vision that comes to mind relates to a condition.

One of the major events which led to the enslavement of African people was the Muslim conquest of Constantinople, which disrupted the spice shipments from India and the East to Europe. In 1441 Portuguese explorers were looking for a safe passage around the continent to India. They became the first nation to participate in the "forced importation" of Africans into Europe. The Portuguese were in search of pepper, nutmeg and cinnamon, but found the black skinned peoples whom they would later call Negroes, curious items of trade. According to Dr. Clarke:

> Some Spaniard or Portuguese took a descriptive adjective and made a noun of it. We, as a people, are neither a noun nor an adjective.

Robert Powell, a Jamaican of African ancestry, also questioned the significance of the word "Negro." In 1927 he authored a book entitled *The Human Side of A People and the Right Name.* Mr. Powell offers the following analysis:

> The word 'Negro' was not only a superfluous term but one that carried with it a connotation of contempt, opprobrium and inferiority.

Mr. Powell's comments were certainly warranted, considering the depths to which historians, theologians and scientists descended in an attempt to substantiate the "inferiority of the Negro." Earl Conrad, author of *The Invention of the Negro,* offers this historical perspective:

> Fifty years before Columbus sailed westward, Catholic Spain and Catholic Portugal were engaged in a rivalry to sack Africa, to seize its inhabitants as slaves and to ship them back to Europe and sell them. Portugal, the first invader, sought and secured the blessings of the Popes and in a series of papal bulls issued from 1443 on, there is the spectacle of the Christian Vatican sanctify-

ing the enslavement of Africans on grounds that they were pagans....

Prince Henry of Portugal...took the Africans...and sold them as slaves in the ports of Portugal. He asked absolution for the seaman...and Pope Eugenia IV in 1442, granted the request. By 1452, Pope Nicholas V gave King Alphonso of Spain general powers to enslave 'pagans.' Pagans meant the African who didn't yet know Christ....

So controlling was the power of the Vatican in the conduct of trade into Africa that in 1481, Edward IV of England asked the Pope for permission to trade in Africa.

Five hundred eleven years after Edward IV's request, in February, 1992, Pope John Paul II visited Goree Island, a slave outpost located off the coast of Senegal in West Africa. The Pope passed through the "door of no return" and he toured cells in the "house of slaves" where tens of thousands of Africans were prepared for their voyage across the Atlantic to the New World. The Pope compared the house to the concentration camps of the 1930's, and begged forgiveness for the Christians involvement in the slave trade. Pope John Paul II remarked:

> How can one forget the enormous suffering inflicted, ignoring the most elementary rights of man, on the people deported from the African continent....From this African sanctuary of black pain, we begged the pardon from above.

Since religion played such a major role in the development and maintenance of slavery, the enslaver had to justify his actions by proving that Africans were less than human and that they had no soul to save. The more successfully scholars and theologians justified the inferiority of the slave, the more readily slavery was accepted within the hearts and minds of the slavemaster. In the nineteenth century it was believed that the Negro was more nonmoral than moral, and more inhuman than human. The following report was presented by the Rev. Dr. Tucker at the American Church Congress in 1883:

> I know of whole neighborhoods...where there is not one single Negro couple, whether legally married or not, who are faithful to each other for a few weeks. In the midst of a prayer-meeting I have known Negroes [to] steal from each other, and on the way home they will rob any hen-roost that lies conveniently at hand....Mention is further made of Negro missionaries guilty of the grossest immorality, living in open

concubinage, addicted to thieving, lying, and every imaginary crime, yet all earnest and successful preachers, and wholly unconscious of hypocrisy. Their sins, universally known, did not diminish their influence with their race.

The 1884 edition of the Encyclopedia Br*itannica* went to great lengths to document the inherent inferiority of the Negro by stating that he

occupies at the same time the lowest position in the evolutionary scale, thus affording the best material for the comparative study of the highest anthropoids and the human species.

In describing the skull of the Negro the editors stated that he possessed an

...exceedingly thick cranium, enabling the Negro to butt with the head and resist blows which would inevitably break any ordinary European's skull.

The Negro's skin was described as

...thick epidermis, cool, soft and velvety to the touch, mostly hairless, and emitting a peculiar rancid odor, compared by Pruner Bey to that of the buck goat.

Of particular interest in this volume were the comments made regarding the Negro's stymied capacity for intellectual thought:

The cranial sutures...close much earlier in the Negro than in other races. To this premature ossification of the skull, preventing all further development of the brain, many pathologists have attributed the inherent mental inferiority of the blacks, an inferiority which is even more marked than their physical differences. Nearly all observers admit that the Negro child is on the whole quite as intelligent as those of other human varieties, but that on arriving at puberty all further progress seems to be arrested. No one has more carefully studied this point than Filippo Manetta, who during a long residence on the plantations of the Southern States of America noted that 'the Negro children were sharp, intelligent and full of vivacity, but on approaching the adult period a gradual change set in. The intellect seemed to become clouded, animation giving place to a sort of lethargy, briskness yielding to indolence. *We must necessarily suppose that the development of the Negro and White proceeds on different lines* [emphasis mine]. While with the latter the volume of the brain grows with the expansion of the brain-pan, in the former the growth of the brain is on the contrary arrested by the premature closing of the cranial sutures and lateral pressure of the frontal bone.'

History books, encyclopedias, scientific journals and other publications are teeming with inaccuracies which were written to demean African people in the eyes of the world. In 1972, the late Alex Haley spoke before a national group of educators and shared with them some of the research that he uncovered while writing his best-seller *Roots.* Haley described the role that the church played in the institutionalization of slavery:

> One of the most perverse things that I have found in my long research was that the people, in what might be called the hierarchy of slavery, the owners, the agents, the captains of those ships, strove in every possible way to somehow manifest that they were functioning in a Christian context....If at all possible, a slave ship sailing should sail on the Sabbath [for] there was a popular saying that 'God will bless the journey.' There was a practice they had, when a slave ship began loading slaves, if at all possible, the first two on board would be male and female who would be recorded in the log as 'Adam and Eve' and the rest were numbered 3, 4, 5 on up to 200 if they [could hold] that many.

Africans were often packed aboard slave ships like sardines stuffed in a can. Some ships were designed to carry 500 or 600 Africans in approximately the same cubic capacity as ten double cabins on the luxury liner *Queen Elizabeth 2.*

Wherever one finds African people outside of the continent, one is witnessing "the visible expression of an economic and political reality as important in its day as Japanese car exports or OPEC oil are today," so says Le Baron Armel de Wismes of Nantes, France. De Wismes is the author of *Nantes Et Le Temps Des Negriers,* a publication which documents the history of the slave trade in Nantes. De Wismes discussed the broader implications of Columbus' "discovery" and the events that led to the enslavement of African people:

> Imagine...what happened after Columbus, when Europeans were first exposed to chocolate! It electrified the imagination and stirred a hunger in every town and city across the continent. They went wild over vanilla, tomatoes, corn, tobacco, potatoes, sugar, coffee, rum and other unheard of tastes from the New World.

> That's what slavery was all about....The man in the street was intoxicated by these things. The London tea rooms, the Paris cafes, the Italian espresso and ice cream parlors, the sweet and pastry shops all over Europe—all were possible only after the New World was

discovered and only through the labor of millions of African slaves uprooted to America.

The injustices of the African enslavement might never have occurred were it not for the diseases and destruction the Spanish brought to the shores of the New World. Within 150 years of Columbus' landing, the native population was reduced from approximately 100 million to ten million, according to most cultural anthropologists. The subsequent decimation of the indigenous population practically destroyed the agriculture and economy of the "New World."

De Wismes continued to recount the role of Europe in the enslavement of Africans after the demise of the native American population:

> To fill the enormous labor void, first Spain, then all of Europe - with the exception of Russia - dabbled in the African slave trade. Farmers, merchants, princes, little old ladies with their life savings, even the hypocrite Voltaire, who railed against slavery in *Candide* - invested in schemes that promised and often delivered returns of 300 percent, 400, even 1,000 percent on their

Nothing about slavery horrified its critics more than the slave auction. The sentimental paternalism of American slaveholders could not get over the inconsistency of treating human beings as a form of real property. And it could not protect black children from being torn from their families under the auctioneer's hammer.

Cultural Atlas of Africa, edited by Jocelyn Murray.

Africans being auctioned in Virginia, 1861.

money. Cities like Liverpool, Seville and Nantes were the European capitals for this slave marketing.

Thus began the "triangular trade" from Europe to Africa to America and back again, which established the first major transnational economy since the fall of Rome. In fact, the buying, shipping and employment of 12 million to 25 million slaves (no one knows how many blacks were forced into the African diaspora) constituted a major part of all international economic transactions in the period 1451 to 1870.

Whether we care to admit it or not, it [slavery] formed the bedrock on which our current world economy is built and...it surely explains in part the social and political frictions and misunderstandings between the world's whites and colored peoples to this day.

Hand in hand with the enslavement of African people came the destruction of African civilization and the loss of a culture, which the European would later say never existed. Dr. Clarke made the following remarks on the subject:

There has been a deliberate destruction of African culture and the records relating to that culture. This destruction started with the first invaders of Africa. It continued through the period of slavery and the colonial system. It continues today on a much higher and more dangerous level. There are now attempts on the highest academic level to divide African history and culture within Africa in such a manner that the best of it can be claimed for Europeans, or at the very least, Asians. That is the main purpose of the Hamitic and the Semitic hypothesis in relationship to African history.

The manipulation of African history has been so thorough that many people now mistakenly believe Egypt is not in Africa. It is as if Egypt has mysteriously detached itself from the continent and floated off to a nebulous place called the "Middle East." The ridiculousness of this issue is mind boggling, particularly when one considers that there are islands in the Mediterranean and the Atlantic (Corsica, Greece and England) that are physically separated from Europe, but are still considered a part of that continent. Any attempt to separate Egypt from Africa is an attempt to disassociate African people from the Nile Valley, and to deny the role that Africans played in influencing Western (European) culture and civilization.

There currently exist hundreds of examples of Africans having lived in Europe, but they are often ignored. There was Pushkin in Russia, Hannibal in Italy, Beethoven in Germany and Aseop in Greece. Traditionally, all of these individuals have been portrayed as European, despite evidence to the contrary. The Moors occupied Spain for more than 350 years, and there was a strong African presence in ancient Britain. People of African descent have had a major impact on European culture for hundreds of years, and yet no one asks whether the Europeans were black.

Diop once stated that cultural alienation has been used as a weapon of domination for thousands of years, but the full impact of his statement didn't hit me until I visited the Museum of Man in Paris. While in the lobby of this museum, I was taken aback by two signs directing patrons to an exhibit on the upper level. One sign read "Black Africa," the other "White Africa," and both signs had arrows pointing in opposite directions.

Why is color used to denote racial diversification on one continent, but not on another? At this moment there are hundreds of thousands of Africans from the Continent and the Caribbean who currently reside in Europe, but one never hears the term "White Europe" and "Black Europe." J.A. Rodgers, in his three-volume work *Sex and Race*, cites the existence of numerous Africans who lived in Europe as kings, queens, popes and saints. Their very presence justifies the use of the term "Black Europe," if history were to be recorded fairly.

But history is not fair; neither is it always true. History is often told from the perspective of the victor in any conflict, and always at the expense of the victim. The French general Napoleon Bonaparte once asked, "What is history, but a fiction agreed upon?" Winston Churchill, former prime minister of Great Britain, was heard to state emphatically that "History is going to be kind to Britain, because I'm going to write it."

Indeed, history has been very kind to Europeans because *they* have written it and in many instances, it has been the fiction (lie) agreed upon. Because of a global system of mis-education which currently exists, the average person honestly believes that civilization began in Europe, and that the rest of the world waited in darkness for the Europeans to bring them the light. For more than 500 years, Europeans have controlled and manipulated the image and information of the world. Consider the following:

- Since the sixteenth century, Europeans have controlled the map making industry and have projected their culture as the primary point of reference.

- The geographic orientation of most maps to "North" exists only because Europe is in the "North."

- If one were to draw diagonal lines from corner to corner across the world map, western Europe would lie at the center.

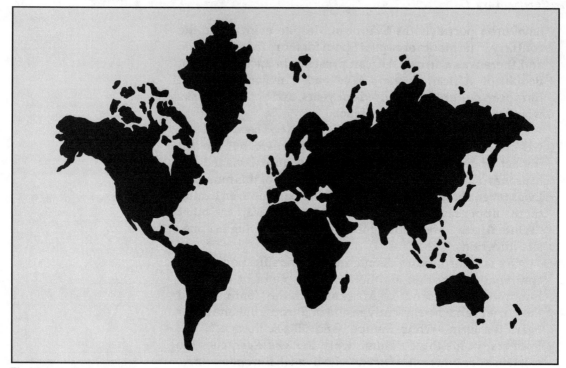

The Mercator Projection Map

Ward L Kaiser, author of *A New View of the World*, provides us with this historical perspective on the map currently in use worldwide.

The typical map in use today is the Mercator map which was developed in 1569 for European navigators by the German cartographer, Gerhard Kremer, whose surname (meaning 'merchant' in English) becomes Mercator in Latin.

Mr. Kaiser goes on to state:

The point is not that Mercator deliberately falsified the picture. He was following almost universal precedent in setting his own land at the center of everything. This had, in fact, a positive effect in this sense: it facilitated the use of his map by European navigators in the age of exploration.

We, however, are not Sixteenth Century European sailors. For us, the continued widespread use of the Mercator as a general-purpose map presents serious problems. We are neither fair to Kremer nor acting in our own best interests when we force his map to function beyond its originally intended use or its capabilities....The Mercator map, as it is most often used today, lends support to the assumption...that nationalism or ethnocentrism or even racism is all right:

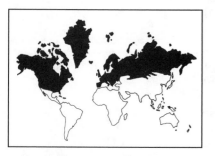

The traditional Mercator map seriously distorts and misrepresents the true shapes and proportions of the landmasses of the world. The Mercator map shows the northern hemisphere (18.9 million square miles of the land above the equator) to be more than two-thirds of the total landmass. It compresses the southern hemisphere (38.6 million square miles) into the remaining one-third. This is not compatible with the objective reality of the modern scientific age.

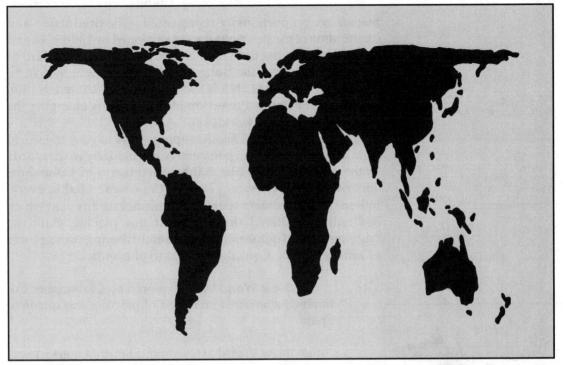

The Peters Projection Map

that it is grounded in geographical realities.... Ethnocentrism or racism is the belief that one's own people or race are superior to all others. To see it in its extreme form, look at apartheid in South Africa. Less obvious, but still significant, forms of the problem exist all around us, and within us. The sources of this dangerous disease are many, but surely one of its subtle supports is the pervasive use of a map that, in spite of all known facts:

-enlarges those areas of the world historically inhabited by whites,

-shifts those same areas to the heart and center of the world's stage, where they do not belong, and

-minimizes the importance of what we think of as 'the South,' including most of what we designate as the 'Third World.'

A new world map was created in 1974 by Dr. Arno Peters, a German historian and cartographer. Dr. Peters' map (appropriately called the Peters Projection Map) represents all land masses according to relative size. For example, Europe is shown in its correct proportion, relative to all surrounding land masses and Africa is accurately shown to be larger than the land mass that was once referred to as the Soviet Union.

The Peters Projection Map does exhibit shape distortion of land area, but it is considered a small tradeoff because all land

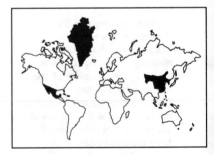

The distortion of the Mercator map can best be shown when comparing Greenland with Mexico and China. The total landmass of Greenland is 0.8 million square miles. It appears much larger than China and almost as large as the whole continent of North America. In reality, China is almost five times larger than Greenland and Mexico is nearly as large as Greenland even though the landmass of Mexico is only a small portion of the total landmass of North America.

masses are proportionally represented. The production and distribution of the Peters map was sanctioned by UNESCO, and it is currently being used by the Vatican, the General Board of Global Ministries of the United Methodist Church, the World Council of Churches, NATO and numerous United Nation agencies. The Peters Projection Map is literally changing the way people view the world.

1992 also afforded us another opportunity to view the world from a new and different perspective, particularly with regards to the quincentenary (the 500th anniversary) of Columbus' "discovery" of America. During the course of this event, billions of dollars were spent to commemorate an event which has radically altered the history of this planet. Both the "discovery" and quincentenary represent the might and power of Eurocentrism. Consider this chain of events:

> -the "New World" was explored by Christopher Columbus, who acted on behalf of the king and queen of Spain

> -the "New World" (North and South America) was later named in honor of Italian born explorer Amerigo Vespucci

> -the "New World" was subsequently divided into a northern and southern zone and colonized by the Spanish, Portuguese, British and French

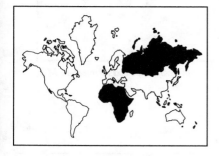

Another example of the skewing of the northern hemisphere where the majority of the population is white, is the landmass of the former Soviet Union.
Compared to the size of Africa, the landmass of the old Soviet Union appears to be more than *twice* the size of Africa. *In reality, Africa is considerably larger.*

The "discoverers of America" were nothing more than an invading force who brought, along with their armies, their language, culture and religious traditions and imposed them upon the native populations. These invading forces subsequently exterminated the indigenous inhabitants and replaced them with an imported and enslaved population. Nowhere in the annals of humanity will you find such prolonged acts of barbarism imposed upon people of a different race.

If there exists a "North America" and a "South America," why could there not also be an "East Asia" and a "West Asia?" What could justifiably be called "West Asia" is now referred to as "Europe." Hundreds of years ago a decision was made to draw an imaginary line through Asia and everything west of that line was called "Europe" and designated as a continent, contrary to the accepted definition. No body of water separates Europe from Asia. It is separated by an invisible boundary, drawn in order to establish the primacy of the continent, which the World Book Encyclopedia describes as:

> ...the birthplace of Western civilization. No other continent has had such great influence on world history. From the time of the ancient Greeks, European political ideas, scientific discoveries, arts and philoso-

phies, and religious beliefs have spread to other parts of the world. The civilizations of the United States, Canada, [and] Latin America...developed largely from European civilization.

The worldwide manipulation of history and maps brings to mind the concept of mental enslavement described by George Orwell in his book *1984*. To paraphrase Mr. Orwell: Whoever controls the image and information of the past will determine what and how future generations will think; and, whoever controls the information and images of the present, will also determine how those same people will view the past.

This interminable cycle of mind manipulation, which has influenced the world for hundreds of years, now appears to be disintegrating in the wake of a tidal wave of multiculturalism that is currently sweeping through the United States and Europe. People all over the world are expressing a need to see the world through a different set of eyes.

The emergence of divergent world views such as Afrocentrism and multiculturalism indicate that we, like Columbus 500 years before, are standing on the threshold of a new age of discovery, and that a shift from a Eurocentric to a more global perspective is rapidly taking place. The events which have set this shift into motion are irreversible. They began with the decimation and enslavement of the first African man, woman and child half a millennium ago.

Pope Urges Whites To Seek Blacks' Forgiveness!

Pope John Paul II recently maintained that Whites must never stop asking the forgiveness of Blacks and Native Americans for past injustices.

The Pope, who made the announcement at the Vatican, said: "This demand for forgiveness has to be made above all to the first inhabitants of the New World, the Indians, and also to those who were deported as slaves from Africa for heavy labor."

JET Magazine
November 9, 1992

Columbus claims the "New World" in the name of Spain and God.

Part One

Nile Valley Civilization

Exploding The Myths
Volume 1

The Major Rivers of the World

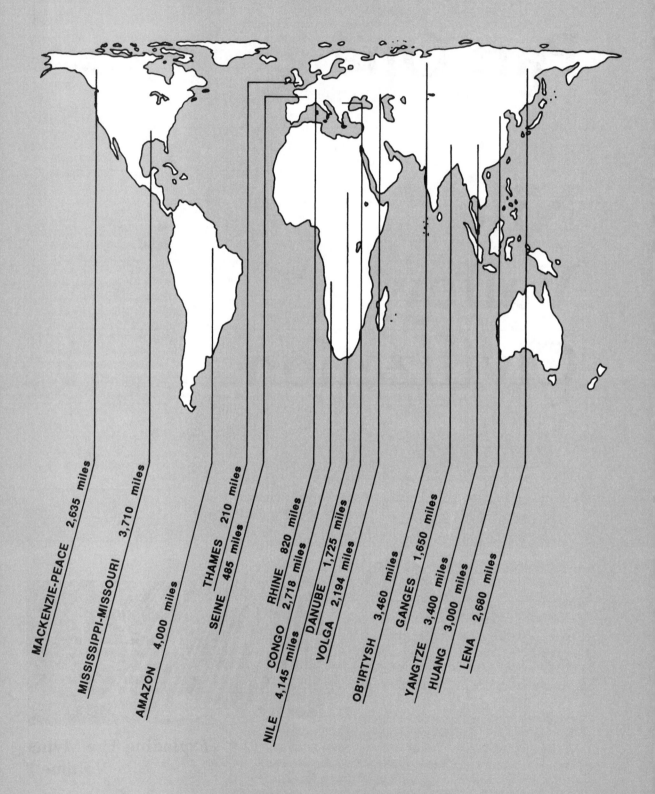

Chapter One
The Nile Valley

The emergence of civilization in ancient Egypt was nothing more than the outgrowth of the culture that developed along the Nile Valley. It is in the Nile Valley where one can find the greatest primary evidence of the earliest beginnings of agriculture, architecture, engineering, language, writing, philosophy, science and religion. In short, all of the essential components that would lead to the development of a great civilization.

The Nile Valley extends over 4,000 miles, from the highlands on the east coast of central Africa to the delta region in the extreme north. The origins of the mighty waterway, which courses through the Nile Valley, have been traced to the twin sources of the Nile River, which are called the Blue Nile and the White Nile.

The Blue Nile begins at Lake Tana, which is located in the mountainous region of northern Ethiopia, near the city of Gonder and the Choke Mountains. This river contains, within its flow, extremely rich mineral deposits (called silt), which played a major role in the physical evolution of the lands to the north and the development of agriculture in Egypt. The Nile Valley and the Nile Delta are among the most fertile farming areas in the world because of the silt which was deposited upon their shores during the annual flood season. An estimated 70 percent of the Nile's water comes from the Blue Nile.

The second major tributary to the Nile Valley River system is the White Nile, which has its beginnings in the Great Lakes region of central Africa along the equator. Approximately half of the water which flows from the White Nile evaporates as it courses through the Sudd, a vast swamp in southern Sudan. The primary source for the White Nile is the body of water originally called "Nyanza" or "Lake" by the indigenous population thousands of years ago.

Nyanza is surrounded by the countries of Kenya, Uganda and Tanzania. It is the largest lake in Africa, and the second largest in the world, exceeded in size only by Lake Superior in the United States. Nyanza was renamed "Lake Victoria" by the English explorer John Speke, who "discovered" it in 1858 and named it in honor of Queen Victoria, the British monarch.

There are numerous lakes and rivers feeding into the White Nile. They are primarily the result of the water runoff from Mount Kilimanjaro, which boarders Tanzania and Kenya. Kilimanjaro, the tallest mountain in Africa, rises to a height of 19,340 feet. The second major contributor to the waters of the

White Nile is the Ruwenzori Mountains, which border the countries of Uganda and Zaire.

For centuries, this area of equatorial Africa has been called "The Mountain of the Moon" by the native inhabitants. As a matter of fact, in the language of Ki-Swahili, *Kilimanjaro* means "Mountain of the Moon," as does the Buganda word *Rwenzori.*

The term "White Nile" describes the raging waters of the southern branch of this mighty river, and "Blue Nile" is an appropriate description for the body of water which is the noticeably calmer of the two. It is in Sudan, in a city called Khartoum, where these two rivers meet and form the singular Nile River, which continues its northerly flow into the delta area of northern Egypt, where it empties into the Mediterranean Sea. The word *khartoum* means "elephant's tusk," and is a geographic metaphor which describes the coming together of the two branches of the Nile.

The Nile Valley River system is the world's longest waterway (4,160 miles), and it irrigates approximately 2,800,000 acres of land in Sudan and 7,600,000 acres in Egypt. An interesting fact about the Nile is that it and the Amazon, which is the world's second longest river, are the only major rivers which flow from south to north. The migratory pattern of the people who navigated the Nile, from "up south" to "down north," was to later play a major role in the development of civilization in ancient Egypt.

The country of Egypt, which lies in the lowlands of the Nile Valley, is nothing more than the extension of the lands that expanded northward from the south. It is generally believed that the delta region of northern Egypt was created by the accumulation of silt from the Blue Nile, which was deposited upon the shore over the course of thousands of years during the annual flood season. The 600 mile narrow strip of fertile land that lies within the boundaries of Egypt (from what is now referred to as the First Cataract to the Mediterranean) exists only because of the waters from the south which led to its development.

Within the singular body of the Nile River are six low-lying areas of rocky waterfalls called cataracts. These cataracts posed the only major impediment to the continued navigation of vessels through the river. Because the Nile flows from the south to the north, to travel "down" the Nile would mean traveling in a "northerly" direction. It was because of the northerly flow of the Nile that southern Egypt was originally referred to as *Upper Egypt* and the north *Lower Egypt.*

The references to the numerical order of the six cataracts plays an important role in determining one's perspective of Egypt in both ancient and modern times. When traveling "down" the Nile in a northerly direction, from south central Africa to the Mediterranean, the ancient Nilotic people encountered the First Cataract in Sudan, north of Khartoum, and

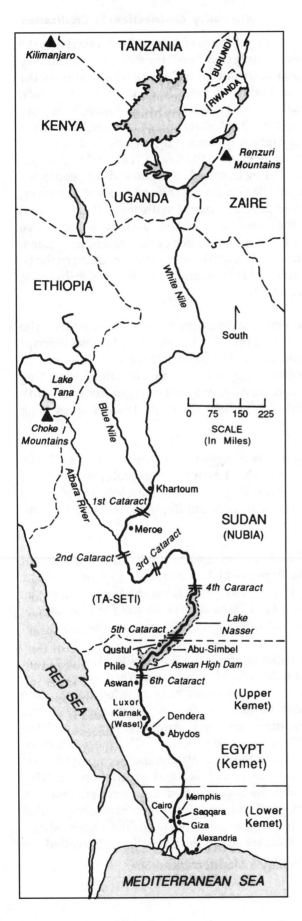

The Nile Valley and Africa

(A Southern Orientation)

TANZANIA

▲ Kilimanjaro

BURUNDI

RWANDA

KENYA

▲ Renzuri Mountains

UGANDA

ZAIRE

White Nile

↑ South

ETHIOPIA

Lake Tana

Blue Nile

▲ Choke Mountains

Atbara River

● Khartoum

1st Cataract

● Meroe

2nd Cataract

3rd Cataract

SUDAN (NUBIA)

4th Cararact

(TA-SETI)

5th Cataract

Lake Nasser

Qustul — Abu-Simbel

Phile — Aswan High Dam

Aswan ● 6th Cataract

Luxor Karnak (Waset)

Dendera

● Abydos

(Upper Kemet)

EGYPT (Kemet)

Cairo ● Memphis
● Saqqara
● Giza
Alexandria

(Lower Kemet)

RED SEA

MEDITERRANEAN SEA

SCALE (In Miles)
0 75 150 225

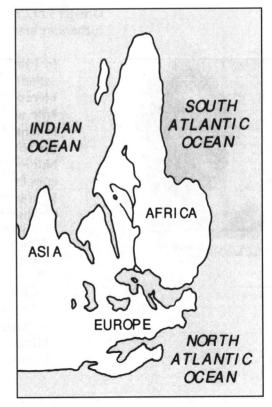

INDIAN OCEAN

SOUTH ATLANTIC OCEAN

AFRICA

ASIA

EUROPE

NORTH ATLANTIC OCEAN

John G. Jackson

Professor G. Jackson was 86 years old when joined the ancestors on October 14, 1993. He was remembered as an "African Scholar-King" by the friends and associates who memoralized him at the DuSable Museum, in Chicago, Illinois, on December 4, 1993.

the Sixth Cataract, in Egypt south of Aswan. However, since the European explorers navigated "up" the Nile, in a southerly direction, they naturally referred to Egypt as the location of the First Cataract and Sudan as the site of the Sixth Cataract. Because of a predilection for a northerly orientation, European explorers coming from the Mediterranean into the Nile Valley literally, and geographically, turned Egypt upside down.

The Nile has often been referred to as a "cultural highway," and has been traveled by hundreds of thousands of people, for thousands of years. Traveling northward "down" the river, the earliest Nilotic people brought with them their cultural traditions, which continued to evolve with each successive migration. In the earliest documents of the ancient Egyptians, their historians often recounted stories of their southern roots. John Jackson, author of *Introduction to African Civilization*, cites a historic reference:

> The Edfu Text is an important source document on the early history of the Nile Valley. This famous inscription, found in the Temple of Horus at Edfu, gives an account of the origin of Egyptian civilization. According to this record, civilization was brought from the south by a band of invaders under the leadership of King Horus.

Jackson's statements of Egypt's southern origin have been echoed numerous times by the eminent Egyptologist, Dr. Yosef ben-Jochannan. Addressing an audience at a lecture before the Greater London Council, London, England, in 1986, Dr. ben-Jochannan stated:

> In (the London Museum) you will find a document called the Papyrus of Hunefer...and I quote from the hieratic writing, 'we came from the beginning of the Nile where God Hapi dwells, at the foothills of The Mountains of the Moon'...Where is 'the beginning of the Nile?' The furthest point of the beginning of the Nile is in Uganda; this is the White Nile. Another point is in Ethiopia. The *Blue Nile* and *White Nile* meet in Khartoum; and the other side of Khartoum is the Omdurman Republic of Sudan. From there it flows from the south down north. And there it meets with the Atbara River in Atbara, Sudan. Then it flows completely through Sudan...into the southern part of what the Romans called 'Nubia,' and parallel on the Nile, part of which the Greeks called 'Egypticus'; the English called it 'Egypt' and the Jews in their mythology called it 'Mizrain' which the current Arabs called Mize/ Mizrair. Thus it ends in the Sea of Sais, also called the Great Sea, today's Mediterranean Sea.

Yosef ben-Jochannan

Hapi unifying the two lands of Upper and Lower Kemet.

Dr. Asa G. Hilliard, III, a widely respected educational psychologist and historian, cites additional references for the southern origins of the early Egyptians:

> Their legends tell of their origins in the south at the sources of the Hapi. Rose...cites the Edfu text as authority for the legend of a southern origin of the predynastic Kemites (Egyptians). The land "up south" was called Ta Ntr, or the land of God. They faced south to get their bearings. The word for "left hand" and the word for "east" are the same, as are the words for "right hand" and "west..."

The only possible way that the left hand could indicate east and the right hand west is if one is oriented to the south and that view served as your point of origin.

Dr. Charles Finch, a distinguished physician and historian, also commented on this interesting aspect of ancient Egyptian cultural and geographical orientation:

> Further evidence is found in the Egyptians' anthropomorphic representations of the passage of sun across the heavens, in which the boat of the sun begins its morning or eastern ascent on the left side of the sky-goddess Nut who thus is in a southern heaven despite Egypt's northern hemispheric location.

Ancient Egypt has often been referred to as the "Gift of the Nile" and it is believed by many scholars, both ancient and modern, that Egypt was nothing more than the extension of the civilization which had its origins in Ethiopia. Chancellor Williams, author of *The Destruction Of Black Civilization*,

Dr. Chancelor Williams made his transition into the ancestral realm on December 7, 1992, at the age of 98. His presence will be surely missed by his family, friends and colleagues.

Chancellor Williams

This map of Africa was drawn by European explorers probably after 1884 because the prime meridian is located in London instead of Cairo. It labels the entire continent "Ethiopia," a name which comes from the Greek word meaning *sunburnt faces*. Ethiopia was formerly called *Abyssinia*, which some think was derived from an Arabic word meaning *mixed*. Others have expressed the belief that it referenced the name of the early inhabitants of the country. Note that the southern Atlantic Ocean is also referred to as the "*Ethiopic* Ocean."

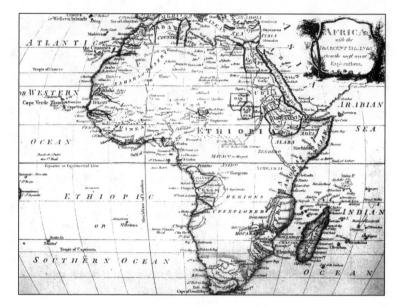

expressed his agreement with this point of view in the second chapter of his book entitled, "Ethiopia's Oldest Daughter: Egypt." John Jackson, author of the monumental book, *Introduction to African Civilization*, has similarly titled the second chapter of his work, "Ethiopia and the Origin of Civilization." In this chapter, Jackson comments on the Greek origins of the word "Ethiopia."

> When the Greeks came in contact with the dusky inhabitants of Africa and Asia, they called them the "burnt-faces." The Greek word for burnt was *ethios* and the word for face was *ops*. So *ethios* plus *ops* became Ethiopian.

Many of the words currently used to describe ancient Egypt, its cities, artifacts and historical personalities, are not indigenous and were derived from Greek, Arabic, French and British interpretations. For example, the word Egypt is of Greek origin and was originally used to describe the ancient capital city of Menes or Memphis. Today, the word Egypt refers to the entire nation. John Jackson provides additional insight on the evolution of this country's name:

> It may be of interest to the reader to know that the ancient Egyptians did not call themselves 'Egyptians'; the name was invented by the Greeks. The first Greek visitors to Egypt, in the Seventh Century B.C., were greatly impressed by the Temple of Ptah, at Memphis. They regarded it as the grandest structure in the Nile Valley and they afterward referred to this ancient land

as *Hekaptah* (The Land of the Temple of Ptah). In the Greek language *Hekaptah* became *Aiguptos*: and under the Roman rule the name was Latinized into Aegyptus, from whence we get the name Egypt.

Memphis was the site of the first capital of Egypt, and named in honor of Menes, the ruler who unified the two lands of Upper (southern) and Lower (northern) Egypt. It is important to note that "Menes" is the Greek name for the African ruler whose name was originally "Narmer" or "Aha." This city was so vast that it was once described by Arab travelers in the Middle Ages as "stretching a day's journey in every direction." Although little remains of this historic site, John Anthony West, author of *The Travelers Key to Ancient Egypt* describes its significance:

King Narmer,
also known as Aha.

> In ancient Egypt, Memphis was called *Ineb-hedj*, the White Wall, possibly referring to the great enclosure wall of Saqqara nearby. In the Middle Kingdom it was called *Ankh-tawy*, That-Which-Binds-the-Two-Lands. Some scholars believe that the name of one of the New Kingdom temples at Memphis, *Hi-ka-ptah*, Temple-of-the-Ka-of-Ptah, is the source of the Greek *Aegyptos* from whence both "Egypt" and "Coptic." "Memphis" is believed to be a Greek corruption of *Men-nefer*, [which means] Established-in-Beauty...

Historically, in the Old Kingdom, Memphis was the seat of the administrative and religious power of ancient Egypt. During this time, the term "Double-White House" was also used to describe the painted mud-brick palace in which the king lived, which was constructed within the "White Wall." The kings of Egypt were later given the title "Pharaoh" by a foreign ruler. It is a word which means "great house," and is derived from the term *Pr-ah*.

Incidentally, the word "Pharaoh" is also of foreign origin. The term was first used in the New Kingdom by an Asian, to describe the king of Egypt.

The word "pharaoh" is of foreign origin and was not used in Kemet until the New Kingdom (1550-1196 B.C.E.). This word was used by an Asian king when referring to his regal counterpart in Kemet. The Kemetic word for king was "Ngu."

John West also described some of the many problems created by the Greeks, who not only renamed the city of Memphis, but numerous temples, deities and historic personalities:

> ...the Greeks appear guilty of any number of severe etymological crimes, producing "Cheops" out of *Khufu*, "Thoth" out of *Djhuiti*...at the same time causing almost inextricable confusion even among scholars, since certain Greek names, such as Memphis, have taken such prominence that the proper Egyptian names are seldom used, while in other cases the Egyptian

names prevail and in still other cases, the Greek and Egyptian are freely interchanged.

Chancellor Williams reminds us of the importance of using the earliest African name to describe the land now referred to as Egypt:

> There was no 'Egypt' before the black king from whose name it was indirectly derived. Before that the country was called Chem (Khem) or Chemi (Khemi) - another name indicating its black inhabitants, and not the color of the soil, as some writers have needlessly strained themselves in asserting.

Prior to the Greek use of the word "Egypt," Africans referred to their land as Kemet, that is, the Black Land. "Kemet" was the strongest term used by the ancients in Pharaonic times to indicate blackness. It meant "coal black." The word Kemet (KMT), written in hieroglyphic form, was represented by a block of wood, which was charred on the end. The name which the people of Kemet called themselves was *Kemmiu*, which literally translates as *"the Blacks."*

The word "Kemiu" was also used to describe the vast population that inhabited a considerable portion of the Nile Valley. In ancient times, there was no physical distinction made between the people who occupied the lands now called Egypt and Sudan. The ancient Egyptians saw themselves as "Blacks," who were portrayed as no different from other blacks in Africa, but were physically and phenotypically, different from the Indo-Europeans (Caucasoids) or the Semites (Mulattos).

Charles Finch informs us that the ancient Egyptian word:

> ...for the African lands to the south of them was 'Khenti' - 'Khentiu' denoting the Sudanic peoples who lived there - and this is also their word for 'first, foremost, beginning, origin, (and) chief.'

Prior to the Greek use of the word "Egypt," Africans referred to their country as Kemet which was written kmt. The first symbol is a biliteral; that is, it stands for two letters and means "black." Pictorially it is a charred piece of wood; phonetically, it represents KM (KM). The second symbol is a monoliteral; that is, it stands for one letter. Pictorially it is an owl, that stands for the consonant M. The third symbol, pictorially a loaf, is another monoliteral that stands for the consonant T. The fourth symbol is a determinative, which represents the plan of a village, city or nation. Thus, the word KMT or Kemet means "the country of the blacks or the land of the blacks" and not "the black soil" as some have suggested.

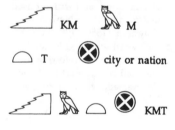

KM   M

T   city or nation

KMT

Since the word *Kemiu* (or *Kemmiu*) was an original term used to describe the people of Kemet, contemporary scholars have elected to use the words *Kemites* and *Kemetic* when referring to the people and things of ancient Kemet. The spelling of certain Kemetic words varies considerably among researchers because the hieroglyphic language (*Medu Netcher*) was written without vowels. We have elected to use Budge's phonetic spelling of the word *Netcher* instead of *Neter*, because it facilitates ease of reading and pronunciation.

Author's Note:

For the purpose of historical clarity we will henceforth use the word "Kemet" to describe "ancient Egypt" - circa 3200 B.C.E. through the third century B.C.E. The word "Egypt" will be used to describe the land after the Greek occupation in 332 B.C.E. The term B.C.E. references incidents which occurred "Before the Common (Christian) Era" and A.C.E. references events "After the Common Era." The Common Era or Christian Era begins with the Birth of Jesus, the Christ, as referenced by those nations which use the Gregorian Calendar.

Chapter Two
The Peopling of Kemet and Egypt

Qustul, The World's Oldest Monarchy

On March 1, 1979, the *New York Times* lived up to its slogan "All the News That's Fit to Print," when it featured a cover story of earthshaking significance. The article was written by Broyce Rensberger, a science writer for the *Times*, and was entitled "Ancient Nubian Artifacts Yield Evidence of Earliest Monarchy." This article recounted the archaeological discovery of the late archaeologist, Dr. Keith Seele, who served as the director of the University of Chicago's Oriental Institute Nubian Expedition in 1962.

Professors Keith Seele and Bruce Williams discovered artifacts in Nubia which supported the predynastic birthplace of a pharaonic civilization in the ancient Nubian city of Qustul. Although the discoveries were made around 1964, the news of the find was not made public until 1979. No publication, other than the *Times*, devoted any appreciable space to Dr. Seele's archaeological research.

Dr. Seele's expedition, in a dramatic race against time, directed its research in an area that was soon to be flooded by the rising waters of Lake Nasser, which was created by the newly constructed Aswan High Dam. The Seele team concentrated its efforts in Upper Egypt, in an area north of the Sudanese boarder, at an ancient Nubian site called *Ta-Seti*, which was euphemistically referred to as "Land of the Bow." This name was the earliest hieroglyphic description for Nubia, the southernmost nome or province of Kemet, and it referred to the skilled archers of ancient Nubia.

More than 5,000 artifacts were unearthed by Seele's team during their digs in Nubia. At that time, the Oriental Institute had no one on staff to catalogue the artifacts. Dr. Williams, an archaeological Egyptologist, changed his area of focus to Nubian archaeology, and assumed the responsibility for organizing the collection. After Dr. Seele's death in 1977, Williams began publishing the findings of the Nubian Expedition and to date he has authored nine volumes, in a continuing series, on Nubian excavations. As a result of his current research, Williams feels that Nubia can no longer be looked upon as an appendage of Egyptology, and a stepsister to Ancient Kemet, but as an independent field of archaeological study.

Recently analyzed artifacts suggests that the first Nubian civilization developed around 3800 B.C.E., and lasted until approximately 652 A.C.E. Although the civilizations of Nubia and Kemet emerged about the same time, the Nubian civilization actually lasted longer. The earliest period of Nubian civilization is classified as the A-Group (ca. 3800-3100 B.C.E.); this culture was succeeded by a second, called the C-Group (ca. 2300-1500 B.C.E.). Both groups are said to have flourished in Lower Nubia, while to the south, above the Third Cataract, a third group called Kerma Culture developed (ca. 2000-1550 B.C.E.). This monarchy was referred to in the Kemetic records of the Old Kingdom as the ancient "Kingdom of Kush."

Although one would not normally associate castles with Africa, during the Twelfth Dynasty (ca. 1900 B.C.E.) fortifications were erected in Nubia near the area now referred to as the Second Cataract. These castles were formidable and were equipped with drawbridges, moats and fortified entrances. These fortresses were like walled cities and contained hundreds of people and facilities for sleeping, cooking and storage.

During the third century B.C.E., the heartland of Nubian civilization was located further south in the city of Meroe. The Meroitic civilization (ca. 200 B.C.E - 300 A.C.E) is well known for its temples at Musawwarat es Sufra, Naga and Meroe and for its many royal pyramid tombs. A 2,000-year-old sandstone tablet, which was discovered in 1963, may hold the key to deciphering the Merotic writing system, which is closely related to the *Medu Netcher* (hieroglyphics). The last known great Nubian culture was the Ballana, or X-Group, (ca. 250-550 A.C.E.). The tombs of this civilization were found in Lower Nubia and excavated in the 1930's.

Another architectural design unique to the Nile Valley was the veranda. Many of the brick homes that were built in Nubia contained porches and patios. "This architectural feature was brought to America from Africa in colonial times" and had a profound impact on the development of architecture in the southern states.

Of all the numerous items discovered in Nubia, the most significant were found in an A-Group grave site, called Cemetery L, which yielded artifacts that were created six to seven generations (approximately 200 years) before the start of the First Dynasty in Kemet (3150 B.C.E.). The most impressive

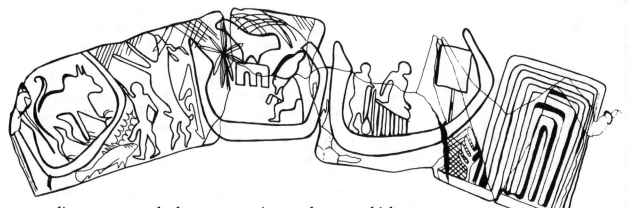

discovery unearthed was a stone incense burner, which was found in the city of Qustul, the ancient capital of the Nubian kingdom, called Ta-Seti. Engravings on the side of the incense burner are scenes depicting the following:

Reproduction of the engravings found on the incense burner in Qustul.

- A *serekh* or paneled palace facade,

- The Falcon God Horus which substantiates the southern (Nubian) origins of the Holy Royal Trinity, which consisted of Osiris, Isis and their son Horus,

- A representation of a king or pharaoh, wearing the traditional beard and crown of Upper Kemet, while sailing in a boat toward the royal palace,

- Elements of iconography, which were later to become an integral part of Kemetic writing and art.

The discovery of this artifact has led Dr. Williams to remark:

> The idea of a pharaoh may have come down the Nile from Nubia to Egypt [and] that would make Nubian civilization the ancestor of Egypt's, at least in one critical aspect.

This segment of the incense burner clearly illustrates a king (wearing the crown, which symbolized Upper Kemet, and a false beard) seated upon a throne and holding in his hand a symbol of royalty. In front of the king is a representation of a falcon standing atop a serekh. Both figures are shown aboard a boat sailing on the Hapi River.

As a result of the reexamination of data concerning ancient Nubia, many scholars have concluded that the Nubians were an extremely sophisticated people who built cities, roads and temples comparable to those of the people of Kemet in the north. It has even been suggested by one researcher that there were more pyramids constructed in Nubia than in Kemet. Unfortunately, the likelihood of further archaeological study at Qustul, or any other site in Nubia, is all but impossible because many of the primary areas of investigation now lie under 250 feet of water, at the bottom of Lake Nasser.

This man-made lake covers an area of approximately 1,550 square miles, and it is the second largest man-made lake in the world. Since 1981, the Nubian Lake, as it is sometimes called, has covered an area which extends from the Sixth Cataract to

The building of the Aswan High Dam flooded the homes of the Nubians, thereby creating Lake Nasser

beyond the Fifth Cataract. It has an average width of six miles and it is 50 miles wide in some areas. One-third of the waters of this lake cover northern Sudan and the remaining two thirds blanket southern Egypt.

During the construction of the Aswan High Dam (1960-1968) and the subsequent creation of Lake Nasser, 40 Nubian villages were relocated further inland. Thousands of Nubians were resettled in and around the city of Aswan and in villages further north; however, an untold number drowned when they refused to leave the lands that their ancestors had occupied for more than 5,000 years.

In addition to the displacement of human beings, a total of 18 ancient temples were dismantled and relocated. Of the 18 temples that were moved, 12 are still in Egypt, and the remaining four can be found in museums in Madrid, Spain; Rome, Italy; Leiden, Holland and New York City in the United States. These temples were presented as gifts to those nations that assisted in the construction of the Aswan High Dam.

There is no way to estimate the total number of temples and tombs which now lie at the bottom of Lake Nasser, nor is there any way of knowing the many secrets that these structures currently hold. One thing is certain, because of the creation of the Aswan Dam, the world will never have an opportunity to study the full impact Africans from the southern Nile Valley had on the development of ancient Kemet and subsequent civilizations.

The Nubians

The Egyptians of today are not the same people as the ancient Kemites of 5,000 years ago, just as the Americans of today are not the same as the Native Americans of 500 years ago. The Egypt of today is an Islamic nation, which is currently inhabited by peoples from Assyria, Syria, Persia, Europe and other areas of the world, who have, through a process of miscegenation over a period of thousands of years, evolved into the Egyptian of today.

In order to correctly address the issue of race in modern Egypt, one must have a clear understanding of the racial makeup of the peoples who originally occupied that land, where they came from and where their descendants currently live. They certainly haven't all disappeared into the modern Egyptian melting pot. These indigenous people are still called Nubians today.

The area called Nubia was divided into two regions, Lower Nubia (in southern Egypt) and Upper Nubia (in northern Sudan). The word Nubia was derived from the Kemetic word *nub* which meant gold. Thus *Nubia* was referred to as the land of gold and its people were called *Nubians,* or people from the land of gold. In addition to gold, ebony, incense, spices, ivory,

Drawing of a Nubian found in the tomb of King Seti I (ca. 1291-1279 B.C.E.)

Contemporary Nubian children

feathers and animal skins were also exported to Kemet from Nubia.

Nubia was much more than a source for the vital mineral resources which were required for architectural, artistic and personal use in Kemet. Nubia was the lifeline of ancient Kemet, and the source of its language, philosophy and religion. For more than three thousand years of Pharaonic rule, Nubia played a pivotal role in the development and maintenance of its daughter nation Kemet, particularly during the New Kingdom (ca. 1550-1196 B.C.E.). During this time, Nubia was ruled by the Kemetic king Amenhotep I and his new providence was administered by an official who was referred to as the "King's Son of Kush."

In recounting "A Brief History of Nubia" in the Spring 1992 issue of *News & Notes* (a newsletter of the Oriental Institute), Emily Teeter, assistant curator of the Oriental Institute Museum, wrote:

> By Dynasty 22, (ca. 945 B.C.), Egypt fragmented into rival states. When Thebes and her allies in Middle Egypt were threatened from the north, the Theban officials appealed to the Kushite kings at Napata who styled themselves the "protectors of the god Amun." In 747 B.C., Nubian troops led by king Piye (Piankhy) marched to Thebes and thereafter, they moved northward, conquering Memphis and restoring unity

to Egypt. This period of Nubian rule in Egypt is referred to as Dynasty 25. With few exceptions, the kings resided at Napata, leaving the administration of Egypt to their sisters and daughters. These *God's Wives of Amun* dwelled in Thebes, and assisted by Egyptian administrators, they served as the theocratic rulers of Egypt.

The Nubian rulers remained in control of Kemet for approximately 100 years, until they were finally overrun by the Assyrian armies of King Ashurbanipal. The Nubian kings retreated into Kush where they continued to rule at Napata. Four hundred years later (250 B.C.E.), they moved the center of Nubian civilization further south where they continued to flourish in the city of Meroe.

Despite their retreat into Upper Kush, the Nubians continued to have contact with European forces. In the first century A.C.E ambassadors of the Roman emperor Nero were given "passports" by the Nubian king, who sent letters to the rulers of cities further south instructing them to give the Romans safe passage into central Africa. The continued contact with the Roman emissaries of Emperor Justinian eventually led to the conversion of the Nubians to Christianity in the sixth century A.C.E.

While much of northern Africa was overpowered by the advancing forces of Islam, the superiority of the Nubian army, particularly her famed archers, held the Arabs in check and defeated them at Dongola in 652 A.C.E. Nubia was able to stave off the ever-increasing advances of Islamic forces longer than any other region in Africa and continued to remain a Coptic Christian nation for almost 1,000 more years.

Unfinished statue of Ausar (Osiris)

The nation which was once ancient Kush is now called Sudan; it is the largest country in Africa. As late as 1909 American Egyptologist George Reisner, curator of the Boston Museum, espoused the view that Nubia was originally governed by "white" Libyans who created this ancient civilization, and later withdrew, leaving it to be governed by "blacks." Many of the early archaeological expeditions were financed by wealthy businessmen, who endowed museums and religiously believed in the superiority of the white race.

Evidence of this outdated view can still be found in the 1986 edition of the *World Book Encyclopedia* which describes the people of the Sudan as:

> ...descendants of African blacks and Nubians (brown-skinned people related to the early Egyptians and Libyans). African blacks who belong to several different ethnic groups live in the south.

Timothy Kendall, the associate curator of the Boston Museum of Fine Arts, has an entirely different view of the Nubians than his predecessor George Reisner had in 1909. Kendall states:

> These controversies over the Egyptians' racial origins obscure the fact that, to the south of Egypt, in Nubia, there was a literate and undeniable black civilization.

One of the world's most respected experts, E. A. Wallis Budge, addresses the issue in his book *Egypt*:

> The prehistoric native of Egypt, both in the old and new stone ages, was an African, and there is every reason for saying that the earliest settlers came from the south....There are many things in the manners and customs and religions of the historic Egyptians that suggests that the original home of their prehistoric ancestors was in a country in the neighborhood of Uganda and Punt.

A lesser-known writer by the name of Lady Flora Shaw Lugard also advanced the notion of a southern "black African" origin of ancient Kemet. In her book, *A Tropical Dependency: An Outline of the Ancient History of the Western Sudan*, Lugard discusses the significance of the role played in the city of Meroe:

> This remarkable spot is regarded by the ancients as the "cradle of the arts and sciences," where hieroglyphic writing was discovered, and where temples and pyramids had already sprung up while Egypt still remained ignorant of their existence.

Contemporary Nubian male

It is most unfortunate that traditional and accepted "experts" are only now beginning to acknowledge the true origins of civilization in the Nile Valley. For many decades African scholars (such as ben-Jochannan, Jackson, Clarke, Hansberry, Du Bois, Dundgee-Huston, Rodgers and numerous others) have intelligently argued their case and provided substantial evidence to support their assertions. Without the benefit of the true history of the indigenous population of modern day Egypt, one would not suspect that the Nubians had any significant role to play in the shaping of early life in the Nile Valley.

Present day Egyptian Nubians live under conditions somewhat reminiscent of conditions of *Negroes* in Jim Crow-era America. In many respects, Nubians are often relegated to the lowest rung of the social, political and economic ladder in Egypt, and a distinction is often made between Nubian and Egyptian people and culture.

Walter B. Emery, Edwards professor of Egyptology at the University of London, made the following remarks concerning the employment expectations of many Nubians in his book *Lost Land Emerging*:

> For generations the Nubians have earned their livelihood as domestic servants or as sailors of the Upper Egyptian Nile, in both of which professions I think they may be considered masters. All the best butlers and cooks in Egypt are from Nubia, and certainly the most reliable janitors of Cairo's great apartment houses, offices, and hotels almost invariably come from somewhere south of Aswan.

In many respects, the Egypto-Nubian population has a historical and cultural relationship that is far closer to the people of Kemet than modern Egyptians. However, because of innate frailties of the human species, irrespective of religious ideology, modern Nubians are often regarded as second class citizens in their own nation and their rich history is often overlooked.

Two Egyptians of Nubian ancestry have played major roles in the development of modern Egypt. The first was General Muhammad Naguib, who led the revolution in 1952 which overthrew King Faruk, thereby ending 2300 years of foreign rule in Egypt. Naguib became Egypt's first president in 1953, but was later overthrown by Gamal Abdel Nasser in 1954. References to Egyptians as Arabs is a relatively recent phenomenon that was instituted by Nasser who formed a United Arab Republic in late 1958.

Following the death of Nasser, in 1970, Anwar Sadat became Egypt's third president, and proclaimed his Nubian ancestry when he declared himself "the first true Egyptian pharaoh in modern times." Sadat was a corecipient of the Nobel Peace Prize in 1978, and Award-Winning African American Actor, Louis

Gossett, Jr., was selected for the starring role in a motion picture depicting the life of Anwar Sadat.

Historians are quick to note that the Nubians were often at odds with the people of Kemet, who often enslaved Nubian prisoners of war. But what is not commonly addressed is that the people of Kemet, while acknowledging geographical and political differences between themselves and the people of Nubia, did not denote any physical differences. Carvings from the tomb of Rameses III (1200 B.C.E.) portray the Nubians and Kemites as identical and Indo-Europeans and Semites as profoundly different in physical appearance and dress.

It is as foolhardy to suggest that the people of Kemet were phenotypically different from their Nubian, Sudanese or Ethiopian neighbors, as it is to suggest that the people of France, Switzerland and Germany are phenotypically different from one another. With the exception of southern African countries, national boundaries have done more to distinguish cultural and political differences than racial differences.

Louis Gossett, Jr.

This reproduction, from the tomb of Rameses III, illustrates distinct races of people. The Kemites portrayed themselves as being no different than the Nubians but distinctly different from the Indo-European (Caucasians) and the Semite.

| *Kemite* | *Indo-European* | *Nubian* | *Semite* |

Khufu (ca. 2575 B.C.E)

A Historical Overview of Kemet and Ancient Egypt

No one knows for certain when civilization in Kemet first began, though oral records indicate that a considerable amount of activity was taking place as early as 20,000 B.C.E. According to Sir Gaston Maspero in his publication *The Dawn of Civilization:*

> ...the Egyptians made their first appearance on the stage of history about 8,000 to 10,000 B.C.E.

It is generally agreed that a number of predynastic kingdoms (Ta-Seti and others) existed hundreds of years before the consolidation of power, which led to the unification of the country that is now geographically referred to as Egypt. The term *dynasty* refers to a family or period of rulership during a specific era.

The practice of dividing the many kingdoms of Kemet into dynastic periods was first established by a Greco-Egyptian priest named Manetho during the third century B.C.E. Manetho was commissioned by Ptolemy Philadelphus to write the definitive history of the country, which he subsequently chronicled in a book entitled *History of Egypt*. Regrettably, much of this history was lost when the library of Alexandria was destroyed; however, the remaining fragments of Manetho's chronology provides us with some clues as to the names of the early rulers.

There is general disagreement among modern Egyptologists and other historians regarding the exact dates of the dynastic periods. Some historians have recorded the establishment of the First Dynasty as early as the fifth millennium B.C.E., and others document it as beginning in the third millennium B.C.E. While most historians have adopted the conservative date of 3150 B.C.E. as the beginning of the First Dynasty, new data is continuing to surface which tends to support earlier dates for the establishment of the First Dynasty in Kemet.

Even though the early history of Kemet remains shrouded in mystery, there is general agreement upon the division of Kemet into 30 dynastic periods, which lasted until the Greek conquest in 332 B.C.E. The Greco-Roman rulership of Egypt extends from 332 B.C.E. to 395 A.C.E., after which all traces of Egyptian culture were suppressed. The dynasties of Kemet have been divided into four kingdoms of stable rulership and three intermediate periods that were either wracked with internal disorder or periods of foreign occupation.

All historical dates prior to the Twenty-sixth Dynasty are approximations and vary considerably from source to source. The following timeline is a very conservative and greatly abbreviated chronology of ancient Kemetic and Egyptian history:

Roman emperor wearing the royal Kemetic headdress (ca. first century A.C.E.)

Pre-Dynastic Kemet (4236-3150 B.C.E.)

4236   Kemetic people using 1,460-year-old astronomical calendar.

3800   Emergence of earliest Nubian civilization.

3400   Nubian Kingdom of Ta-Seti.

Dynasties 1-2 (3150-2649 B.C.E.)
Old Kingdom

3150   King Narmer (Menes) unifies Upper and Lower Kemet and establishes Memphis as the state capital.

Narmer

Dynasties 3-6 (2649-2150 B.C.E.)
Old Kingdom: Pyramid Age

2630   Zoser builds Step Pyramid and Saqqara complex.

2575-2465   All the great pyramids at Dahshur and Giza built.

2465-2323   Great sun temples and mortuary complexes built.
Pyramid Texts inscribed in tomb of King Unas.

First Intermediate Period (2150-2040 B.C.E.)
Kemet experiences widespread political upheaval

Zoser

Dynasties 11-12 (2040-1763 B.C.E.)
Middle Kingdom: Literary Age

2040   Mentuhotep II unifies Kemet and relocates the capital to Waset (Thebes/Luxor).
Art, literature and religion all flourish during this era as prosperity and stability are restored to the land.

1897   Senwosret establishes a colony in Greece and founded the city of Athens.
Construction of the great Kemetic Labyrinth by Amenemhet.

Mentuhotep III

Dynasties 13-17 Second Intermediate Period (1783-1550 B.C.E.)
First Asian invasion of Kemet by Hyksos "rulers of foreign lands." Invasion begins period of widespread destruction.

Dynasties 18-20 (1550-1170 B.C.E.)
New Kingdom: Temple and Imperial Age

1550   King Ahmose defeats the Hyksos and reunifies Kemet.

1504   Thutmose I expands the imperial rulership from the Upper Nile to the Upper Euphrates (Persia/Iraq).

1473   Hatshepsut rules Kemet as first female pharaoh.

1391   Amenhotep III rules Kemet at the height of its military power. Queen Tiye rules by his side.

1353   Amenhotep IV (Akhenaton) introduces concept of the Aton as the sole god to be worshiped in Kemet. Queen Nefertiti rules by his side.

1333   Tutankhamen ascends the throne of Kemet.

Senwosret

Tiye

Amenhotep III

Rameses II

Taharqa

Alexander

1306   Seti I, the father of Rameses II builds magnificent tomb in the Valley of the Kings.

1290   Rameses II (Rameses the Great) rules Kemet for 67 years.

Nefertari the Nubian queen reigns as Rameses II chief wife.

During this period, Kemet experiences enormous prosperity and a phenomenal resurgence in temple construction, literature and art.

Dynasties 21-24 Third Intermediate Period   (1070-750 B.C.E.)

Deterioration of political authority and a general period of social, political and religious decline.

Dynasty 25 (750-675 B.C.E.)

Late Kingdom

750   Piye (Piankhi), Nubia king conquers Upper and Lower Kemet and reestablishes central authority in Kush.

712   Shabaka reunifies all of Kemet and rules from Waset (Thebes/Luxor).

690   Taharqa leads military invasion of Spain and Palestine.

667   Assyrians conquer Lower Kemet.

664   Assyrians conquer Upper Kemet.

Nubian kings reestablish central government in Upper Kemet until they are conquered by Assyrian forces.

Dynasty 27 (525-404 B.C.E.)

First Persian Invasion

525   Kemet invaded by Cambyses and becomes a part of the Persian Empire; capital is moved to Babylon.

Dynasty 28 (404-399 B.C.E.)

404-   Persians are expelled from Kemet; capital is moved to
399   Sais in the Western Delta.

Dynasty 30 (380-343 B.C.E.)

Last period of rulership by native-born Kemetic kings.

Second Persian Invasion   (343-332 B.C.E.)

Greek Period (332-30 B.C.E)

332   Alexander of Macedonia (Alexander the Great) defeats the Persian army and conquers Kemet.

323   Ptolemy I establishes the Ptolemic Dynasty of Egypt.

285   Ptolemy II commissions Manetho to write History of Egypt, hereby establishing the only surviving record of Dynastic rulership.

69-30   Cleopatra VII born and rules Egypt until her death.

Cleopatra VII

Roman Period (30 B.C.E-323 A.C.E.)

30   Augustus Caesar claims Egypt as a province of Rome.
B.C.E. Degenerate elements of the ancient Kemetic religion are popularized in Rome.

Augustus

Byzantine Period (323-642 A.C.E)

323   Constantine becomes first Christian Emperor of Rome and convenes the first Nicaean council in Nicaea, Turkey, in 325 and declares Christianity the official state religion in 333.
391   Christian Emperor Theodosius bans the ancient religious systems of Egypt and orders the closing of all Egyptian temples.
394   Last recorded date of Egyptian hieroglyphic inscriptions.
527   Christian Emperor Justinian finally succeeds in closing the last Egyptian temple at Philae.

Bonaparte

Islamic Period (651 A.C.E-Present)

642   Conquest of Egypt by Arabs and the introduction of Islam.
1250 The Mamelukes (former Turkish and Circassian slaves) conquer Egypt.
1517 Egypt conquered by the Turks of the Ottoman Empire.
1798 Egypt conquered by Napoleon of France.
1881 British and Ottoman troops seize control of Egypt.
1952 Egyptian officers force King Faruk to give up the throne.
1953 General Muhammad Naguib becomes the first Nubian to rule Egypt since 343 B.C.E.
1954 Muhammad Naguib overthrown by general Gamal Abdel Nasser who forms the United Arab Republic in 1958.
1970 Anwar el-Sadat becomes president after death of Nasser.
1981 Hosni Mubarak becomes president after assassination of Sadat.

Nasser

Sadat

Mubarak

Western Asiatic immigrates from area that was home to the Hyksos and later the Persians.

Summary

With the discovery of the ancient city of Ta-Seti, it can now be said with impunity that the "oldest monarchy in the world" and indeed the progenitor of the monarchies of Kemet were of indigenous African (black, Negroid, etc.) stock. The first 12 dynasties (3150-1783 B.C.E.) were also African. It was during this time period that Kemet was unified as one nation. All the pyramids were built and the great literary texts (which comprise the *Book of the Dead*) were written.

The first military and foreign occupation of Kemet was the Hyksos invasion, 1783-1550 B.C.E. The Hyksos were foreigners from Palestine and surrounding areas who immigrated into Lower Kemet and gradually seized control. The word Hyksos is of Kemetic origin and means "chieftains of foreign countries." Historians credit them with introducing the horse and chariot into Kemet, but it is important to note that this foreign conquest was totally destructive, and that no architecture, art or literature was produced during the period that Kemet was under siege.

After approximately 233 years of rulership, the Hyksos were driven out of Kemet by native African forces from the south, who not only moved the seat of government back to Waset (Thebes/Luxor), but extended their boarder into Asia to minimize the possibility of further invasion from the north. It was during the Eighteenth and Nineteenth Dynasties of the Middle Kingdom that Kemet instituted the greatest architectural and military expansion in its entire history. The wonderful temples at Luxor and Karnak are a living testament to this grand epoch in human civilization.

For the next 500 years Kemet experienced unprecedented growth and development, which was followed by 300 years of internal turmoil and political instability. While teetering once more on the brink of uncertainty, the ruling body of Kemet looked to the south for leadership. Salvation came in the personage of the Nubian King Piankhi, who secured the northern boarders and once again unified the two lands, thus paving the way for Kemet to experience what would inevitability be her final years of glory.

In 525 B.C.E., Kemet experienced the first of two devastating invasions by the Persians. The Persian rulers were merciless and after a brief defeat by the army of Kemet in 380 B.C.E., they returned with a vengeance in 343 B.C.E. From that fateful day onward, Kemet would never again be ruled by an indigenous African population.

The Persians were driven from Egypt by Alexander of Macedonia in 332 B.C.E. After securing the country, Alexander began developing plans to build a great city on the Mediterranean coast in honor of his latest conquest, but he died before this dream was realized. All of the lands that had been conquered by Alexander's troops were subsequently divided

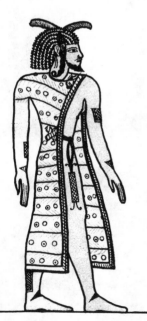

Libyan

among his generals. Egypt fell into the hands of the general Ptolemy who honored his fallen commander by completing the plans for the construction of the new city, which he named *Alexandria* in honor of his former commander-in-chief.

The rulership of the Ptolemaic kings was unique because of their desire to immerse themselves into the traditions of Ancient Kemet. Following an age-old custom, these Greek rulers married into the Egyptian royal families in an attempt to maintain dynastic rulership, which was passed on by the queen to her offspring. The last of the Ptolemies to rule Egypt was Cleopatra VII, who wooed both Julius Caesar and Marc Antony in an attempt to prevent Roman control and occupation of Egypt. Cleopatra was unsuccessful in her attempts to maintain Egypt's sovereignty, which became a colony of Rome in 30 B.C.E. after her death.

The Romans, like the Greeks before them, saw great value in the civilization of Kemet and incorporated those elements most easily discernable into their culture. Egypt's greatest gift to Rome was her ability to supply unlimited food to her mighty army. During this period, Egypt was referred to as the "Bread Basket of the Roman Empire." But in the final analysis it was not the Roman army that ultimately brought Egypt to her knees and destroyed her, it was the newly emerging religion of Christianity. From its earliest beginnings, Christianity was embraced more readily in Egypt than anywhere else worldwide, primarily because of its similarity to the ancient religion of Kemet. Coptic, which became the official language of the early Christians, is essentially nothing more than the language of Kemet (hieroglyphs) written in Greek letters.

The *ankh* was the ancient Kemetic symbol for life. It represented the unification of the feminine and masculine forces in the universe and the creation of new life. It portrayed both the physical and spiritual aspects of life. Symbolically, the oval represents the womb, the vertical shaft depicts the phallus and the horizontal bar expresses the coming into existence of a new life, resulting from the union of man and woman.

The *cross* is a symbol common to Christianity. During the Middle Ages, the cross was a symbol of the Christian belief in the resurrection of Jesus the Christ. Much later, Christians began to emphasize the death and suffering of Jesus and portrayed his image on crucifixes. A crucifix is a cross with an image of the dying Jesus.

Within the Ipet Isut there is an interesting statue which shows King Thutmose III standing between images of Mut and Amon-Ra. This statue was one of many structures defaced during the conquest of Kemet by the Christians. The upper and lower body parts of Mut and Amon-Ra were strategically chiselled away so as to form a crucifix.

Aset and Heru

In 333 A.C.E., Constantine declared Christianity the official religion of the Roman empire and ordered the closing of all Egyptian temples, in an attempt to eradicate any and all competing religious systems. The *African Trinity* of Ausar, Aset and Heru (Osiris, Isis and Horus), which existed for more than 4,000 years, was replaced with a Trinity, which consisted of *The Father, Son and Holy Ghost.* In 325 A.C.E., the Christian bishops who met at the Council of Nicea introduced a new religious theology which contained doctrines similar to the African concepts of a *virgin birth, resurrection* and *salvation.* This new version of Christianity lacked significant African elements, which where viewed as competitive and were subsequently outlawed by the Byzantine emperors.

Sometime during the reign of the Emperor Justinian (527-565 A.C.E), the last of the Egyptian priests were driven out of the Temple of Philae in Upper Egypt. The structure was then converted into a Christian church. During this same time the written languages of the ancient Kemites (Medu Netcher and demotic) were so totally repressed that the ability to read them would remain shrouded in mystery for more than 1,300 years.

During the next 1,500 years, Egypt was systemically raped and pillaged by an untold number of foreign rulers and explorers, who destroyed monuments, robbed tombs and wreaked havoc throughout the land. Napoleon's conquest of Egypt in 1798, and the subsequent publication of *Description de L'Egypte,* ignited a new interest in ancient history which led to the development of the science of Egyptology.

More has been learned about ancient Kemet within the last two hundred years than any other time within the past two millennium. No other nation on earth has had the privilege of 3,000 years of cultural and historical continuity, nor has been the object of such intense international scrutiny. Modern archaeologists, geologists and other scientists are constantly uncovering treasures and reevaluating their knowledge of ancient Kemet. Based upon their new findings, it is certain that the length and breadth of this great civilization is yet to be fully realized.

Many reputations have been made, and others shattered, with the discovery of each new tomb and artifact or reinterpretation of ancient papyrus texts. Very few scholars are willing to relinquish old views in light of newly discovered data which contradict the norm. Ancient artifacts not only have to be unearthed, they sometimes have to be rescued from contemporary misinterpretations. John Anthony West discusses the reticence some scholars express when they are exposed to new theories:

> Nobody likes being proved wrong, but in the case of the scholar or scientist, a sound theory that contradicts views held and pursued for a lifetime pulls the rug out from under his or her ego and a familiar paradoxical

situation develops. The people professionally engaged in discovering the "truth," are those, psychologically, least capable of accepting the "truth" if it happens to contradict what they already believe. Nowhere is this more apparent than in Egyptology. As we examine the many controversial theories, it will become obvious that most of them could be easily tested, and either accepted or refuted, if only the parties involved, be they in the orthodox or unorthodox camps, would take the trouble to consider the evidence presented by the opposition.

The modern Egyptian is the by-product of countless peoples who have occupied, invaded and traded in North Africa for thousands of years. The Persians, Greeks, Romans, Arabs, Turks, French, British, Germans and countless other nationalities, have intermingled with the native African population to produce a new people who have inherited, by right of possession of the land, the legacy of African peoples. The Egypt of today is not the Kemet of yesterday. Yes, the land is still the same and the monuments evoke memories of ages long gone, but the people and their spirit are profoundly different.

Chapter Three
The Historical Accomplishments of Kemet

One of the two "aker lions" which symbolically guard the entrance to the New York Public Library.

New Perspectives of an African Civilization

The nations of the "First World" are often held in high esteem for the rest of the world to idolize, and with good reason. Modern technology has created rockets which have taken man to the moon and has launched satellites to explore the furthest regions of the galaxy. The marvelous advances in computer sciences now make it possible to store the contents of libraries onto discs no larger than a long-playing record. But despite these technological advances, modern man cannot recreate the technology that built the Great Pyramid, mummified the kings of Kemet, or built the Temple of Ipet Isut (Karnak).

The admiration of the accomplishments of Kemet has given rise to an entire field of study named in its honor-*Egyptology*-and the unearthing of her priceless treasures, which has brought wealth and fame to archaeologists and their financial backers. No nation in the history of civilization has had a greater influence on the arts and sciences than Kemet and it is there where one can still find the only remaining one of the "Seven Wonders of the World."

The lion was a symbol of great importance in the Nile Valley and has had a profound influence on contemporary society. The twin lions that flank the entrances to most buildings represent concepts which had their origin in Kemet. The image of the *aker lions* (below) shows two lions with their backs turned to the sun on the horizon. They both represent "two aspects of the sun: that which goes to sleep behind the mountain and that which rises from it in the morning." The lion on the left corresponds to "yesterday" and faces west, the lion on the right faces east and represents "tomorrow." The presence of two lions on either side of a doorway (left) represents the role of the lions as the "keepers who open and shut the gate" into the worlds yesterday, today or tomorrow. This same concept is symbolized by statues of lions that flank the entrances to libraries, museums, bridges or other buildings.

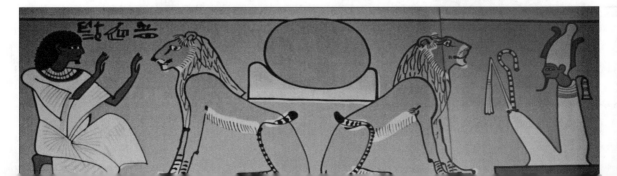

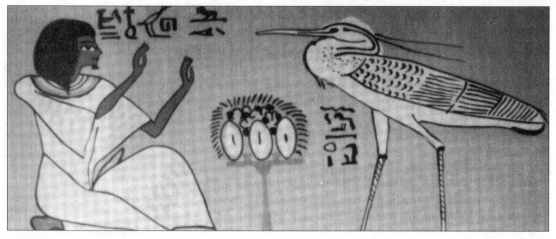

The *Benu bird* is an ancient mythical symbol which represents the regeneration of the soul. In the scene above, the soul of Ani makes an offering to the benu. The relationship between the *benu* of Kemet and the *phoenix* of Greece is strikingly similar. In both myths, only one bird lived at a time, and it was always a male. According to the fable, the bird lived for 500 years and was burned on a funeral pyre. A young and new bird rose from the ashes, carried the remains of its father in an egg of myrrh and placed it on the alter of the the sun Netcher in the *City of the Sun* (Heliopolis) in Kemet. The long life of the benu, and later that of the phoenix, became symbols of immortality and spiritual rebirth. Both birds represented the sun, which dies in its flames each evening and is resurrected each morning. The phoenix became the symbol of Atlanta, Georgia after 1865 when the city was rebuilt following its burning during the Civil War. It is also used in the city seal of Phoenix, Arizona.

For thousands of years various European leaders have held Egypt in high esteem and looked to her as the progenitor of world civilization and as the seat of ancient knowledge. Admiration for the accomplishments of the ancient Egyptians was so strong that it prompted the following remarks from Henry H. Gorringe, lieutenant commander of the United States Navy in 1882:

> Egypt itself is a book of history, one of God's great monumental records....It was the birthplace of literature, the cradle of science and art, the garden and garner of the world....In the branches of decorative art and the science of architecture they were undoubtedly far in advance of us at the present day....The architectural types of all other structures of antiquity sink into insignificance when compared with those of Egypt. The Egyptians were the first to observe the course of the planets, and their observations led them to regulate the year from the course of the sun. They were a wonderful race, combining within themselves all the branches which adorn, beautify, and add to the reputation of a people when directed in the right channel.

Since the development of the Black Studies movement in the 1960's and the expansion of Negro History Week into Black History Month, February has come to be regarded as a time for the official recognition of the accomplishments of African people. Over the years, a number of major corporations have helped to promote "Black History Month" by sponsoring scholarships and creating calendars, posters and advertisements depicting the many accomplishments of African people.

Of the many ads produced for Black History Month, one has generated particular interest within the African American community. This ad depicts four unmistakably black Egyptian figures and a caption which reads "Before There Was American History, There Was Black History." One of the reasons for the

Before There Was American History, There Was Black History.

People of Kush, from a wall painting in the tomb of Seti I, around 1300 B.C.

History, it's been said, is biography. Yet some of the world's greatest biographies, black biographies, are all but lost to history.

Sundiata. Mansa Musa. Sunni Ali. Askia Muhammad. Not exactly household names, but they were honored in their time as leaders of empires. Yet it appears their honors have vanished along with their empires.

But they weren't the end of black history. Only the beginning. Because black history is an ongoing entity; a progression of brilliant biographies still being written.

And this time, they won't be lost. American history could itself be said to have begun with a piece of black history when the death of Crispus Attucks in the Boston Massacre made him the first of America's 600,000 war dead.

Dr. Daniel Hale Williams made black history, if not world history, when he performed the first successful open heart surgery. Edward M. Bouchet made history when Yale made him the first black in America to be awarded a doctorate. James B. Parsons went into the history books as the first black federal judge in the continental U.S.

Charlotte Ray joined black history when she became America's first black woman lawyer. Madame C.J. Walker, when she became America's first millionaire black woman.

Black biographies have made and will continue to make black history in more cities than even Eastern Airlines flies to, which is more cities in Latin America, Florida, and the Caribbean than any other airline. That's a lot of cities. But that's a lot of history, too.

EASTERN
We've Got Your Ticket.

© 1988 Eastern Air Lines, Inc

The myth of Ausar (Osiris) was the earliest recorded story of a god-man who was symbolically crucified, resurrected from death and reigned eternally in heaven. The people of the Nile Valley believed if they lived righteously, in harmony with the teachings of Ausar, they would inherit eternal life. In the Nile Valley he became a powerful symbol and was associated with the physical and spiritual rebirth of man. Later, Ausar was associated with the essential element of nature, which represented the physical rebirth of vegetation. This concept of a "resurrected Christ" was the prototype for the numerous religious beliefs which later surfaced throughout the world.

The figure to the right is a portrait of the first "Trinity" (Holy Royal Family) in human history. It portrays Heru, Ausar and Aset.

ad's popularity is its portrayal of Egyptians as "Black" Africans and its association with a "legitimate" corporate entity, the now defunct Eastern Airlines.

This specific advertisement has also been reproduced on T-shirts sold throughout the United States, and on papyrus scrolls which are sold in Cairo, Egypt. The cultural exclusivity associated with the marketing of these two products is most interesting. In Egypt, the aforementioned papyrus art is displayed solely to groups of African American tourists; while in America, the ad ran only during Black History Month - and only in *black* publications. It is as if the only time one can be interested in Black History is during the month of February and the only people interested in black history are black people. The history of Kemet should be important to everyone, not only because it is the history of *Black* people, but because it is the history of a people who have had a profound impact on world civilization.

Every culture has had its classical period, a time of high achievement which provided the social, moral and intellectual impetus for succeeding generations. For Western culture, its classical period began in ancient Greece. For the ancient Greeks, their classical period began in Africa, in a country called Kemet. Herodotus, the reputed "father of history," provided us with a written testimonial of Egypt's relationship to Greece in the fifth century B.C.E.

Early Astronomy and The Creation of the Calendar

Practically all of the art, science, architecture, religion and philosophy of Nile Valley civilization was directly related to man's interpretation of his immediate environment. The sun, stars, moon, plants and animal life all appeared to have a relationship with one another; and after observation over a period of hundreds of years, it became clear that the movement and position of the sun and the moon had a direct effect on all objects on the planet earth.

The drawing above illustrates the Netcherw ascending the "Stairway to Heaven" which leads to the observatory located on the roof of the temple at Dendera. The 14 figures represent the 14 days of the waxing (growing) moon. On the right of this scene is a symbol which illustrates the full moon on the 15th day, to the right of the moon stands the figure of the Netcher Djhuiti, who is associated with the full moon.

After studying the heavens, the astronomers of Kemet developed stellar, lunar and solar calendars as a means of regulating agricultural, religious and civic activities. They also predicted eclipses, plotted the movement of numerous stars, described the method for determining the phases of the moon, and identified five planets. They called Mercury, *Sebku*; Venus, *Bennu-Asar*; Mars, *Heru-Khuti*; Saturn, *Heru-Ka-per* and Jupiter, *Heru-Ap-Sheta-Taui*.

The effectiveness of any calendar is determined by its accurate timing of the cyclical appearance of a specific heavenly body. The moon was easy to identify because of the apparent changes in its shape. The lunar month was determined by the interval between successive full moons, which is a period of precisely 29 days, 12 hours, 44 minutes, and 2.7 seconds. The word "month" is derived from the word *mona*, which means "moon". This lunar calendar was useful, but it had shortcomings because of its differences with the solar year. Twelve lunar months is approximately 354 days which is about 11 days shorter than the true solar year, and 13 lunar months is about 383 and 1/2 days, which is 18 and 1/2 days longer than the solar year.

The daily apparent motion of the sun provided a more accurate unit of measurement. Eventually, the solar day and the changing seasons of the year gave rise to the development of a calendar based on the solar year. The solar year is defined as the time it takes the planet Earth to make one complete revolution around the sun, which is a period of exactly 365 days, 5 hours, 48 minutes and 46 seconds.

The astronomers of Kemet were the first to develop a solar calendar which divided the year into 365 days, consisting of 12 months of 30 days each. Five additional days were added to the end of the year, which corresponded to the birth of the Gods (Netcherw) Osiris, Isis, Horus, Set and Nephthys, who were the progenitors of the human race (12 X 30 + 5 = 365 days).

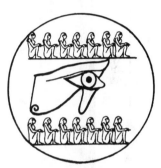

The 14 Netcherw who were associated with the 14 days of the waning moon.

The astronomical knowledge that emerged from Kemet was responsible for giving the world the calendar year of 365 days, the division of a circle into 360 segments and the designation of the second, minute and hour as measurements of time. The word *hour* is derived from the word *Horus* (Heru,) who was a Netcher associated with the sun. The right eye of Heru represents the sun and the time of day is determined by the position of the Earth relative to Heru (the sun). Various timekeeping devices, such as the tekhen, clepsydra and shadow clock, were developed to record the passage of time.

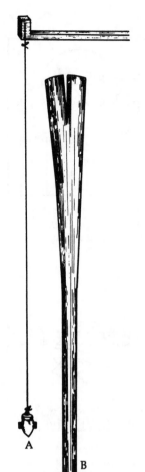

The astronomical instrument (above) is the oldest known tool used to survey the stars. It is now housed in the Berlin Museum. The plumb line (A) was attached to a handle and the other instrument (B) was held over a designated point on the ground while the astronomer viewed through the slit at the top toward a celestial body. While looking over a rod, which was held between the observer and the observed object, until the rod was aligned with the object, the scientist could determine the exact meridian and observe each star that crossed it. This process allowed for the precise measuring of time and led to the development of accurate star maps and other celestial data.

The year was subsequently divided into three seasons of four months duration, which were called the *inundation*, the *cultivation* and the *harvest*. Each 30-day month was divided into 3 weeks of 10 days, and each day was then divided into 24 hours. The word *hour* is derived from the name of the God (Netcher) *Horus* (Heru), who was associated with the sun. The hour of the day represents the position of the sun (Horus/Heru) relative to the planet Earth at any given time of the day or night. This particular calendarial system was based upon the civil year of Kemet. Otto Neugebauer, author of *The Exact Sciences in Antiquity*, referred to it as "the only intelligent calendar that has ever existed in human history."

The Kemites realized that their civil calendar was imperfect because it lacked a quarter of a day each year relative to its *sidereal orbit* - the exact period in which the earth makes one complete revolution around the sun. To correct this error, a more precise *sidereal* calender was introduced around 4236 B.C.E. This new calendar alleviated the necessity of adding one day every four years (leap year) by adding a *new year* every 1,460 years (4 X 365 = 1,460). Both the civil year calendar and the astronomical year calendar were used simultaneously and were in synchronization with one another every 1,460 years when the first day of each calendar coincided with the helical rising of the "dog star," Sothis (Sirius), which also coincided with the inundation - the annual flooding of the Nile.

Successive civilizations found it difficult to maintain these complex time-keeping systems and created their own. The Roman calendar, which was introduced around 738 B.C.E., was said to have been borrowed from the Greek calendar; it consisted of 10 months and a year of 304 days. The 10 months were named *Martius, Aptilis, Maius, Janius, Quintilis, Sextilis, September, October, November* and *December*. The last six names were derived from the words for the numbers, *five, six, seven, eight, nine* and *ten*.

In 452 B.C.E., the Emperor Numa added the month of January to the beginning of the year and February to the end of the year in an attempt to make the Roman calendar correspond to the solar year. Numa then created a new month called *Mercedinus*, which had 22 or 23 days, and inserted it between February 23 and 24 every other year. This manipulation of the calendar caused the Roman year to shift three months ahead of the seasons, thereby causing autumn to appear in July and winter in September.

In 46 B.C.E., at the invitation of Julius Caesar, Cleopatra visited Rome and was accompanied by their son Caesarion, her brother Ptolemy XIV and numerous servants and scientists. Cleopatra's astronomers corroborated with the Roman astronomer Sosigenes and made recommendations for the improvement of the old Roman calendar. A new calendar was then developed which consisted of 365 and 1/4 days. The year was divided into 12 months of 30 and 31 days, with the exception of February, which had 29 days and 30 days every four years. The beginning of the new year was also moved from March 1, to January 1.

In honor of the new *Julian calendar*, the Romans renamed the month of Quintilis after Julius Caesar and called it *July*, which was also the month of his birth. Upon the death of Caesar in 44 B.C.E., the month of Sextilis was renamed *August* after the new emperor Augustus. Not to be overshadowed by the memory of the late emperor, Augustus removed a day from the month of February and added it to August in order to make his month as long as Julius Caesar's. As a result of these two maniacal manipulations, July and August are the only consecutive months with 31 days each, while the other months alternate between 30 and 31 days. February, the obvious exception, has been reduced to 28 days per year, with an additional day added every four years. All of these changes created so much confusion that a rhyme was written to remind us of the number of days in each month - *Thirty days hath September, April, June and November...*

Augustus

The Julian calendar remained in use for more than 1,500 years, but because it was actually 11 minutes and 14 seconds longer than the solar year, it eventually led to a shifting of the dates of the seasons; and by the year 1580 A.C.E., the spring equinox fell on March 11, instead of March 21. In order to correct this error, a new calendar was introduced in 1582 by the Roman Pope Gregory XIII. This calendar is supposed to be based on the year that Jesus the Christ was born (although the actual date is unknown). Dates before the birth of Jesus are listed as B.C., or *before Christ*. Dates after that year are listed as A.D., or *anno Domini* (in the year of our Lord). Non-Christian references to dates are written B.C.E., for *before common era* and A.C.E, for after *common era*.

The Gregorian calendar corrected the difference between the sun and calendar by deleting ten days from the month of October, which restored the next equinox to its proper date. Pope Gregory further decreed that February would have an extra day only in century years divisible by 400. In years that cannot be divided by 400, such as 1700, 1800 and 1900, the extra day in February is not added. This calendar is based on the tropical year of 365.2425 days and is so accurate that the difference between the calendar and solar years is now only approximately 26 seconds. All of this pales in comparison when one considers that the Kemetic calendar, which was introduced approximately 6,228 years ago, was based upon a year of exactly 365.2422 days.

Other calendars currently in use worldwide

The Hebrew calendar, which was said to have begun with the Creation 3,760 years and 3 months before the beginning of the Christian era. This calendar is based on the moon and consists of 12 months that are alternately 30 and 29 days long. An extra 29-day month is added 7 times during every 19-year period. The year 1992 in the Gregorian calendar corresponds to the year 5752 in the Hebrew calendar.

The Islamic calendar begins with Muhammad's flight from Mecca to Medina, which occurred in 622 A.C.E. by the Gregorian calendar. This is a lunar calendar which has 12 months, alternately 30 and 29 days in length. The Islamic year has 354 days, and divides time into cycles of 30-years long. During each cycle, 19 years have the regular 354 days, and 11 years have 355 days each. The Islamic calendar is considered to be as accurate as the Gregorian calendar. The year 1992 in the Gregorian calendar corresponds to the year 1412 in the Islamic calendar.

Astronomy, Astrology and Agriculture

The study of the heavens and the mapping of the stars is an age-old science which requires centuries of observation and analysis. The early inhabitants of the Nile Valley identified groups of stars which were stretched across the sky, and whose rising followed each other by a period of ten days. These stars were associated with various Gods and called *decans*. The division of the Kemetic year into 36 weeks of ten days each meant that each week was ruled over by a specific decan or constellation. This is the process by which it was determined, thousands of years ago, that a circle would consist of 360 degrees (36 X 10 = 360).

The people of Kemet further divided the heavens into 12 divisions in the southern sky, 12 divisions in the northern sky and 12 divisions in the central sky. These 36 divisions were then divided among the three seasons and from that delineation emerged the regions for the 12 signs of the zodiac. Each zodiacal sign was associated with a decan who was referred to as one of the *watchers of the hours;* they were regarded as messengers of the greater gods or of Horus himself, hence the origin of the word *horoscope.*

The association of each zodiacal sign was purely symbolic, and represented the relationship between the appearance of certain stars overhead and specific activity taking place on the earth below. According to John Jackson, in his book *Introduction to African Civilization:*

> When the agriculturists of the Archaic Civilization of Africa were faced with the problem of determining the proper seasons for planting their crops by observing the motions of the stars, they projected the animal symbols of the totemic hunters into the skies, to become the Signs of the Zodiac.

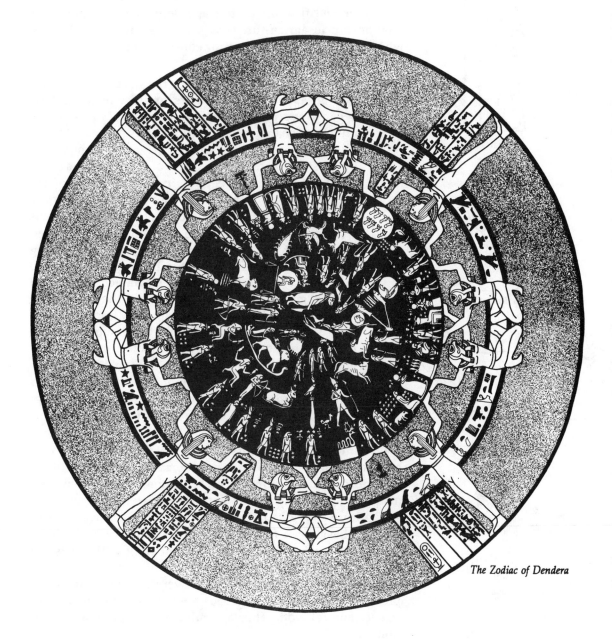

The Zodiac of Dendera

The original zodiac was located in the ceiling of an observatory in the Temple of Dendera. It was "discovered" by Napoleon's troops in 1799 and dynamited from the ceiling. After a series of owners, it was sold to Louis XVIII for 150,000 francs and is now located in the Louvre Museum. The inner circle of figures, which move counterclockwise like the stars, shows the astrological signs of the zodiac circling around the North Pole, which is symbolized by the jackal. The outer circle of figures represents the 36 decans, each one symbolizes the ten-day weeks of the Kemetic year. The 12 figures outside of the circle represent the 12 months of the year and their arms, the 24 hours of the day.

Aquarius

Taurus

Leo

Further clarification of the astrological signs and their relationship to agriculture was presented by Count Volney who offered us the following for consideration:

> The Ethiopian of Thebes named the stars of the inundation or *Aquarius*, those stars under which the Nile began to overflow; stars of the ox or bull *(Taurus)*, those under which they began to plow; stars of the lion *(Leo)*, those under which that animal, driven from the desert by thirst, appeared on the banks of the Nile; stars of the sheaf, or of the harvest virgin *(Virgo)*, those of the reaping season; stars of the lamb *(Aries)*, stars of the two kids *(Gemini)*, those under which these precious were brought forth....In the same manner he named the stars of the crab, those where the sun, having arrived at the tropic, retreated by a slow retrograde motion like the crab or *Cancer*. He named the stars of the wild goat or *Capricorn*, those where the sun, having reached the highest point in its annuary tract...imitates the goat, who delights to climb to the summit of the rocks. He named the stars of the balance, or *Libra*, those where the days and nights being equal, seemed in equilibrium, like that instrument; and the stars of the *Scorpion*, those where certain periodical winds brings vapors, burning like the venom of the scorpion.

Virgo

It is important to understand the relationship that exists between the astrological signs of the zodiac and agriculture. The ability to plant, grow, harvest and store food is essential to maintaining stability among a people who were once nomadic. Agriculture gave rise to the development of culture. Once a people's basic need for food is satisfied, they can then focus attention on other critically important philosophical issues such as *who am I, where did I come from and what is my reason for being?* It was the attempt to answer these and many other profound questions that led to the development of writing, science and religion. Thus agriculture is the path to civilization.

Some scholars, including the noted Egyptologist Budge, assert that the Egyptians borrowed their knowledge of the signs of the zodiac from the Greeks who, in turn, derived their astronomical knowledge from the Babylonians.   Albert Churchward strongly disagreed with Budge and offered the following rebuttal:

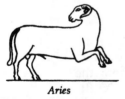

Aries

> The Egyptians had worked out all the architecture of the heavens, and their priests carried all of the same with them to all parts of the world....The Babylonians copied and obtained all their knowledge from the Egyptians, we are surprised that Dr. Budge should write that they

Cancer

borrowed from the Greeks; they were old and degenerating in decay before the Greek nation was born! Well may he say that "it is a subject of conjecture at what period the Babylonians first divided the heavens into sections, etc.," because they never did; what they knew they borrowed either direct from the Egyptians or Sumerians—the latter obtained it from Egypt.

Gemini

Astronomy and Religious Architecture

Astronomy, the calendar and astrology all played a major role in the development of myth, ritual and religion in the Nile Valley. The impact that Nile Valley religion and temple architecture had on world civilization will be discussed in a later chapter, but it is important to establish the relationship between astronomy and religious architecture.

Many of the primary Gods (Netcherw) of the Nile Valley were associated with celestial bodies. A primary component of temple architecture was the precise alignment of these religious structures to either the sun or the moon; the four cardinal points, the summer solstice or winter solstice; the spring equinox or autumn equinox; or star systems (constellations). The purpose for this exact orientation was to align the temple to a heavenly body in such a manner so as to capture the light (or spirit) of that body inside the "Holy of Holies," which was the most sacred shrine in every temple. This was the place where the priest or king could meet the spirit of God face to face.

Capricorn

There are a number of temples in Upper Kemet, Sudan and Ethiopia which are oriented to the bright star Alphi Centuri. The great Temple of Ipet Isut (Karnak) is oriented to the setting summer solstice sun, and the Temples of Edfu and Philae are oriented to sunrise at the autumn equinox. The pyramids of Lower Kemet are oriented on an east and west axis to the sun and the pyramids of Upper Kemet are oriented on a southeast solar axis.

Libra

Very little is known as to how the ancient Africans plotted the sun, moon and stars, but Cheikh Anta Diop makes it very clear that the method of astronomical observation of these architectural structures represent "the existence of a sound astronomical science." Diop further states that "the number of monuments that are oriented in relation to the four cardinal points, with an error always below one degree to the true north, eliminates any notion of chance."

Scorpio

The stars of the sign of Pisces, which follows Aquarius, indicate the fertilization of the land following the inundation. The fish represent fecundating aspects of the Nile River. The stars of Sagittarius portray a being with two heads, one looking forward and the other looking backward. It is a symbol associated with the completion of a successful harvest season and the anticipation of a productive harvest next season.

Sagittarius

Pisces

Maat is associated with the seven cardinal virtues, the keys to human perfectibility: truth, justice, propriety, harmony, balance, reciprocity and order. The symbolic representation of Maat as a human figure with outstretched hands and wings is the prototype of the image of the angel found in the world's major Western religions. The ostrich feather and the balance are also symbols of Maat and the precepts she represents. The seven virtues and the 42 admonitions of Maat were the guidelines of correct behavior and the standard against which the soul of the deceased would be judged. People who lived their lives in accordance with the principles of Maat were guaranteed a just reward in the afterlife after the judgement of their soul.

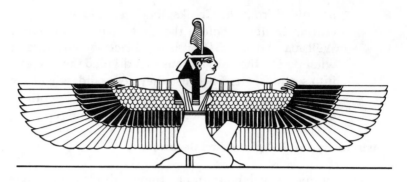

The Development of Symbols and Symbolic Thought

...Man having remarked in the beings which surrounded him certain qualities distinctive and proper to each species, and having thence derived a name by which to designate them, he found in the same source an ingenious mode of generalizing his ideas: and transferring the name already invented to every thing which bore any resemblance or analogy, he enriched his language with a perpetual round of metaphors.

Count Volney,
Ruins of Empires

The divine atributes of Maat were the prime inspiration for the concept of the angel in Christian theology. The fifteenth-century painting of "St. Michael Weighing Souls" (below) portrays the winged image of a male weighing the soul of a man on the scale of judgement.

Symbols and symbolic thought played a vital role in the development of all aspects of Nile Valley civilization. There was no dimension of life that was devoid of it. Architecture, religion, science, medicine, clothing, jewelry, philosophy, writing and many other facets of everyday living were influenced by varying forms of symbolic expression. It was a language which communicated on several levels simultaneously. The degree to which one understood the abstract and or practical aspects of symbolic thought was determined by the extent of one's education.

The development of agriculture required the services of individuals who were capable of plotting the heavens and identifying the appearance or disappearance of certain stars which foretold the return of the annual floods, the rainy season and of the precise times to sow the various grains. These early astronomers were invaluable to their community and were exempt from the rigors of manual labor. Their responsibilities were to study the heavens, to catalog and codify their findings and transmit the information to the appropriate officials.

Over a period of many generations, the astronomers/priests became well acquainted with the "secrets of the universe." They discovered the movements of the stars and planets, the relationship between their phases and their influence on vegetation, human beings, animals and many of the various elements and minerals of the planet. As their knowledge grew, new areas of specialized interest evolved, thus allowing man to better understand his relationship with the infinite power that is called God.

The universe was viewed as the omnipotent expression of one great Supreme Being, which manifested itself within all of the functions and principles that govern the universe and maintain balance and harmony. These facets of the one supreme God were referred to collectively as *Netcherw* and individually as *Netcher*. Each manifestation of a Netcher was associated with a divine aspect of God, and was represented by a specific symbol. As time passed, the Netcherw became known as the many forces of *nature,* for example., the God of water, the God of air, the God of the earth, etc.

Animals were usually selected to represent the qualities of a specific Netcher because the nature of an animal was unique to that particular creature and remained constant over the years. The following are examples of animal traits and their association with specific Netcherw:

Djhuiti

The *falcon* is a symbol for the sun and light, because of its rapid flight and its ability to soar into the highest regions of the air where the light abounds. The Netcher Heru is represented by the falcon and his right eye symbolizes the sun and the sun's ability, like that of God, to see all things at all times. The eye is also the organ which perceives light and represents the process of spiritual awareness. Similar attributes have been incorporated into native American names such as *Hawk Eye* and *Eagle Eye.*

The *ibis* is a bird that sleeps with its head folded beneath its wing and its body assumes the shape of a heart, which was regarded as the seat of the soul and true intelligence. The footstep of an ibis was said to be equal to one cubit, which was considered a sacred unit of measurement. The Netcher Djhuiti was portrayed with an ibis head and he represented divine articulation of speech and intelligence. He was the keeper of the sacred cubic and the creator of science, writing and medicine. He was known to the Greeks as Thoth and Hermes. The Romans identified him with Mercury.

The *scarab* beetle symbolizes the resurrection and immortality of God as represented by the sun. The scarab lays its eggs in a ball of dung, which it rolls across the ground in a direction that follows the path of the sun. The heat of the sun warms the eggs inside the dung ball, which undergo a metamorphosis through the larva and nymph stages before emerging into the light of day as winged scarabs. The ball of dung symbolizes *matter,* the eggs *spiritual potential* and the newly born scarab represents *spiritual rebirth.* The Netcher Kheprea symbolizes this transformative quality and becomes an excellent metaphor for the process of resurrection.

The eyes of the falcon (and other birds of prey) are so keen they can spot their quarry at distances of over a mile. Their eyes act like telescopes which magnify objects with crystal clarity. This ability is due to the structure of the interior of their eyes where vision cells give off electrical signals that travel through the optic nerve to the brain. The eyes of birds of prey contain more than one billion vision cells while the human eye contains only about 130 million. This enhanced capacity for sight is due to the unique structure of the eye of the falcon, and thus was used as the perfect symbol to represent spiritual vision within man.

Scarab beetles

Set

Anpu

The _ass_ is a stubborn, passoniate and often overburdened animal. It symbolizes the recalcitrant personality of humans. This personality, like the ass, bears the weight of our suffering and carries us through life but often refuses to go in the direction we think is best. The ass symbolizes the Netcher Set because, like that animal, he is also of a reddish color. Set represents the rebellious nature of the spirit and that which is often referred to as evil. We see this symbol in the gospels when Sampson defeats his enemies with the *jawbone of an ass* and when Jesus the Christ rides into Jerusalem mounted on the Ass.

The _jackal_ (dog) feasts on carrion which must be consumed at a specific point of decay in order for it to be of sustenance. This natural instinct of the jackal symbolizes the qualities of *fine judgement.* The jackal is represented by the Netcher Anpu (Anubis) who was responsible for adjusting the balance of the scale that weighed the heart/soul of the deceased at judgement. The natural homing instincts of the jackal are also reflected in Anpu who prepares the corpse to serve as a receptacle for the reincarnated spirit before guiding it through the underworld.

Aspects of God were also attributed to the Netcher associated with the Nile River who was called *Hapi.* The annual flooding of the Nile was a guarantee from the creator that water would be available for farming, fishing, drinking and other enterprises so vitally important to the maintenance of life. Hapi was portrayed as an elderly male with large flabby female breasts that symbolized one who had nursed or breast-fed an entire nation. Hapi was the original "Old Man River," and his name is probably the source of the word *"happy."*

Hapi

One of the most significantly important symbols in the Nile Valley was the sun. The worship of the sun was a very complex affair, which continued to evolve throughout the ages. The people of Kemet not only deified the physical structure of the sun, but also considered its many different aspects: its light, its heat and its rays. Various Netcherw were designated to represent the physical sun, the intellectual sun, the power of the sun, the sun in the heavens and the sun in its resting place.

The representation of the sun as a supreme Netcher is understandable when you examine the importance of its relationship to the Earth. This planet, and all life on it, exists because of the sun. The sun's light illuminates the sky during the day and overpowers the light of the stars (Netcherw/Decans), which are always present, but cannot be seen because of the intensity of the sunlight. After the sun sets, its presence can still be seen reflecting off the surface of the moon and the planets that are millions of miles away. The sun, therefore, makes a fine symbol for the omnipresent power of a Netcher.

The most significant sun-Netcher was Ra or Re, who represented the creative aspect of God, and whose visible expression is the sun. He was the principal responsible for all creation and was referred to in the sacred text as self-created and all-powerful. The term "a ray of light," refers to this Netcher. Another significant sun-Netcher was Amen or Amon, the personification of the sun after setting, when it was hidden from view in the underworld. Amen was depicted as a man with the head and horns of a ram. In the Medu Netcher (The words of God, later referred to by the Greeks as hieroglyphs, sacred carvings) the word "ram" means "concealment" and one of the common names for Amen was "the Concealed One." In modern language the word "Amen," which is often used at the conclusion of prayers, also means "the Hidden One." These two concepts are identical, but what has been lost over the ages is the deeper meaning of the symbolism and the power of the word.

The awesome force of the sun was recognized as the primary activator for life. When the sun rose on the eastern bank of the Nile all life began. Birds would sing its praises, man would begin his work, flowers would blossom and insects would fly about. Likewise, when the sun set on the west bank of the Nile all activities would cease - until the next morning. This drama of death and rebirth was played out daily in the sky and the east and west banks of the Nile became physical representations of the life and death principles associated with the sun.

The sun was born each morning in the east; therefore, all activities pertaining to life were conducted on the east side of the river where cities, temples and palaces were constructed. The sun was said to die each night when it set in the west so, consequently, the dead were buried on the west bank of the Nile, which is where we find the tombs of the kings, queens and nobles. Upon closer examination, all activities associated with

Amen

The ancient Kemmiu recognized three forms within their language structure, *singular, plural* and *dual*. The singular and plural forms are self-explanatory, the dual is used to refer to a pair of complementary objects or persons. For example:

Netcher	singular
Netcherw	plural
Netcherwy	dual

Tekhen	Singular
Tekhenw	Plural
Tekhenwy	Dual

life and death had a symbolic and spiritual relationship with the forces of nature, which were called the Netcherw.

Nile Valley Religion

From the beginning of time Africans have always had a belief in one god, self-created and all-powerful. Upon observing the wonders of the universe, man began to see the many manifestations of the one *Creator* reflected in all that existed and identified them as aspects of the One, or Netcher. This monotheistic viewpoint saw *everything* as a part of the whole. A Netcher is not God, it is an integral part of that which is God. Similarly, a transmission is not an automobile, but it is an essential component to the function of that automobile, as is every part of that vehicle.

Attempts to portray African religion as polytheistic, anthropomorphic or idolatrous are as repugnant as those who seek to condemn it. Modern religion has angels, archangels, messengers and saints who carry out roles similar to those of the Netcherw. References to Jesus the Christ as "the lamb" is just as anthropomorphic as Amon's association with a ram. References to the spirit of God as a dove is just as anthropomorphic as Het-Heru's (Hathor's) association with a cow.

John Anthony West provided the following commentary on two fundamental aspects of Kemet and world religion, creation myths and the role of man:

> Egyptian religion may be divided into two distinct but complementary and intertwined themes: the creation of the universe, and the creation of man and his role in the universal scheme. The Egyptians expressed their religious ideas through myth and symbolism, not through philosophical explanation. In many ways, myth and symbol are superior means for expressing metaphysical concepts, but it is first necessary to be privy to the inner meaning of the symbolic language employed. The keys to Egypt died with their religion. That is why the subject is so prone to controversy.

In both the Nile Valley account and the Christian account, God is self-created, creates heaven and earth, divides the waters, creates the light and separates it from darkness and creates man. The parallels between these two religious systems are numerous and striking, but because much of the early research on Kemet was conducted by Christians, historical information was doctored to suit their particular religious beliefs. John Jackson gives us an example:

The anthropomorphic representation of team mascots and the naming of sports teams after animals (Chicago Bulls, Denver Broncos, Atlanta Falcons, etc.) does not represent animal worship. On the contrary, these animals merely symbolize the attributes the owners want to project into the consciousness of the team and their fans.

Imagine anthropologists 3,000 years from now digging up the remains of Washington, D.C., uncovering the National Zoo, and discovering that hundreds of animals had been sheltered and fed in this facility while thousands of homeless persons walked the streets. Without knowledge of the role of the zoo in twentieth century society, the social scientists of the future might believe this structure was a multimillion dollars temple complex built for the adoration of animals at a time when humans were allowed to suffer.

The late Professor James Henry Breasted (1865-1935) considered the civilization of Egypt the oldest in the world, and dates the First Dynasty of that country as beginning about 3400 B.C. Sir Flinders Petrie (1853-1942), an equally eminent Egyptologist, dates the beginning of Dynasty I in the year 4777 B.C. There is a discrepancy of nearly two thousand years. How do we account for this? Breasted studied for a doctorate in Egyptology under Professor Eduard Meyer (1855-1930) at the University of Berlin. Meyer, being a Christian, assumed that the world began about 4004 B.C., according to the biblical chronology. Breasted adopted Meyer's chronology, and criticized Petrie and other authorities for adopting an earlier date. The building of the Great Pyramid was begun during... the Third Dynasty. According to Petrie, Dynasty III lasted from 4212 to 3998 B.C. If these dates are correct, the Great Pyramid was erected before the creation of the world according to the Christian chronology. Breasted's dates for the Third Dynasty are 2980-2900 B.C. This fits into the biblical tradition.

The people of the Nile Valley were the first human beings to express a profound belief in a doctrine of everlasting life. They preserved the bodies of their dead by a yet undiscovered process of embalming, and entombed these bodies in elaborately inscribed funerary monuments. Prayers and litanies played a major role in preparing the soul of the recently departed for its journey through the underworld and guaranteed its safe passage to God in the next world.

The so-called "Book of the Dead" was a compilation of the prayers that were inscribed on the walls of the tombs or written on papyrus scrolls, which were buried with the dead. These sacred pronouncements were discovered by the grave robbers who violated these tombs in search of fame and glory, and regarded these writings as "the books of the dead." According to Wallace Budge, celebrated translator of the *Book of the Dead*,

> "these texts were...known to have existed in revised editions and to have been used among the Egyptians from about B.C. 4500 to the early centuries of the Christian era."

Budge admits that the correct name for the "Book of the Dead" is derived from the words *pert em hru*, which has been translated as "coming forth by day," a reference to the rebirth or resurrection of the soul of the deceased, a concept that first existed in the Nile Valley.

Inscriptions carved on the walls of the Pyramid of Unas of the Fifth Dynasty (ca. 2465 B.C.E.)

These writings were later referred to as the *Pyramid Text*. They were combined with other writings found in numerous coffins and tombs and incorporated into a publication called *The Book of the Dead*.

There are a number of significant religious references which have emerged from the "Book of the Coming Forth by Day," they include:

- The conception of heaven
- The soul of man going to heaven
- The soul of man sitting on a throne by the side of God
- The heavenly blessed eating from the tree of life
- God molding man from clay
- God breathing the breath of life into man's nostrils
- The concept of creation through the spoken word
- Moral concepts of good and evil
- Traditions of hell and hell fire

The Weighing of the Soul

One of the most celebrated Netcherw in all of Kemet was Ausar, who is commonly known by his Greek name Osiris. It has been written that at the time of his birth, a voice was heard to proclaim that the lord of creation was born. The story of Ausar is long and quite involved. He is recognized as a great mythical king of Kemet who brought civilization to his people and established a code of laws and instruction for the worship of God. He ruled Kemet along with his wife Aset, who is better known by her Greek name Isis.

According to legend, Ausar was slain by his cunning (and evil) brother Set, who cut his body into 14 pieces and scattered them throughout Kemet. After a long search, Aset found all of the parts of her husband's body except the phallus, which, as legend has it, was consumed by a catfish when it was discarded into the Nile. Aset recreated the missing member of Ausar in the form of a tekhen (obelisk), which later became a symbol representing the resurrection of Ausar.

Aset was without child before the murder of Ausar, but by means of certain powerful words given to her by the Netcher Djhuiti (Thoth), who represents divine articulation of speech, Aset resurrected her slain husband. Shortly thereafter, Aset conceived a child upon being immaculately impregnated by the spirit of her husband and gave birth to a son, Heru (Horus), who avenged the death of his father by slaying his uncle Set.

After Heru reached adulthood, he ruled as "king on Earth" and Ausar journeyed to the underworld, where he reigned as king. Some of the titles conferred upon Ausar were Lord of Eternity, Ruler of the Dead and Lord of the Underworld. Images of Ausar in his new position of rulership portray him as a mummified, bearded king who carries the shepherd's crook and the flail, and sits on the throne of judgement, which was ornamented with a checkerboard pattern that represented the good and evil who were to come before him. Ausar also becomes the representation of the deceased king, as well as all deceased individuals. He was commonly referred to as the "good shepherd," and is the personification of the cycles of death and rebirth, and of spiritual salvation.

The components in the scene of the *Weighing of the Soul* can be described as follows:

1. The soul of the man to be judged stands between two figures of Maat; one the personification of physical law and the other represents moral virtues.

2. The heart (soul) of the deceased is weighed on the left balance against the feather of Maat, which is on the right balance. Heru and Anpu oversee this delicate procedure.

3. Djhuiti records the event in the Book of Judgement.

4. This beast is often described as the "Devourer of the Souls of the Unjustified" and awaits the verdict.

5. Ausar is seated upon the Throne of Judgement and prepares to render his decision. Directly in front of Ausar, standing upon a lotus flower, are the four children of Heru.

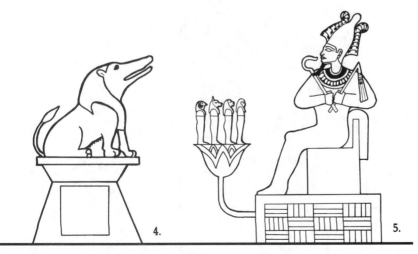

Ausar's role as judge of the souls of the recently departed was of paramount importance, because his decision determined where and how the soul would spend eternity. The heart of the deceased was believed to be the seat of the soul and it was weighed on the scale of the Netcher Maat, against a feather, which represented the principles of truth and righteousness. This scene of judgement is referred to as "The Weighing of the Soul," and each participant plays a critical role.

1. The person whose soul is to be judged stands before Maat and declares his innocence.

2. The scale of Maat was attended to by the Netcherw Heru and Anpu (Anubis) who verify its accuracy. On the left side of the balance was a vessel which represented the heart/soul of the deceased, and on the right balance was an ostrich feather, which represented Maat, and the principles of truth, justice, righteousness and reciprocity. This symbolic weighing of the heart against the feather of truth was performed to establish the righteousness of the deceased. If the scale remained balanced, after the recitation of the "42 Declarations of Innocence," it was an indication that the soul was righteous and deserving of its heavenly reward in the afterlife. The concept of one's heart being "as light as a feather" is derived from this ancient ritual.

3. The Netcher Djhuiti (often identified by his Greek name Thoth) is the principle associated with science, writing, literature and divine speech. Djhuiti's role was to record the outcome of the weighing in the book of life.

4. All of this activity took place in the presence of Ausar who was seated on the throne of judgement and made the final decision regarding the deceased.

Khunum is one of the oldest Netcherw in the Nile Valley. His name means "to mould" or "to model." He is often portrayed seated at a potter's table and before him stands the Ba and Ka of the human being whom he has just fashioned from clay. This story surfaces, thousands of years later, in Genesis when we witness God *molding* Adam from clay. The word *Adam* means "man from the earth."

The statements uttered by the deceased as he stood before the Netcherw were called the *Declarations of Innocence* or *Admonitions of Maat*. These were the 42 laws by which the person was to have lived his life and the standard by which he would be measured at the time of judgement. They are referred to in Budge's translation of "The Book of the Dead" as negative confessions, and are listed as follows.

1. I have not done iniquity.
2. I have not robbed with violence.
3. I have not stolen.
4. I have done no murder; I have done no harm.
5. I have not defrauded offerings.
6. I have not diminished obligations.
7. I have not plundered the Netcher.
8. I have not spoken lies.
9. I have not snatched away food.
10. I have not caused pain.
11. I have not committed fornication.
12. I have not caused shedding of tears.
13. I have not dealt deceitfully.
14. I have not transgressed.
15. I have not acted guilefully.
16. I have not laid waste the ploughed land.
17. I have not been an eavesdropper.
18. I have not set my lips in motion (against any man).
19. I have not been angry and wrathful except for a just cause.
20. I have not defiled the wife of any man.
21. I have not defiled the wife of any man. (repeated twice)
22. I have not polluted myself.
23. I have not caused terror.
24. I have not transgressed. (repeated twice)
25. I have not burned with rage.
26. I have not stopped my ears against the words of Right and Truth (Maat).
27. I have not worked grief.
28. I have not acted with insolence.
29. I have not stirred up strife.
30. I have not judged hastily.
31. I have not been an eavesdropper. (repeated twice)
32. I have not multiplied words exceedingly.
33. I have not done neither harm nor ill.
34. I have never cursed the king.
35. I have never fouled the water.
36. I have not spoken scornfully.
37. I have never cursed the Netcher.
38. I have not stolen.
39. I have not defrauded the offerings of the Netcherw.
40. I have not plundered the offerings to the blessed dead.
41. I have not filched the food of the infant, neither have I sinned against the Netcher of my native town.
42. I have not slaughtered with evil intent the cattle of the Netcher.

Ba

The *Ba* and *Ka* were considered to be two primary aspects of the soul which exists within man. The *Ba* was represented by the bearded head of a man on the body of a hawk. It symbolized the "world-soul," which existed within man and the universe. The bird's body represented the soul's ability to move between heaven and Earth. It is the life-giving power of the Netcherw, and death comes to the body when the breath (Ba) exits.

The *Ka* is represented by two arms, held at 90-degree angles, symbolizing the animating forces within the body. The Ka is also seen as containing all of the powers of creation and is an activator of cosmic forces. A person's Ka determined their inherited and personal character as well as their destiny. On a higher level, the Ka represented spiritual free will, on a lower level it represented the fetters that bind one's physical being to Earth. A soul becomes enlightened when it is liberated by both the Ba and the Ka.

This concept has been incorporated into aspects of Islam which have come to view the *Kaaba*, in Mecca, as the most sacred shrine of the Islamic faith.

Ka

By conservative estimates, the 42 Declarations of Maat were written approximately 1,500 years before the writing of the Ten Commandments. By comparing the two documents, one will find striking comparisons. The following list reflects the numbering most commonly used in English-language references to the Ten Commandments, and those which are similar to the 42 Declarations are highlighted by parenthesis.

1. I am the Lord thy God. Thou shalt have no other gods before me. (41)
2. Thou shalt not make unto thee any graven image...
3. Thou shalt not take the name of the Lord thy God in vain... (7, 37, 41)
4. Remember the Sabbath day, to keep it holy...
5. Honor thy father and mother. (1, 12, 28)
6. Thou shalt not kill. (4)
7. Thou shalt not commit adultery. (11, 20, 21)
8. Thou shalt not steal. (2, 3, 5, 6, 7, 9, 39, 40)
9. Though shalt not bear false witness against thy neighbor. (8, 13, 18, 29)
10. Thou shalt not covet thy neighbor's house or wife... (13, 20, 21, 29, 33)

There are many mysteries concerning the historical life of Moses. Most of the important questions, concerning the extent of his education in Kemet and his reasons for leaving, have yet to be satisfactory answered. Moses is credited with giving the Hebrews the *Ten Commandments*, but a close examination of their content reveals they were derived from the 42 *Admonitions of Maat* (Negative Confessions,) which Moses was exposed to while living in Kemet. There is a growing body of evidence among archaeologists and Old Testament scholars which has lead many to conclude that the exodus was a mythical event, recorded in allegorical form.

Moses, the law giver

When one thinks of the Ten Commandments an association is automatically made with Moses, the law giver. But we must ask ourselves, who was Moses and where did he acquire the laws that he gave? We are told that Moses is credited with the declaration and dissemination of monotheism, and we are also told that he was raised and educated in Egypt. Exodus 2:9-10 states:

> And Pharaoh's daughter said unto her, Take this child away, and nurse it for me....And the child grew, and she brought him unto Pharaoh's daughter and he became her son. And she called his name Moses: and she said, Because I drew him out of the water.

The infant Moses had been placed in an ark among the bulrushes by his mother, where he was found by a handmaiden of the king's daughter. We are informed by Budge that the ark of "bulrushes" was nothing more than a small papyrus boat. Papyrus is a plant which is abhorred by crocodiles and thus is excellent material for a boat; papyrus was also a plant which symbolized Lower Kemet. Acts 7:22 informs us that "Moses was learned in all the wisdom of the Egyptians, and was mighty in words and in deeds."

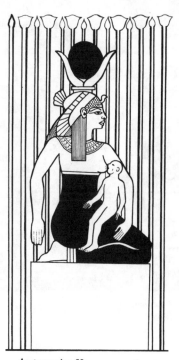

Aset nursing Heru among the bulrushes.

Peter Tompkins, author of *Secrets of the Great Pyramid*, references Moses' presence in ancient Kemet:

> Heliopolis, the On of the Bible, was considered the greatest university in the world. It had existed since much earlier times under the domination of the priests, of whom there were said to be 13,000 in the time of Rameses III, 1225 B.C. More than 200 years earlier, Moses was instructed at Heliopolis "in all the wisdom of the Egyptians," which included physics, arithmetic, geometry, astronomy, medicine, chemistry, geology, meteorology and music.

Moses is said to have been raised in the Pharaoh's household as the grandson of the Pharaoh, and to have lived with him in Egypt for forty years. John Jackson, in his book *Ages of Gold and Silver*, suggests that Moses was educated as a young priest and received his theological education at the Temple of Heliopolis, where he was a disciple of Akhenaton. Akhenaton was the Pharaoh who broke with the long-standing Kemetic religious tradition of acknowledging the Netcherw, and focused the nation's attention on a singular personification of God whom he worshiped as *Aton*.

The infant Moses being delivered to the daughter of the king.

Amenhotep IV
(Akhenaton)

Amenhotep IV was the son of Amenhotep III and Queen Tiye. Upon ascending the throne of Kemet, he changed his name to Akhenaton, instituted a new religious order and moved the capital to a new location called *Akhenaton*, which is now referred to as *Tell-el-Amarna*. He was married to Queen Nefertiti and was reputed to have been the brother of the young King Tutankhamen.

Akhenaton is often referred to as "the Heretic" because of his obsession with the new deity "Aton," which he introduced into Kemet. After his death, many of the records of Akhenaton and Aton were obliterated from the written history by his successors.

Akhenaton's religious conversion was not accepted by the established priesthood and after his death (some suspect that he may have been murdered), Moses led a group of heretics out of Kemet and reestablished this new religious doctrine in Palestine. Jackson, ben-Jochannan and other scholars have maintained that not only was Moses' teachings of "One God" a direct result of his theological training in Kemet, but the Ten Commandments represent less than one-third of the original document, The 42 Declarations of Maat. Akhenaton's influence on the Old Testament texts can be seen in a careful analysis of the similarity between *Akhenaton's Hymn to the Aton* and "Psalm 104."

Comparison Between Akhenaton's Hymn To The Aton and Psalm 104

Akhenaton's Hymn (ca. 1353 B.C.E.)	Psalm 104 (ca. 1000 B.C.E.)
The world is in darkness like the dead. Every lion cometh forth from its den: all serpents sting. Darkness reigns.	Thou makest the darkness and it is night, wherein all the beasts of the forest do creep forth. The young lions roar after their prey...
When Thou risest in the horizon...the darkness is banished...Then in all the world they do their work.	The sun riseth...Man goeth forth unto his work and to his labour until the evening.
All trees and plants flourish...the birds flutter in their marshes...All sheep dance upon their feet.	The trees of the Lord are full of sap...wherein the birds make their nests...The high hills are a refuge for the wild goats.
The ships sail up stream and down stream alike...The fish in the river leap up before thee: and thy rays are in the midst of the great sea.	So is this great and wide sea, wherein are thing creeping innumerable, both small and great and beasts...There go the ships.
How manifold are all Thy works!...Thou didst create the earth according to Thy desire, men all cattle...all that are upon the earth.	O Lord how manifold are thy works! In wisdom hast Thou made them all...The earth is full of thy creatures.

In 1984, at the *Nile Valley Conference* in Atlanta, Georgia, Dr. Charles Copher, professor of Old Testament at the Interdenominational Theological Center in Atlanta, discussed the role of Egypt and Ethiopia in the Old Testament. He stated the following:

> In the King James and Revised Standard versions of the Bible, the word "Egypt" (Mitzraim in Hebrew) along with cognates, occurs some seven hundred forty times in the Old Testament. The word translated Ethiopia and/or Cush (Cush in Hebrew) along with cognates, and including three instances of duplication in the references, appears fifty-eight times in the King James Version. In this version the translation "Ethiopia" is used thirty-nine times; "Cush" (untranslated) with cognates, nineteen times. The numerous references to Egypt led one Old Testament scholar to remark, 'No other land is mentioned so frequently as Egypt in the Old Testament'....To understand Israel one must look well into Egypt.

The story of Ausar, Aset and Heru is the first story in the recorded history of man of a holy royal family (the Trinity), immaculate conception, virgin birth and *resurrection*. Evidence of this Trinity is known to have existed in ancient Nubia as late as 3300 B.C.E. Carved on the walls of the Temple of Luxor (circa 1380 B.C.E.) are scenes which depict the following:

1. The Annunciation - The Netcher Djhuiti is shown announcing to the virgin Aset the coming birth of their son, Heru.

2. The Immaculate Conception - The Netcher Kneph, who represents the Holy Ghost, and the Netcher Het-Heru (Hathor) are shown symbolically impregnating Aset by holding ankhs (symbols of life) to the nostrils of the virgin mother-to-be.

3. The Virgin Birth - Aset is shown sitting on the birthing stool and the newborn child is attended by midwives.

4. The Adoration - The newborn Heru is portrayed receiving gifts from three kings, or Magi while being adored by a host of gods and men.

Heru in the form of a falcon wearing the crown of Amen.

Samuel Sharp, author of *Egyptian Mystery and Egyptian Christianity*, made the following comments upon viewing this scene:

> In this picture we have the Annunciation, the Conception, the Birth and the Adoration as described in the first and second chapters of Luke's Gospel; and as we have historical assurance that the chapters in Matthew's Gospel which contain the miraculous birth of Christ are after additions not in the earliest manuscripts, it seems probable that these two poetical chapters in Luke may also be unhistorical and borrowed from the Egyptian accounts of the miraculous births of their kings.

Gerald Massey reproduced these images in his book *Ancient Egypt: the Light of the World, Vol. II*, which was published in 1907. In this work Massey cited more than 200 similarities between the lives of Ausar and Heru and the life of Jesus the Christ, who was born at least 3,300 years later.

Comparison Between The Lives of Heru and Jesus The Christ

Heru (ca. 3200 B.C.E)	Jesus (ca. 1 A.C.E)
Horus had two mothers: Isis the Virgin, who conceived him, and Nephthys, who nursed him. He was brought forth singly as one of five brothers.	Jesus had two mothers, Mary the Virgin, who conceived him, and Mary the wife of Cleophas, who brought him forth as one of her (five) children.
Horus was with his mother, the Virgin, until twelve years old, when he was transformed into the beloved son of God as the only begotten of the Father in Heaven.	Jesus remained with his mother, the Virgin, up to the age of twelve years, when he left her "to be about his Father's business."
From twelve to thirty years of age there is no record in the life of Horus.	From twelve to thirty years of age there is no record in the life of Jesus.
Horus, at thirty years of age, became adult in his baptism by Anup.	Jesus, at thirty years of age was made a man in his baptism by John the Baptist.
Horus in his baptism made his transformation into the beloved son and only begotten of the Father, the Holy Spirit, represented by a bird.	Jesus in his baptism is hailed from heaven as the beloved son and the only begotten of the Father, God, the Holy Spirit, represented by a dove.

Jocelyn Rhys, author of *Shaken Creeds: The Virgin Birth Doctrine,* has thoroughly researched the history of virgin birth stories and discussed their African origins:

> Horus was said to be the parthenogenesis child of the Virgin Mother, Isis. In the catacombs of Rome, black statues of this Egyptine divine Mother and Infant still survive from the early Christian worship of the Virgin and Child, to which they were converted. In these, the Virgin Mary is represented as a black Negress and often, with the face veiled in the true Isis fashion....Statues of the goddess Isis with the child Horus in her arms were common in Egypt, and were exported to all neighboring and to many remote countries, where they are still to be found with new names attached to them—Christian in Europe, Buddhist in Turkestan, Taoist in China and Japan.

As an adult, Heru becomes a symbol for good overcoming evil after he avenges the death of his father by slaying his wicked uncle Set. Cosmologically, Set (Satan) represents the setting sun (sunset), which brings on darkness (evil, fear and ignorance). Set also represents the destructive forces of nature. Heru personifies the forces of life and his symbol (the rising sun) banishes the night and overpowers the forces of evil.

In the final analysis, Heru becomes in life what his father Ausar is in death, prototypes for the living and the dead respectively. As other cultures infused elements of Nile Valley symbolism, philosophy and religion into their society, names were changed and symbols were modified, but not all of the original African components were lost. One has only to develop a finely tuned eye to rediscover the remnants of Nile Valley Civilization, which can be found in the symbolism and religions of today.

Scenes at the Temple of Edfu depict Heru battling his uncle Set and avenging the death of his father Ausar. During the battle, Set transforms himself into a hippopotamus and is speared by Heru.

The battle between Set and Heru was the prototype for the classic confrontations between the hero (Heru/light) and the villain (Set/Darkness), which have come down to us over the ages. The fables of knights slaying dragons can be traced back to this famous confrontation, and the old English myth of Saint George slaying the dragon provides an excellent example.

Saint George was the contemporary personification of Heru in the Middle Ages and the dragon was synonymous with Set. Saint George slays the dragon/serpent (darkness) with a lance, symbolic of a piercing ray of light from the sun, which destroys the forces of evil. A similar parallel can be found in the story of Dracula, who is called the "Prince of Darkness," and preys on his victims at night. He can only be destroyed by sunlight or by a small lance (stake) driven through his heart.

St. George slaying the dragon

The architectural form of the *arch* was considered by many to have been introduced by the Romans. But this example of an arched ceiling, at the Temple of Abydos, was built around 1300 B.C.E., approximately 700 years before the founding of Rome.

The Architectural Masterpieces of Kemet

Architecture is one of the most powerful expressions of human creativity. Incorporated within it are elements relating to art, the physical sciences, psychology and religion. Architectural structures serve numerous functions; they provide shelter and serve as gathering places where people work, play, pray and are entertained.

Thousands of years after the architects are dead and forgotten, the structures they created live on and tell the story of their entire civilization. The philosophy of a nation is often reflected in its architecture. Nowhere is this statement more accurate than with respect to ancient Kemet. Before the Medu Netcher (hieroglyphics) were deciphered, and hundreds of years before the complexities of the science, religion and philosophy of Kemet were known, her ancient temples, pyramids and tombs commanded the respect and admiration of millions of awestruck visitors. Numerous questions have been asked as to why, and how, these monuments were built? Many of these questions remain unanswered to this very day.

Not only does the architecture of Kemet reflect the values and philosophies of its people, it also has incorporated within its physical structure aspects of ancient knowledge which can easily be interpreted, and other elements which defy analysis. The architecture of Kemet is exoteric and its powerful images overwhelm the senses. This same architecture transmits a subliminal message into the consciousness of any individual who is spiritually and mentally prepared to receive it.

Upon examining the architecture of Kemet, it becomes obvious that tremendous energy was expended during the planning, design and construction of these ancient structures. Buildings were not arbitrarily located on just any site and they could not have been built without teams of skilled craftsmen and professionals. The notion that many of these structures were built by slave labor is not only unfounded but totally unrealistic. The same organizational skills necessary to build the Sears Tower in Chicago, or the World Trade Center in New York City, were also required to build the ancient monuments in the Nile Valley.

The mortuary temple of Queen Hatshepsut is considered one of the finest architectural structures ever created. It was built into the mountains on the west bank of the city of Waset (Luxor) around 1470 B.C.E. The original name of the temple was *Zosert-Zosru*, which means "The Holy of Holies." This structure is now called "Dier el-Bahari," which was the name given it by the Arabs.

The colonnaded hall of the Ipet-Isut offers an impressive view of Kemetic architecture. One can still see the clerestory windows and the vivid colors of the Medu Netcher carved into the stone.

In archeology, whenever a temple or ancient monument is aligned to a specific rising or setting position of the sun, moon or other heavenly body, that site is usually referred to as an observatory or a solar or lunar structure. From this perspective, practically every pyramid and temple in the Nile Valley served some astronomic purpose. These ancient buildings were designed not only to accommodate the physical needs of the people, they were also astronomically oriented to facilitate their spiritual needs as well.

Temples were designed to create a sense of grandeur and to inspire greater faith within the priests and the general population. The harmonic proportion of the structure, its orientation to celestial bodies and the location of the sacred alter (Holy of Holies), were all part of the design to create an environment where the "spirit" of a specific Netcher would dwell. Every component within a temple—the soaring height of the columns, the number of columns, the clerestory windows, the positioning of the walls, the paintings and carvings on the walls and columns—all reflected an intense desire to establish a sacred place for a dialogue between the human form and its spiritual essence.

This view of the Ipet-Isut illustrates various plants which were incorporated into two styles of columns. In the foreground one can see the truncated remains of circular papyrus bundled columns. In the background stand two square columns, the one on the right has lotus carvings and the one on the left has papyrus carvings.

The use of columns in temple construction was first recorded in the Nile Valley, where it was not uncommon to find them carved to resemble palm trees, papyrus reeds or lotus blossoms. These three plants represented man's physical, mental and spiritual relationship with the creator. The fruit of the palm tree provided nourishment and its leaves and trunk were used to create shelter. The stem of the papyrus plant was used to make paper, thus allowing man to record his thoughts and deeds for posterity. The lotus flower symbolizes the mind, and its potential for receiving knowledge and spiritual enlightenment.

Every building tells a story in stone, and says something about the culture that created it. How historians interpret an ancient architectural monument is determined by their willingness to dismiss their prejudices and by their ability to see the edifice through the eyes of the people who created it. The architecture of Kemet requires such an analysis.

The Step Pyramid

The Step Pyramid of Saqqara

Ancient Kemet is a land of many firsts, and chief among them is the distinction of being the home of the world's first skyscraper. The first stone building ever constructed still stands majestically within the vast complex of temples at Saqqara. It is called the Step Pyramid. There is a total of 15 royal pyramids at Saqqara. Most are in varying stages of disrepair, but they were all developed from the same prototype.

The Step Pyramid was built around 2630 B.C.E., for a king of the Third Dynasty named Zoser. His pyramid rises to a height of 197 feet in a series of six box-like steps called mastabas (an Arabic word which means *mud benches*). The early mastabas were small rectangular tombs in which the bodies of nobles were buried during the early dynastic period in Kemet. The Step Pyramid of Zoser represents a profound shift in the construction of the traditional tomb. In this instance, six mastabas were built, one on top of the other. Each of the five mastabas was smaller than the one beneath it. This created a tiered monument that symbolically represented a stairway to heaven. The completed structure was encased in polished limestone-thus the first pyramid was born.

The Step Pyramid is but one of a number of structures comprising the largest stone complex ever built under the rulership of one leader. The uniquely stylized architecture of the enclosure wall, and the adjoining colonnade, gives the impression that you are viewing a contemporary structure, not one that was built more than 4,500 years ago. The architectural designs employed at this site set the architectural standard in Kemet for the next 3,000 years.

King Zoser

The enclosure wall of the Saqqara Complex with the Step Pyramid in the background.

Detail of the engaged columns at the temple complex

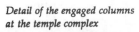

Note the similarity between the enclosure wall at Saqqara and the detail of the palace facade from the Nubian incense burner found at Qustal (ca. 3400 B.C.E.)

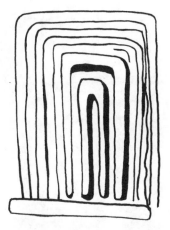

Imhotep

The enclosure wall at the Saqqara complex was originally nearly 1800 feet long and 900 feet wide. This wall rose to a height of over 30 feet, and enclosed more than a square mile of land. Upon entering the pyramid complex of Zoser, one must walk through a colonnade consisting of 40 columns believed to represent the 40 provinces or states of early Kemet. The design of these columns is quite reminiscent of the architectural style that would be attributed to the Greeks more than 2,000 years later.

The architect responsible for designing the Step Pyramid and its surrounding compound was referred to by Manetho in 285 B.C.E. as "the inventor of the art of building with hewn stone." This architect's name was Imhotep and he is described as "the world's first multigenius." Imhotep's brilliance superseded his architectural ability, for he was also revered as an astronomer, philosopher, poet and physician. He was recorded in history as the world's first physician, a title that was later bestowed upon a Greek named Hippocrates who was born some 2,200 years later.

During his lifetime, Imhotep was given many titles, among them: *Chancellor of the King of Lower Kemet, the First after the King of Upper Kemet, High Priest of Heliopolis* and *Administrator of the Great Palace,* just to name a few. He was deified 2,000 years after his death by the residents of Kemet and was later referred to as *Asclepius,* the god of medicine, by the Greeks. As a philosopher, Imhotep is credited with having written many poems and proverbs, the most famous of which is: "Eat, drink, and be merry for tomorrow we shall die."

Very rarely is a noble man more popular than the king he serves. But in the case of Imhotep, he was worshiped in early Christianity as the *Prince of Peace* and described as the "first Christ," a title meaning "the anointed one."

The colonnaded hall inside of the Saqqara temple complex

The Pyramids of Giza

The Great Pyramid of Khufu (extreme right), the Pyramid of Khafre (center) and the Pyramid of Menkaure (left). In the extreme foreground are the three pyramids of the queens.

The Great Pyramid of Giza

Ten miles west of Cairo, at the geographical center of the Earth's landmass, is a man-made limestone plateau which is one mile square and rises one hundred thirty feet above the Nile Delta. This area, which today is called Giza, is unmistakably the most important archaeological site on the planet. It is at the Giza Plateau that we find the ancient remains of a vast industrial complex comprising ten pyramidal structures, the most famous of which is the *Great Pyramid*. This Great Pyramid is the largest, oldest and only remaining of the *Seven Wonders of the World*.

When it was originally constructed, the Great Pyramid rose to a height of 481 feet, in 201 stair-stepped tiers. Unfortunately, the last twelve courses of stone and the capstone were removed at some undisclosed point in time. All that remains today is a 20 X 20-foot platform at its apex and a wood frame which indicate its original height. Since its construction, the Great Pyramid has withstood two ruinous assaults at the hands of Arabs, who had little or no regard for its historic significance. These attacks were an obvious indication that this structure represented a culture that was foreign to the Arabs; and in their eyes was, therefore, unworthy of their respect.

The first major assault on the Great Pyramid occurred in 820 A.C.E., when a Persian caliph, by the name of Abdullah Al Mamun, burrowed into its interior in an attempt to find the great treasures rumored to have been stored inside its secret chambers. After tunneling more than 100 feet through the solid core of the pyramid, Al Mamun's men finally broke through into a narrow passageway. The men scurried about in the various rooms and corridors of the pyramid. They were unable to find any treasure and they abandoned their search in disgust. As a result of Al Mamun's forced entry into the pyramid, its interior was made accessible to outsiders for the first time in more than one thousand years.

The second major attack against the pyramid occurred in 1356 A.C.E., when its polished limestone exterior was removed and used to rebuild the city of Cairo after a devastating earthquake. Originally, the entire outer surface of the pyramid was covered with polished white limestone, giving the appearance of one smooth and continuous surface reflecting the light of the sun and moon.

Over the course of several decades, the entire 22 acres of 100-inch-thick limestone casing was removed and used in the construction of the mosques of El Hasan, El Rifai and the fortress of Qalat El Gebel in Cairo. The stripping of the limestone covering left the pyramid's outer core of masonry exposed. These same blocks now provide enthusiastic tourists easy access to climb to the pyramid's apex.

The Great Pyramid has stirred the imagination of man for countless years. It is mentioned in no less than ten thousand documents and has been the subject of many commentaries and theories as to its construction and purpose. There are many who believe the Great Pyramid was built as a tomb for King Khufu, while others maintain it was used as a water purifier. There are those who say it was built by beings from Atlantis, or by aliens from outer space. The truth is, there are neither paintings nor carvings in the pyramid to attest to its purpose, nor has any history of its construction survived the passage of time.

One of the greatest misconceptions regarding the Great Pyramid is that it was constructed by Jews during their enslavement in Kemet. Examination of a time line will show the error of this belief. Abraham, who was the founder of Judaism and the ancestor of both the Arabs and Jews, was said to have been born around 1675 B.C.E., which was at least 900 years *after* the Great Pyramid is believed to have been constructed.

It is not the intent of this work to discuss the controversy and confusion surrounding the building of this structure or its intended use. The purpose here is to present empirical data, and examine its logical implications. One must be extremely careful when examining the Great Pyramid and other aspects of ancient Kemet, for they have been misinterpreted by "arm-chair Egyptologists" who have never been to Egypt, and others

King Khufu

who, having visited Egypt, brought with them their prejudices and a profound disdain for the history of Africa and its people.

As researcher and author John Anthony West noted in his book, *Serpent In The Sky* :

> Egyptian knowledge is a whole, no part of it is meant to be studied divorced from the rest. Since there is no other way for us to study it except piecemeal, we must always bear in mind that any conclusions we come to must be related to the whole from which they have been extracted. Egyptian knowledge is always implicit, never explicit. Egypt did not talk about its knowledge, but rather incorporated it into its art and architecture, allowing it to exercise its effect emotionally: Egypt talked to the mind of the heart.

Mr. West's statements regarding Kemet can just as easily be applied to most investigations of traditional African history and culture. It is very difficult for anyone to "know" that which they do not understand. And when understanding is further hindered by arrogance and prejudice, true knowledge often gives way to distorted perceptions of reality which, is oftentimes accepted as legitimate scholarship.

Many Egyptologists are of the opinion that the Great Pyramid was built by pagan primitives to house the body of a deceased king. They believe its measurements were made by crude instruments and that a slave labor force of thousands of men was used to quarry, transport and position the approximately two and one-half million stones, that make up this great structure. These beliefs persist, despite the lack of evidence to fully support them.

The Great Pyramid may not be the largest stone structure ever created, but it is still, many thousands of years after its construction, the most perfectly aligned building to true north. The alignment is only one-twelfth of a degree off true north. This misalignment has been attributed to the shifting of the Earth's crust since the pyramid's construction, and not an error on the part of those who constructed it.

The Paris Observatory is the most perfectly aligned structure built in modern times, and it is aligned six minutes off true north. How is it possible that "slaves" or primitive workers accomplished a feat, thousands of years ago, which "skilled" technicians would have difficulty duplicating today? This question has not been answered, so it is ignored.

The pyramid's precise alignment to true north is a confirmation that its builders possessed a working knowledge of geography, which is essential to the development of any nation. From the earliest of times the inhabitants of the Nile Valley had to continuously survey and reestablish the agricultural boundaries that were washed away with the annual flooding of the Nile. The designation of national and domestic

The Great Pyramid

Astronomy, [Gr. *astronomia*, from *astronomos*; *astron*, star, and *nomos*, from *nemein*, to arrange, distribute]. The science which deals with the heavenly bodies-fixed stars, planets, satellites, and comets-their nature, distribution, magnitudes, motions, distances, periods of revolutions, eclipses, etc.

Geography, [Gr. *geographia*, geography; *ge*, the earth/ *graphein*, to write]. The descriptive science dealing with the surface of the earth and its various divisions into continents, countries, states and cities.

Geodesy, [Gr. *geodaisia*, the art of mensuration; *ge*, the earth, and *daiein*, to divide]. That part of applied mathematics which has for its object the determination of the magnitude and figure either of the whole earth or of a large portion of its surface, or the locating exactly of points on its surface.

Webster's New Twentieth Century Dictionary, Unabridged Second Edition

With a working knowledge of astronomy, geometry and geodesy, the scientists and engineers of the Nile Valley were able to establish a perfectly aligned meridian of 30 degrees latitude, which exceeded a distance of 2,000 miles and extended from the Mediterranean Sea to the equator.

boundaries, construction of temples and the undertakings of trade and commerce all require a working knowledge of geography and geodesy.

Today, the basis of geography is the system of latitude and longitude used to measure the size of our planet and to chart its surface with supreme accuracy. Most people think of this as an invention of the modern world because it requires a working knowledge of a higher form of mathematics such as spherical trigonometry. However, we find this exact knowledge incorporated into the interior and exterior measurements of the Great Pyramid.

The pyramid's perimeter (the sum of its base lengths) is 3,023 feet, which is precisely equal to one-half minute of a degree of latitude at the equator, or one forty-three thousand two hundredth (1:43,200) of the polar circumference of the Earth. A measurement of the pyramid's perimeter, including the outermost sockets upon which it rests (which incidentally are recessed eight inches below the surface), yields a length of 3,043.8 feet which is precisely equal to one-half minute of a degree of longitude at the equator, or one forty-three thousand two hundredth (1:43,200) of the equatorial circumference of the Earth.

The entire pyramid rests on a platform which is more than 755 feet in length, and level to within four-fifths of an inch. The height of the pyramid plus the height of its base platform, 482.7571 feet, is equal to one forty-three thousand two hundredth (1:43,200) of the polar radius of the Earth, or the distance from the center of the Earth to the North Pole.

It should be noted here that the repetition of the formula 1:43,200 in the three measurements is intentional, and relates to the size and shape of the Earth. There are 360 degrees in a circle, 60 minutes in a degree and two half-minutes in one minute. Simply put, 360 X 60 X 2 = 43,200. These three basic measurements of the pyramid, all on the same scale, represent the three essential geodetic values of our planet, with a precision matched only with contemporary satellite or space shuttle surveys.

These measurements, in addition to other geographic facts about the Great Pyramid-its placement at the center of the Earth's landmass, its position at the apex of the Nile Delta and its orientation to the cardinal points of the compass-all support the idea that whoever built the Great Pyramid knew the precise circumference of the planet, and was aware of the flattening at the poles and equatorial bridge. This knowledge was not rediscovered until the eighteenth century A.C.E.

The fact that the Great Pyramid was engineered with accuracies measured to the hundredths of an inch, is a testimonial to its builders having possessed an advanced knowledge of mathematics. To cite another example, the pyramid's height relates to its perimeter as the radius of a circle does to its circumference. Dividing the perimeter of the pyramid's base

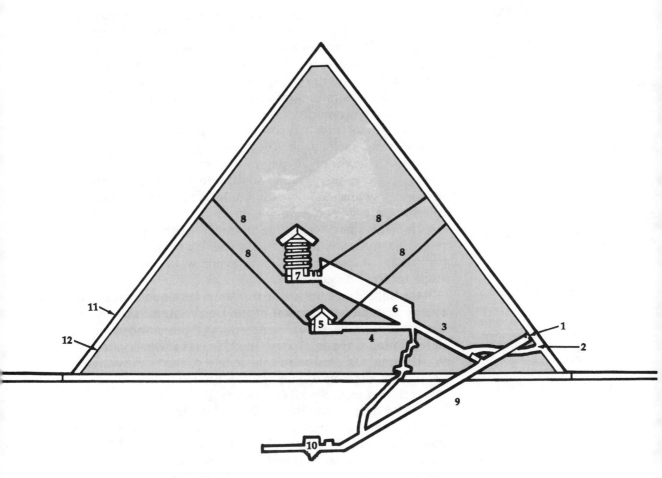

1. Original entrance
2. Al Mamun's forced entrance
3. Ascending passageway
4. Passage to Queen's chamber
5. Queen's chamber
6. Grand Gallery
7. King's chamber
8. Observation shafts
9. Descending passageway
10. Underground chamber
11. Limestone covering
12. Current outer surface

by twice its height yields 3.1428, which is a working approximation of *pi* often used by contemporary engineers in construction design. The area of a face of the Great Pyramid is also the same as the square of its vertical height. The square of the vertical height is also the same as one-half the pyramid's base width, times its slant height. This fact indicates that the pyramid's design is in accordance with *phi* (1.618), also called the "Golden Number."

Math is an integral part of astronomy, the science of observing the stars and planets. Astronomy is vital for the calculation of the length of the year and the precise moment of the solstices and equinoxes, which leads to the creation of a calendrical system. It is a commonly accepted fact that the Egyptians were responsible for the development of a 365 1/4 day year, a 24-hour day and the "second" as a unit of measure for the hour. Clues as to how this information was obtained can be found in the interior passages of the Great Pyramid, which were used as astronomical observatories for watching and clocking the heavens.

One of the most precisely constructed passages in the pyramid is the Descending Passage. The passage points to the northern skies at an angle of 26 degrees 17 minutes which, when subtracted from the pyramid's latitudinal angle of nearly 30 degrees, provides a view within 3 degrees 43 minutes of the celestial pole: a perfect angle for watching the transit of circumpolar stars across the entrance opening. Another passage, the Ascending Passage, angles off from the Descending Passage at 26 degrees 17 minutes and would be the precise angle for light reflection.

If the light from a transiting star shone on a pool of water or mirror at the juncture point of the Descending Passage, the light would be reflected up the Ascending Passage and observed in the Grand Gallery. Today, the U.S. Naval Observatory in Washington, D.C., calculates the length of the year by timing the light of a transiting star across a limited field of vision as it is reflected from a pool of mercury.

Located deep inside the confines of the pyramid is a room referred to as the "King's Chamber." It was given this name for purely chauvinistic reasons - because it is the largest of the two rooms in the pyramid, it had to have been built for the king, and the smaller one was, obviously, built for the queen. The Queen's Chamber is made of limestone and the King's Chamber is made of granite, which is believed to have been quarried in Aswan, some 600 miles to the south.

The dimensions of the King's Chamber (34'4" in length x 17'2" in width x 19'1" in height) are most significant because they express two ratios of "Pythagorean Triangles" ($A^2+B^2=C^2$) and 3:4:5. The pyramid builders were obviously familiar with these sacred triangles thousands of years before Pythagoras was supposed to have introduced them. These same basic geometric principles were referred to by Plato as the building blocks of the cosmos. Elmer D. Robinson, a world-renowned mathematician at Johns Hopkins University in Baltimore, Maryland, studied the Great Pyramid in detail and made these remarks:

> The analysis and mathematical modeling of the Great Pyramid indicates that the ancient Egyptians had a knowledge of geometry and mathematics which few historians and archaeologists will give them credit for. The evidence is strong that they knew of and used quadratic equations and the quadratic formula...they most certainly had a system of logarithms, used com-

> binations of integers with an irrational number [and] used an infinite geometrical progression having many unique properties.

This is a level of mathematical knowledge equaled only within the past two hundred years.

Despite the references to the King's Chamber as the site where the body of Khufu was buried, no *body* has ever been found there. As a matter of fact, evidence indicates that no *original burial* has ever been found in any of the approximately 72 pyramids in Egypt. The Great Pyramid, in stark contrast to the hundreds of tombs which have been unearthed in Egypt, contains no paintings, carvings or images traditionally associated with the burial of royalty.

The association of this pyramid with Khufu is also something of a mystery. The only surviving image of the great Pharaoh Khufu is a small ivory statuette four inches in height. This figurine was found, not in Giza but in a "toilet" 300 miles to the south of Giza, in the temple at Abydos. Further investigations of the King's Chamber continue to shed some light as to some of its possible uses.

Inside the chamber there are two shafts which were cut through 200 feet of solid masonry to the outer surface of the pyramid. These shafts, which face in a northerly and southerly direction, have long been regarded as "air shafts" that ventilated the King's Chamber. New evidence has been presented which shows the so-called air shafts are inclined, within one degree of accuracy, to the northern celestial pole, and to the three stars of Orion's Belt to the south.

It has been suggested that these openings were meant as symbolic guideways for the soul, guiding it either towards the Circumpolars in the northern sky or to the constellation of Orion in the southern sky. Lucie Lamy, author of *Egyptian Mysteries* offers additional insight on this interesting theory:

> Egypt, it was said, is in the image of Heaven. The emphasis placed on north and south then leads us to investigate the regions of the sky, of which earth is only a reflection....It is actually a matter of two ways being offered to each individual: that of final liberation and eternal life (the north), or that of reincarnation in a mortal body and the commencement of a new experience (the south).

The main star viewed through the northern shaft is called Alpha Draconis. Around it turned the Circumpolars (often called the "Indestructibles" because they never disappeared below the horizon). It was for this reason that these stars symbolized immortality. A soul which had chosen this path in life was said to ascend into the imperishable dominion of the northern heavens.

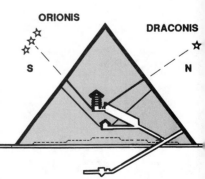

The southern shaft was oriented to the 36 stars (constellations, also referred to as decans) whose consecutive helical risings occurred approximately every ten days, hence the name decan, which is derived from the Latin prefix *dec* meaning "ten." Each decan rose above the horizon after a period of seventy days of invisibility—the seventy-day mummification process corresponds to this phenomenon. Among the stars within this southern hemisphere are Osiris (Orion) the symbol of resurrection and Isis-Sothis (Sirius), which was associated with the annual regeneration of the Nile.

The most impressive aspect of the Great Pyramid is its sheer size and volume. It is composed of approximately two and one-half million stones which weigh an average of two and one-half tons each. There are several located above the King's Chamber that weigh as much as 70 tons—the equivalent of a railroad locomotive. Its base covers an area of 13.11 square acres or seven city blocks. It is perfectly level to within one-half inch.

There is more stone in the Great Pyramid than in all the cathedrals, churches and chapels built in England since the time of Christ. In more contemporary terms, the Great Pyramid was built to a height equaling a 45- story building and with enough stone to build 30 Empire State buildings. So vast is this structure that, if all of its stones were cut into one-foot blocks and laid end to end, they would stretch two-thirds of the distance around the Earth at the equator. The cement used to bind these stones in place is 1/50 of an inch, the thickness of two sheets of paper, and it is nearly invisible when compared to the one-half inch of mortar used in traditional brick construction.

If you were to give a modern construction engineer the task of building a structure 85 million cubic feet in volume, composed of over two and one-half million blocks of limestone and granite—weighing from two to 70 tons apiece, with a joint tolerance of no more than 1/50 of an inch, and an orientation of true north—the engineer would probably tell you that what you are asking for is impossible to build by any means known today.

There is very little creditable data concerning the construction of the Great Pyramid. The one source commonly referenced is Herodotus, who visited Kemet in 443 B.C.E., and reported that 100,000 men built the Great Pyramid in a period of twenty years, during the three-month period of the annual flood season. This account seems to be highly improbable considering the fact that the data suggested translates into only 1,800 working days, at 12 hours per day, which equals a total of 21,600 man hours. If this sum is divided into the 2,300,000 blocks, it means that the builders had to position "about 1,200 blocks a day, or 100 blocks an hour or almost a block every minute." We must remember that the "father of history" visited the pyramids about 2,000 years after they were constructed and many primary sources were not available to him.

As recently as 1978, the Nippon Corporation of Japan attempted to construct a miniature pyramid at Giza utilizing the methods attributed to the original builders. The plan was to quarry the stones using crude implements, transport them by rafts down the Nile, drag them from the river's edge, and then lift them into place with simple levers. However, once construction began the workmen were confronted with innumerable problems. The tools used to quarry the stones proved to be useless and were replaced by modern jackhammers; the rafts used to transport the stones sank in the Nile and steamboats were employed; finally, trucks were used to transport the stones to the work site after the use of manual labor proved to be fruitless.

Once at the work site, the laborers proved to be unsuccessful at lifting and positioning the stones. Power cranes and helicopters were called in to finish the job. Finally, the workers damaged more stones than they used, and those used in the construction of the pyramid were so poorly aligned that it became obvious to the engineers of the Nippon Corporation they had bitten off more than they could chew. Eventually, the Egyptian government intervened and ordered the dismantling of the pyramid because of the "unauthorized" use of heavy duty construction equipment.

This failed attempt to construct a pyramid once again raised the question as to how the Great Pyramid was built. Not only were the Japanese unable to duplicate the building of this structure using the ancient theorized means of construction, they were not able to build it using the technologically advanced equipment of today. Throughout the ages, numerous individuals have sought to unravel the mysteries of the Great Pyramid's construction. Who built it? When was it built, and how was it constructed?

Although the knowledge which produced the Great Pyramid has been shrouded in secrecy for more than 5,000 years, new discoveries are being made which may soon reveal the purpose and method of construction of this "Seventh Wonder of the World," the most ancient of mysteries. When those questions are answered, do not be surprised if all the proponents of the "tomb theories" are looked upon in the same light as those who once thought the world was flat, and that the Earth was the center of the universe.

Her-Em-Akhet: The Great Sphinx

Kemet has long been regarded as a land of many mysteries, but one of the most enigmatic structures which has baffled mankind throughout the ages is the statue called the Sphinx. Carved "in situ" out of one single mass of stone, which was formerly a part of the physical geography of the Giza Plateau, the Sphinx stares majestically towards the eastern horizon.

The Sphinx is the largest and oldest monument ever sculpted from a single rock. It has the head of a person and the body of a reclined lion. As late as the Eighteenth Dynasty (ca. 1550 B.C.E.), this monument was called *Her-em-akhet* (Heru-of-the-horizon). This name was a direct reference to *Heru* the sun Netcher (child of Ausar and Aset), and the *akhet*, which means "places where the sun rises and sets." Her-em-akhet faces the rising sun and its strategic positioning at the foot of the Great Pyramid provides a clue to its symbolic meaning.

This great statue is 240 feet long and 66 feet high, it has a shoulder span of 38 feet, a head that is almost 14 feet wide and a 7-foot smile. Her-em-akhet represents a perfect blend of art and architecture, mystery and magnificence. It aesthetically integrates the essence of man and animal in such a way that it expresses the divine relationship between the two. This is not your typical anthropomorphic statue.

Symbolically, the body of the beast represents the animal

nature which exists in man, and the lion exemplifies the royalty and power of the divine spirit that exists in its lower physical form. The head of a man symbolizes the intelligence of the mind which must be cultivated in order to elevate the consciousness into a higher spiritual state so that it may become divine. Metaphorically speaking, it is the suppression of the lower animal nature and the refinement of the thought process that leads to the spiritual evolution of man. Spiritually speaking, it is only by conquering the "beast" within that one is capable of truly knowing God.

Knowledge comes from enlightenment-light (good/God), which vanquishes the darkness-ignorance (evil/devil). Heru represents the conquest of good over evil (Set/Satan) and Her-em-akhet exemplifies the eternal conquest of good over evil because he faces the eastern horizon and is physically *en-lightened* by the sun as it rises each morning.

The Sphinx has been called the "soul of Egypt" by Zahi Hawass, the director of the Egyptian Antiquity Organization; but in order to understand the depth of its soul, one must go back to its Kemetic roots. A simple analysis of the names that foreigners have used to describe this statue helps to explain how they misinterpreted its spiritual meaning. In Arabic the Sphinx is called *Abu-Hol* which means "Father of Terror." This concept was derived form the Greek word *sphinx* which means "the strangler."

In Greek mythology, the Sphinx was a winged monster with a lion's body and the head and breasts of a woman. This beast was perched upon a rock near Thebes (in Greece, not Kemet) and asked a riddle of every passer-by. All those who were unable to answer the riddle correctly were strangled by the Sphinx. This myth is derived from the tragedy *Oedipus Rex*, which was written by the Greek playwright Sophocles. The riddle asked by the Sphinx was:

> What has one voice
> And goes on four feet on two feet and on three
> But the more feet it goes on the weaker it be?

Oedipus answering the Riddle of the Sphinx.

In the myth, Oedipus is traveling to Thebes when he is confronted by the Sphinx who asks him the riddle. Oedipus responded: "Man—who crawls on all fours as a baby, then walks on two legs as an adult, and walks with a cane in old age." Having solved the riddle, the Sphinx immediately committed suicide by jumping off a cliff and Oedipus continued his journey to Thebes where he was later proclaimed king for having outsmarted the great beast.

This myth vividly illustrates how the Greeks borrowed, plagiarized and distorted elements of Kemetic art, symbolism and philosophy. Before the statue of Her-em-akhet, there were no images of human-headed lions in the world. Since its creation in Kemet, sphinxes have been found among the remains of ancient civilizations such as Assyria, Phoenicia and those of Asia Minor. As was the case with the other nations, sphinxes began to surface in Greece only after contact was made with the people of Kemet. Interestingly, when the Greeks created a statue similar in design to Her-em-akhet, they defiled it by making it evil and portraying it as female because of their low regard for women.

Another interesting element in the concept of the "stolen legacy" of ancient Kemet is the close proximity of the monstrous sphinx to the Greek city of Thebes. Thebes was an ancient city in Boeotia, a region in central Greece, which was founded by the Phoenician King named Cadmus, around 500 B.C.E. Fifteen hundred years earlier, the capital of Kemet was located in a city called "Waset," which was regarded as the greatest city in the richest and most powerful nation of the ancient world. The Greeks later renamed this city "Thebes."

The Greeks derived the name "Thebes" from the African word Apet (or Ipet), which was the original name for the Temple of Karnak in Waset. The Greeks then added a feminine prefix to Apet which became "Tapet," from which they derived "Thebai" which later became Thebes.

Within Waset, there existed two magnificent temples, the Shemayit-Ipet (Luxor Temple) and Ipet-Isut (Karnak Temple). The two temples were connected by an avenue of 2,000 sphinxes spanning a distance of two miles. Homer, the Greek poet, praised the glory of this great city in *The Illiad* (ca. 750 B.C.E.) and referred to it as the "hundred gated" city. Historical data shows that the Greeks visited Waset and renamed this great city "Thebes." They later built a city in Greece which they named "Thebes" and associated a "sphinx" with it. The likelihood that the Greeks developed these associations independent of any direct contact with Kemet is totally preposterous.

The Temple of Her-Em-Akhet

A short distance east of the paws of Her-em-Akhet stands an ancient temple which was one of the last major monuments to be discovered at Giza. Although excavation of the site was not begun until the 1920's, it wasn't until forty years later that the temple was studied in detail and the results of the study were revealed to the world. Herbert Ricke, a Swiss archaeologist, spent three years researching the structure and concluded that it was the oldest solar temple ever built in Kemet.

An article published in the April, 1986 issue of *Smithsonian* magazine reviewed Mr. Ricke's findings:

> He identified niche-sanctuaries on its east and west sides dedicated to the rising and setting sun, a colonnaded court with 24 massive pillars marking the 24 hours of the day, and ten or 12 statues of the pharaoh [Khafre]. Ricke further concluded that the Sphinx was

Not only was the Sphinx portrayed as a beast that terrorized man, but the medical profession has also perpetuated the negative use of the term by designating the orifice that regulates the expulsion of fecal matter from the body the *sphincter muscle*. There is also a company which manufacturers manila envelopes featuring a clasp that holds the flap secure. The brand name for this product is also called "Sphinx." The continued desecration of the image of Heru is unconscionable. It is tantamount to a company manufacturing a line of "crucifix" staples or nails.

not placed to guard the Giza necropolis, as some Egyptologists had surmised, but instead was a symbol of the sun-god himself, peering over the colonnade into the sanctuaries below.

This temple is perfectly oriented to the astronomical midpoint of the year, the vernal and autumnal equinoxes. It is during the spring and fall equinoxes that the earth experiences 12 hours of daylight and 12 hours of darkness. This temple is so precisely aligned to the movements of the sun, that anyone standing in the eastern sanctuary at the equinox will see the sun trace the outline of the head of Her-em-Akhet while illuminating the sanctuary as it sets behind the shoulder of this great statue. The same scene can be witnessed in the sanctuary of another temple, as the sun sets during the winter solstice.

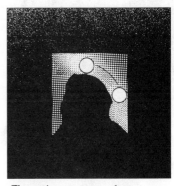

The setting sun traces the outline of Her-em-akhet during the equinox as viewed from the Temple of Her-em-akhet.

The *Smithsonian* article also describes other fascinating discoveries made by Ricke:

> Two other astonishing alignments were revealed as the study went on, both involving the Egyptian hieroglyph *akhet*, which means "places where the sun rises and sets." The *akhet* is rendered as a sun between two mountains. Viewed from the Sphinx at the time of the summer solstice when the sun is at its greatest distance north of the celestial equator, it sets directly between the pyramids of Khufu and Khafre, thus writing across the horizon an *akhet* "on the scale of acres"....This is a clear reference to Horus [Heru] the god and the *akhet* sign, because anyone approaching from ancient Memphis would have seen the head of the Sphinx silhouetted between the two pyramids.

Her-em-Akhet is separated from the Pyramid of Khafre by

The sun on the evening of the summer solstice creates an akhet sign on the Giza horizon as it sets between the Pyramids of Khufu and Khafre.

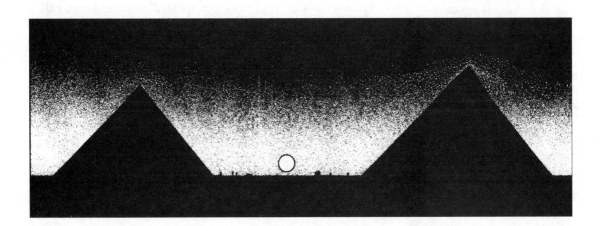

Johnny Carson as Carnak the Magnificent.

The knowledge and power of the priest of the Ipet-Isut (Karnak Temple) was often humorously parodied by Johnny Carson, former host of the *Tonight Show* in a series of skits in which he played "Carnak the Magnificent: the Great Sage from the East." During this routine, Carnak would gaze into the future and provide the answers to questions *before* they were asked.

The questions were secured in envelopes which had been "hermetically sealed in a mayonnaise jar." Once the answer was devined by Carnak, the contents of the envelope (the question) was revealed to the audience. For example, the last answer in the sealed envelope one evening was, "sis, boom, bah." And the question was, "What is the sound of a sheep exploding?"

This routine was so popular that President George Bush did a parody of it at the 107th Annual Gridiron Dinner, which was held at the Capital Hilton Hotel on March 28, 1992. An article describing the gala appeared in the March 30 issue of the *Washington Post*.

George Bush presented himself as *Tarmac the Magnificent* and wowed an audience of "648 normally unbowlable high-powered journalists and their equally

a distance of more than 1,500 feet and the solar temple, which is located directly in front of Her-em-Akhet, was built 70 feet *below* it. Yet despite these vast distances the architects, engineers and designers of this human headed statue, the solar temple and the second pyramid were able to orient all three structures to the solstices and equinoxes with a skill that is unimaginable by today's standards. To many, the buildings at Giza are much more than monuments to the dead. These ancient edifices are the signatures of Godlike men, written in stone across the sky and, they serve as a physical reminder of what man once was and the level of Godliness he must aspire to attain.

The Great Temples of Waset

Four hundred miles south of modern day Cairo, there exists a city once heralded as the seat of government for the most powerful nation in ancient times. This city was called "Waset," or "Wo-Se," a word in the ancient Kemetic language which meant "The Scepter." During the Eighteenth and Nineteenth Dynasties, Waset was the center of an educational, spiritual and architectural renaissance, which continues to have a profound influence upon contemporary life.

It has been said that more than 80 percent of the remains of ancient Kemet can be found in Waset. The tombs on the west bank of the city have yielded some of the greatest treasures in archaeological history and the temples on the east bank are regarded as some of the most remarkable monuments ever created.

So impressive was this great city that foreigners were often awestruck by its magnificence. The Greeks renamed this ancient city "Thebes," and at one point even referred to it as "the city of Zeus," the home of their great god. The Arabic name for Waset is "L'Ouqsor," a word which means "The Palaces," and refers to the great temples the Arabs assumed to be palaces built for royalty. Eventually, the name L'Ouqsor was Westernized to "Luxor," which is the current name for the city and the origin of the word "luxury."

Two of the most magnificent temples in ancient Waset were the "Shemayit-Ipet" (the Southern Ipet), which the Arabs called the "Temple of Luxor," and the "Ipet-Isut," which is now called the "Temple of Karnak."

The Ipet-Isut

The Temple of Ipet-Isut (Karnak) was the largest complex ever constructed in ancient Kemet. It is nearly a quarter of a mile in length and consisted of a series of temples built over a period of nearly 2,000 years, at the behest of numerous kings. Ipet-Isut is an ancient Kemetic word which meant "the most select of places," or "the holiest of places," an obvious reference

unbowlable and high-powered guests" as he masqueraded "as a mystic pressing envelopes to his forehead *a la* Johnny Carson," reported the *Washington Post*. The article continued, "Tarmac holds the envelope to his forehead and gives the answer: Saddam Hussein, Arnold Schwarzenegger and Paul Tsongas. Then he opens the envelope and reads the question: (Name) A scud, a stud and a fud."

A reconstruction of the outer pylon of a temple entrance.

to the sacredness of this site.

This temple also contains the largest colonnaded hall ever constructed. The colonnaded hall comprises 136 columns which stand in 16 rows. The central aisle of the temple contains 12 columns (in two rows) which are 69 feet in height. The papyrus shaped capital adorning each of these 12 columns is large enough to accommodate "a group of 100 men standing crowded atop it at the same time." This great hall measures 338 feet in width and 170 feet in length and the area of its floor space is equal to that of the Cathedral of Notre Dame in Paris.

The English astronomer Sir Norman Lockyer discovered that the axis of this temple was accurately oriented to the summer solstice, and that the colonnaded hall was designed in such a manner as to funnel sunlight between the two rows of columns, in a manner similar to that of a telescope. After numerous summer visits to Egypt, Lockyer's research revealed that the sun temple of Amen-Ra at Karnak was so perfectly aligned to the summer solstice that:

> ...a beam of light coming through a narrow passage some 500 yards all the way to a properly oriented sanctuary would remain there no more than a couple of minutes, then pass away. What's more, it would come in a crescendo and go in a diminuendo with an observable peak at the precise solstice.

It is believed that this phenomenon allowed the astronomer/priest of the temple to be able to determine the precise length of the year to within a minute, or four points of a decimal (365.2422).

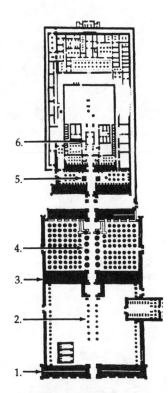

The floor plan of the Ipet-Isut.
1. The Outer Pylon
2. Colonnade of Taharqa
3. Inner Pylon
4. The Great Hall
5. Tekhenwy of Hatshepsut and Amenhotep III
6. The Holy of Holies

Her-em-akhet-like statue with the face of Amenhotep III.

The Shemayit-Ipet

The Ipet-Isut and the Shemayit-Ipet-"the southern place," were connected to one another by a grand avenue of 2,000 sphinxes, which spanned a distance of two miles. These human-headed sphinxes bore the likeness of Amenhotep III, and once a year this avenue was lined with thousands of people who witnessed the annual procession of a statue of Amon as it was carried by the temple priests from the Ipet-Isut to the Southern Ipet.

By contrast, the western entrance to Ipet-Isut (Karnak Temple) was lined with a long row of ram-headed sphinxes and each statue had a small figurine of the king nestled between its paws. These ram-headed edifices represented the Netcher "Amen" who was also referred to as "Amun" or "Amon." This name means *"hidden"* and refers to the hidden or unseen presence of God. This word is still used today at the conclusion of many prayers, and is a lasting reminder of the powerful influence of ancient Kemetic religion.

Coptic Chapel with scenes of the Last Supper, which are barely visible in the upper left corner.

The Southern Ipet is currently referred to as the Temple of Luxor and it was originally dedicated to the Netcher Mut. The greater part of this building was constructed during the reign of Amenhotep III (ca. 1380 B.C.E.), but Rameses II expanded upon the work of Amenhotep III about a century later and added the Great Courtyard and an impressive outer pylon. Rameses is more closely associated with this temple today because of the numerous statues bearing his likeness which now adorn it. Flanking the entrance to this temple are two colossal statues of Rameses and one of an original pair of tekhenwy.

Throughout the centuries this temple has been the site of a great deal of religious activity. During the time of Amenhotep III, images were inscribed upon the walls of this temple depicting the annunciation, immaculate conception, virgin birth and adoration of the Kemetic Trinity of Ausar, Aset and Heru. During the Coptic occupation (ca. 450 A.C.E.), a chapel was erected in the rear of the temple, and the original Kemetic images were covered with plaster and replaced with a mural of Jesus the Christ and the 12 disciples at the Last Supper.

Reconstruction of the Shemayit-Ipet (Luxor Temple).

A support beam of the Shemayit-Ipet, which now serves as a ceiling of the Mosque of Abu el-Haggar. Note the remains of Medu Netcher carvings, from the original structure, that have been painted over in recent years.

The former entrance to the Mosque of Abu el-Haggar as seen from the courtyard of the Shemayit-Ipet.

In the twelfth century A.C.E., the Mosque of Abu el-Haggar was built among the rubble of the Luxor Temple, which was, at that time, buried under a minimum of 15 feet of sand and debris. This mosque makes for a most unusual sight today because its former entrance is now several yards above the current ground level of the temple. Because the mosque rests upon the foundation of this ancient temple, Egyptologists have petitioned for its removal so that the temple can be fully restored. Islamic leaders have fought such recommendations and have argued that the mosque has as much right to this sacred site as the temple.

An elevation of the Shemayit-Ipet clearly shows the extent to which el-Haggar's mosque is fused into its foundation.

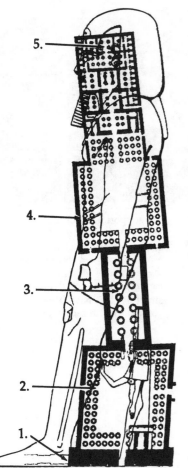

Floor plan of the Shemayit-Ipet (Luxor Temple) with figure of Rameses II superimposed upon it, which illustrates the concept of "The Temple in Man." The basic layout consists of:

1. Feet - The Outer Pylon
2. Legs - Open Courtyard
3. Thighs - Hypostyle Hall
4. Abdomen - Peristyle Court
5. Head - Holy of Holies

One of the most thorough and impressive analysis of Luxor Temple was provided by the Alsatian philosopher R. A. Schwaller de Lubicz and his wife Isha. Mr. de Lubicz was a highly respected mathematician and his wife was an accomplished Egyptologist and writer. Over a course of 15 years (1937-1952), this husband and wife team (aided by their daughter Lucie Lamy) measured, recorded and drew every inch of the temple, including each stone, wall carving and statue. Their research was compiled in three massive volumes entitled *Le Temple de l'Homme (The Temple in Man)*.

Their combined research suggested that the temple was dedicated to the creation of man, and that the floor plan of the temple was representative of the anatomical structure of man. Lucie Lamy superimposed the skeletal framework of a statue of Rameses II over the floor plan of the temple and discovered some interesting similarities. The open courtyard represents the legs; the hypostyle hall represents the thighs; the peristyle court represents the abdomen and the inner temple represents the head.

Within each segment of the temple, activities took place which were related to specific body functions. In the hall that corresponds to the center of perception, there are designs that emphasize time, space, measurement and orientation. This hall also contains 12 columns which correspond to the 12 hours of the day. In the hall that corresponds to the mouth, we find written all the names of the Netcherw and the creation of the God by Ptah via the *spoken word*. Under the chin, at the site of the vocal cords, the king is baptized and given his new name; it is also in this hall where we find the scene of the marriage of the mother of the king to the god Amen.

Through a skillful interpretation of the Kemetic Medu Netcher (hieroglyphics) and symbolism, the de Lubicz family discovered that the architectural forms in Kemet embodied a level of knowledge they described as *sacred science*. This sacred science was regarded as the grand synthesis of Kemetic art, science, religion, philosophy and architecture whose expression was unique with each pharaonic temple that was constructed.

The Significance of Tekhenw

For more than 4,400 years the Great Pyramid held the distinction of being the tallest structure ever made by man. On December 6, 1884, another Nile Valley-inspired architectural structure was completed, which, at 555 feet, became the tallest man-made structure on the planet. This edifice was called the "Washington Monument," and it was created as a tribute to the first president of the United States of America. But, in reality, this monument was nothing more than a replica of an African tekhen.

It has been estimated that the Ipet-Isut contained as many as 64 tekhenw, of which only two are currently standing. Of the two tekhenwy which originally stood at the entrance to the Southern Ipet, only one remains. Its companion was given as a gift to King Louis Philippe of France in 1836, by Muhammad Ali of Turkey, in exchange for a clock which never worked. This relocated tekhen now stands at the eastern end of the Champs Elysees in the Place de la Concorde (Square of Peace) in Paris, France.

During the reign of Thutmose III (circa 1450 B.C.E.), two tekhenwy were erected at the entrance of the Temple of Re at Heliopolis. They were moved to Alexandria around ten B.C.E. by the Romans, and in the 1870's they were given as gifts to the United States and Great Britain. One now stands in Central Park in New York City and the other was erected along the Thames River in London. Currently there are 13 tekhenw in Rome, including one which stands in St. Peter's Square in the Vatican. Tekhenw may also be found in Turkey, Germany and many other locations throughout the world.

The European fascination with tekhenw dates back to the times when the Greeks first visited Kemet. They referred to these monuments as *obelisks*. Dr. Labib Habachi discusses this topic in greater detail in his publication, *The Obelisks of Egypt: Skyscrapers of the Past*:

The remaining tekhen at the first pylon of the Shemayit-Ipet (Luxor Temple).

> Obelisks were known to the ancient Egyptians as *Tekhenw*, a word whose derivation is unknown. When the Greeks became interested in Egypt, both obelisks and pyramids attracted their attention. To the former they gave the name *"obelisks,"* from which the modern name in almost all languages is derived. *Obeliskos* is a Greek diminutive meaning "small spit"; it was applied to obelisks because of their tall, narrow shape. In Arabic, the term is *Messalah*, which means a large patching needle and again has reference to the object's form.

The symbolic significance of the tekhen has undergone interpretations over the ages. Originally, this structure was associated with Ausar (Osiris) as referenced in Volume 2 of The Gods *of the Egyptians* by E.A. Wallis Budge:

> Isis was never able to recover the privy member of Osiris, which having been thrown into the Nile immediately upon its separation from the rest of the body....In order, however, to make some amends for the loss, Isis consecrated the Phallus, made in imitation of it, and instituted a solemn festival to its memory...

The tekhenw of Hatshepsut (left) and Thutmose I at the Ipet-Isut.

The Unfinished Tekhen was being carved *in situ* at a quarry near Aswan when a crack was discovered in the stone and it was abandoned. It is believed that it was being built under the direction of Hatshepsut. If completed, it would have stood 137 feet high and 13 feet wide at the base. It would have weighed an estimated 1,168 tons.

From the earliest of times, the tekhen represented the regenerative powers of Ausar and his resurrection after death. In later years tekhenw were associated with the benben stone and the *Benu*-bird. The Benu-bird was said to be self-regenerating, and like its namesake the phoenix, it would live for 500 years, consume itself in a ball of flames, and later arise from the ashes to live for another 500 years.

It was also believed that the tekhenw were meant to resemble the rays of the sun. Oftentimes the pyramidions (capstones) of the tekhenw were covered with gold or silver (or some combination of the two metals) in order to reflect the light of the sun. The date that tekhenw were first erected is not known, but it is believed that the kings of the Fifth Dynasty (2494-2345 B.C.E.), who were fervent worshipers of the sun Netcher, may have been the first kings to erect these monuments. Two tekhenwy often flanked the entrances to temples and their presence was representative of the complementary, male and female, aspects of the Netcherwy.

The tekhen was a massive monument which was carved from a single block of stone. Most were made from highly polished granite and inscribed with Medu Netcher, which recorded the accomplishments of the ruler who was responsible for their construction. These structures were also used as time keeping devices, and the length of their shadow was measured to determine the time of day. These early sundials also played a key role in ascertaining the precise moment of the solstice and the equinox.

No records have survived which explain how tekhenw were quarried, moved or erected. The tallest tekhen currently standing in Egypt can be found in the Temple of Ipet-Isut. It was erected during the reign of Hatshepsut (1473-1458 B.C.E), is 97 feet high and weighs an estimated 320 tons.

A Survey of Nile Valley Education

Every temple built in Kemet was designed to certain specifications and oriented to a specific celestial body. Each temple was decorated with elaborate wall carvings that were painted in brilliant colors. Most temples contained numerous statues, some were life-size and others were several stories high. It's quite obvious that in order to create a temple, a vast array of skilled technicians was required for the planning, construction and maintenance of each edifice. These individuals had to be skilled in math, architecture, engineering, drafting, painting, sculpture, art, design and a number of assorted disciplines.

In order to facilitate the enormous demand for such technicians, institutions had to be established in order to train them. Within these institutions, there also had to exist a faculty with specialists in various fields of study, along with a support staff. Of course, there had to be administrators who were responsible for maintaining the infrastructure necessary for the continued existence of each institution. Numerous records exist which show that the Africans in the Nile Valley, particularly those in ancient Kemet, had created such an educational system, the likes of which have yet to be duplicated.

Every temple in Kemet had vast libraries equipped with thousands of papyrus scrolls which contained dissertations on law, medicine, philosophy and numerous other subjects. Issac Myer, in the publication, *Oldest Books in the World*, gives an account of the libraries of the Old Kingdom:

> In one of the tombs at Gizeh [Giza], a great functionary of the Sixth Dynasty...takes the title of "Governor of the House of Books." This simple mention thrown incidentally between two or more elevated titles would be sufficient in fault of others coming to show us the extraordinary development at the time of Egyptian civilization. Not only had they a literature, but that literature was also large enough to fill libraries, its importance was so great that to one of the functionaries of the court was especially attached the preservation of the royal library.

In the Kemetic literature, the world was created by the *Ennead*, a group of nine Netcherw. The Netcher Atum (Atom), whose name means "All and Nothing," projected himself into cosmic existence and then produced from his body four complementary pair of Netcherwy. They were:

1. Shu (Air)
2. Tefnut (Moisture)
3. Geb (Earth)
4. Nut (Sky)

These four Netcherwy were said to have given birth to four other Netcherwy. They were:

5. Ausar (the Principle of Omnipotence)
6. Aset (Female Complement of Ausar)
7. Set (Principle of Opposition)
8. Nebt-Het (Female Complement of Set)

This process of halving is the basis of Nile Valley mathematics and the contemporary biological science which is associated with the process of cellular division called mitosis. This concept was expressed in an ancient text which stated:

I am One that transforms into Two
I am Two that transforms into Four
I am Four that transforms into Eight
After this I am One

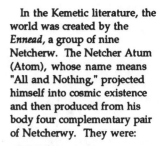

One of the earliest stories of the creation of the world was recorded in the literature of Kemet in a document now called the *Greenfield Papyrus*. This text shows the Netcher Shu separating Nut from Geb.

Shu separating the "Earth" from the "sky."

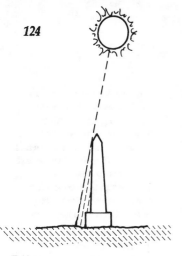

Tekhen

A variety of timekeeping devices were developed in the Nile Valley. The length of the shadow of a *tekhen* was measured to determine the precise moment of the solstice or equinox. The hours of the day or night were determined by measuring the amount of water remaining in the *clepsydra*. The *shadow clock* was referred to by Breasted as: "The oldest clock in the world....It was from the introduction of such Egyptian clocks that the twelve-hour day reached Europe....This clock is about thirty-four hundred years old. Nearly a thousand years later such clocks were adopted by the Greeks."

In 1984, at the *Nile Valley Conference,* Dr. Asa Hilliard presented a paper on the Kemetic Concepts in Education and cited the significance of Ipet-Isut as a center of learning during the Eighteenth Dynasty:

> It was both a center of religion and education, since the two could not be separated in the minds of the Kamites. It housed an elite faculty of priest-professors. It has been estimated that at one time there were more than 80,000 students at all grade levels studying at Ipet Isut University (Abdullah, 1984). Temples were at the center of religion, politics, and education.
>
> The faculty were called Hersetha or "teachers of mysteries," and were divided into departments (Meyer, 1900), as follows: (1) Mystery Teachers of Heaven (astronomy and astrology); (2) Mystery Teachers of All Lands (geography); (3) Mystery Teachers of the Depths (geology); (4) Mystery Teachers of the Secret Word (philosophy and theology); and (5) Mystery of Pharaoh and Mystery Teachers who examined words (law and communication).

Much has been written about the "Mystery Schools" of the Nile Valley, but one important factor must be remembered; these schools, and the subjects taught within them, were a mystery only to those who were unfamiliar with that system of education. The purpose of education in the Nile Valley was to create a society where the citizens would understand the relationship which existed between themselves and the universe. In the truest sense of the word, the educational centers in the Nile Valley were the first "universities." Upon closer examination of the complexities of Nile Valley education, one can begin to understand why they were called "Mystery Schools" by the many foreigners who came there seeking enlightenment.

Clepsydra

The shadow clock told time by turning the crossbar (A) toward the east, which caused its shadow to fall on the perpendicular bar (B). As the sun rose higher in the sky it caused the shadow to shorten, thus marking off the hours on bar (B) in six-hour increments. At noon the crossbar (A) was turned around 180 degrees to the west and the time was measured for six additional hours.

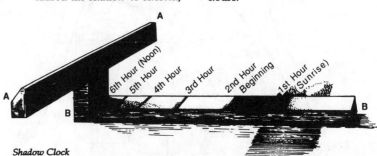

Shadow Clock

Medicine

The *Edwin Smith Papyrus* is the oldest medical treatise in existence, and it is believed to have been written in the Eighteenth Dynasty (ca. 1550 B.C.E). Many regard this papyrus as a copy of an original document that was created as early as the First Dynasty. Depending on what time line one uses to date the First Dynasty of Kemet, this medical text could have been written as early as 4200 or as late as 3100 B.C.E.

In any event, the appearance of a highly sophisticated text had to have been preceded by hundreds of years of observation, research and refinement. The ancient physician/priests of the Nile Valley were said to have been instructed in temples which were called "Per Ankh." In today's language they would be called the "House of Life." Of the thousands of medical papyri originally written, less than a dozen have been discovered, and of that number, the Ebers Papyrus and the Edwin Smith Papyrus are deemed the most profound.

The *Edwin Smith Papyrus* was published in 1930 by James Henry Breasted, who had spent ten years translating the document. This papyrus describes 48 different injuries to the head, face, neck, thorax and spinal column and the appropriate surgical methods for attending to them. It is suspected that the Eighteenth Dynasty scribe who was responsible for copying the original text only wrote the first 48 cases dealing with the upper third of the body. There are more than 90 anatomical terms referenced in the *Edwin Smith Papyrus*, and there are more than 200 terms listed in various Nile Valley medical literature. This papyrus is also of great importance because of its use of the word "brain" and references to the neurological relationship between the brain (spinal cord and nervous system) and the body.

The *Ebers Papyrus* (ca. 1500 B.C.E.) explores a broad range of medical science and includes chapters on the pulse and cardio-vascular system, dermatology, dentistry, gynecology, ophthalmology, obstetrics, tumors, burns, fractures, intestinal disorders and much more. There is also considerable evidence that physicians in Kemet practiced circumcision, brain surgery and were extremely well versed in gynecology and obstetrics.

By 2000 B.C.E. physicians in Kemet had already created an effective organic chemical contraceptive. This product consisted of acacia spikes, honey and dates, which were mixed in a specific ratio, and inserted into the vagina. Modern science has since discovered that acacia spikes contain lactic acid, which is a natural chemical spermicide.

Pregnancy and fetal sex tests were conducted by Nile Valley physicians who soaked bags of wheat and barley in a sample of a woman's urine. Urine from a pregnant woman was known to accelerate the growth of certain plants; if the barley sprouted,

Imhotep
(ca. 2700 B.C.E.)

Imhotep, the earliest-known physician, was a minister of state, a scribe, a seer, an architect, astronomer, magician and physician. He was deified under the Eighteenth Dynasty and a temple was erected in his honor on the Island of Philae. Imhotep was venerated as "the great physician of the gods and men," "the god who grants life to all who turn to him" and "the god who protects men." He is believed to be the author of what is known as the *Edwin Smith Papyrus*, the oldest document on surgery. The document is notable for its accuracy and high scientific standard.

This notation was taken from the placard of Imhotep in the Hall of Immortals at the "International College of Surgeons" in Chicago, IL.

Hippocrates
(460?-377? B.C.E.)

The Hippocratic Oath
I swear by Apollo, the
physician, and Asclepius and
Health and All-Heal and all the
gods and goddesses that,
according to my ability and
judgement, I will keep this oath
and stipulation.

So reads the first paragraph
of the *Hippocratic Oath*. Not
only was the science of
medicine first developed in the
Nile Valley, but an analysis of
the opening lines of the *Oath*
provides further evidence of its
Kemetic roots and the
personalities associated with its
early development.

Apollo was the Greek version
of the African Netcher *Heru*
and *Asclepius* (who was the son
of Apollo) was the Greek name
for Imhotep. The sacred
symbol of Asclepius was a
snake entwined around a staff.
This symbol was first used in
Kemet and was associated with
Djhuiti the Netcher of medicine.

Asclepius

it meant that the woman was pregnant and was going to give
birth to a female child, and if the wheat sprouted it meant that
she would give birth to a male child. The urine pregnancy test
was not rediscovered by modern science until 1926 and the
wheat/barley sex determination test was not developed until
1933.

In 1987, the National Academy of Sciences published a report
by the National Academy of Engineers entitled *Lasers: Invention to Application*. This publication featured on its cover
a photograph of a stella of Akhenaton and his wife Nefertiti
basking in the soothing rays of the sun disc, the Aton. The
cover art is quite interesting because one of the rays of sunlight
is chromatically highlighted so as to give the suggestion of a
laser beam.

In a chapter titled "Lasers in Medicine," the author, Rodney
Perkins, M.D., suggests that a form of laser therapy was actually
used in the Nile Valley. Dr. Perkins states that:

> The use of the laser in medicine and surgery has a
> relatively short pedigree of less than two decades.
> Although the range of laser radiation extends both
> below and above the visible portion of the electro-
> magnetic spectrum, that radiation is, in a sense, only a
> special form of light. The use of other forms of light in
> medicine has a longer history. There is documentation
> that the ancient Egyptians recognized and used the
> therapeutic power of light as long as 6,000 years ago.
> Patches of depigmented skin, now referred to as vitiligo,
> were cosmetically undesirable. Egyptian healers re-
> portedly crushed a plant similar to present day parsley
> and rubbed the affected areas with the crushed leaves.
> Exposure to the sun's radiation produced a severe form
> of sunburn only in the treated areas. The erythema
> subsided, leaving hyperpigmentation in the previously
> depigmented areas.

Residents of the Nile Valley who often journeyed in cara-
vans across the desert were advised to chew a root called "ami-
majos," which provided extra protection from the intense sun
by increasing the amount of melanin in the skin. Modern
scientific research has shown that the ami-majos root contains
an organic chemical substance called 8-methoxypsorate, which
stimulates melanocytes and increases skin pigmentation.

Medical practitioners in Kemet were often specialists who
treated specific disorders. Archaeologists have discovered
cancerous tumors in some ancient mummies and evidence
that the ancient physicians were removing tumors with knives
or red-hot irons as late as 1600 B.C.E. Historical records have
also provided the name of the earliest female physician, Prechet,
a woman who also held the title of "chief physician."

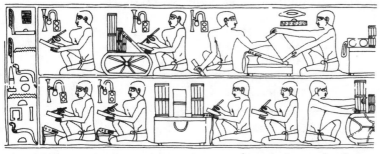

Accountants assessing the estate of a deceased person from the mastaba of Ti at Saqqara.

Mathematics

Much of what is known about Nile Valley mathematics can be found in a document called the *Rhind Mathematical Papyrus*, which was purchased by the Scottsman Alexander Rhind and brought to London. This ancient papyrus was discovered in the mid nineteenth century and was believed to have been written during the Middle Kingdom (ca. 1900 B.C.E.) by the scribe Ahmose. The text consists of more than 80 mathematical problems and their solutions. This papyrus is said to be a copy of a much earlier document which was originally written as a mathematical textbook for children.

Cheikh Anta Diop holds this document in the highest regard. He states:

> ...exercises 56, 57, 58, 59, and 60 of the Rhind Papyrus show us that the Egyptians, two thousand years before the Greeks, studied the mathematics of the pyramid and of the cone, and that they even used the different trigonometric lines, the tangent, the sine, the cosine, the cotangent, in order to calculate their slopes.

Some of the problems addressed in this papyrus include the surface of the sphere, the square root (Pythagorean Theorem), the quadrature of the circle, the volume of a sphere and the methods for determining the surface of the circle, rectangle, trapezium and triangle.

One of the most interesting elements of the *Rhind Papyrus* is problem 79, which deals with a geometric progression of a ratio of seven. In the text this problem is called "The inventory of goods contained in a house." It states:

> There are seven houses,
> in each house there are seven cats.
> Each cat kills seven mice,
> each mouse had eaten seven grains.
> Each grain would have produced seven *hekat*.
> What is the sum of all the enumerated elements?

The eyes of the Netcherw were considered to have been the two symbols of light in the heavens, the sun and the moon. The right eye was called the "Eye of Heru," and represented the sun. The left eye was associated with Djhuiti and symbolized the moon.

Arithmetic in the Nile Valley was based on *dimidiation,* halving rather than addition. The components that comprise the "Eye of Djhuiti" were given a numerical value and were used when writing the fractions one-half to one-sixty fourth. The symbols for the various fractions of the eye were called the *hekat*, which was also a unit of volume used when measuring grain. Thus, the *hekat* and Djhuiti both symbolized *measurement*.

The relationship between the lunar eye, the moon, and measurement is quite profound because the passage of time was noted by adding the various fractions of the moon (quarter moon, half moon, full moon, etc.). The astronomers of ancient Kemet knew that the moon reflected the light of the sun and that it became invisible (a new moon) when it was in conjunction with the sun and that it was fully visible (a full moon) when it was directly opposite the sun.

The solution to the problem is as follows:

7	houses
49	cats
343	mice
2,401	grains
16,807	*hekat* of grain

19,607	Total

This problem is designed to show that in each of seven houses there are seven cats, each cat caught seven mice, each mouse ate seven grains of corn and each grain of corn would have produced seven *hekat* of grain. Another way of writing the problem is:

$$7 \qquad 7$$
$$7 \times 7 \qquad 7(1 +7) = 56$$
$$7 \times 7 \times 7 \qquad 7(1 + 56) = 399$$
$$7 \times 7 \times 7 \times 7 \qquad 7(1 +399) = 2,800$$
$$7 \times 7 \times 7 \times 7 \times 7 \qquad 7(1 + 2,800) = 19,607$$

The concept of the *Pythagorean Theorem* and the "magic 3-4-5" triangle existed centuries before Pythagoras founded his aristocratic *brotherhood* in 529 B.C.E. This formula had been used in Kemet as late as 1143 B.C.E. and an image representing it was carved in the tomb of Rameses VI. Incorporated within this symbol are the major constants necessary for geometry and the "sacred 3-4-5 triangle." This 3-4-5 triangle is also referred to as the "Golden Section," which is expressed mathematically as *phi*, or 1.6180.

At each stage of the problem the sum is obtained by increasing the previous sum by one and multiplying by the common ratio. The sum of the series of four terms was 2,800, when this is increased by one it becomes 2,801 and by multiplying 2,801 by seven gives the sum to five terms.

Most people will recognize a profound similarity between problem 79 and the well-known Mother Goose nursery rhyme, *As I was going to St. Ives:*

> As I was going to St. Ives
> I met a man with seven wives
> Each wife had seven sacks
> Each sack had seven cats
> Each cat had seven kittens.
> Kittens, cats, sacks, wives.
> How many were going to St. Ives?

This rhyme is more of a riddle then an algebraic problem because the answer is "one." The traveler is the only one *going to* St. Ives, while the group that he encounters is *returning from* St. Ives. If one is unaware that this is a trick question one would probably attempt to solve the geometric progression. This version of problem 79 was introduced into Europe approximately 3,500 years after its creation.

Although similar mathematical problems can also be found in the Papyrus of Moscow there are many who wish to attribute the development of higher mathematics to the Greeks, despite their proclaimed indebtedness to the priests of the Nile Valley. Gay Robins and Charles Shute offer the following conclusions

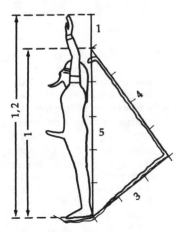

in their book *The Rhind Mathematical Papyrus: an ancient Egyptian text:*

> Proclus in his *Commentary on Euclid,* following Herodotus, wrote that geometry had an Egyptian origin arising out of the necessity of resurveying the land after each inundation. Aristotle (*Metaphysics* I, i, 16), on the other hand attributed the birth of mathematics in Egypt to the existence of a priestly leisured class. Perhaps the most enduring effect of Egyptian mathematics was the stimulus that it gave to the Greeks, who then traveled beyond mere calculation into the realms of abstract thought. In which case, the Greek achievement will have owed something to the learning meticulously and patiently handed on by the Egyptians from generation to generation since early times.

Mineralogy

Visitors to the various Egyptian museums found throughout the world often marvel at the priceless treasures that were created in ancient times. Aside from the numerous papyri, monumental architecture and phenomenal paintings, the artisans of the Nile Valley were also skilled jewelers who fashioned works of art made of gold, silver and semi-precious stones. One area that is often overlooked is the development of mining precious metals in Kemet and Nubia.

Scientists acknowledge that there are more than 90 ancient Egyptian gold mines in the Egyptian desert, but there were probably hundreds of mines in Nubia, which was the primary source of that precious ore. In fact the word *Nubia* makes reference to a region with abundant gold reserves.

Modern geologists have discovered some interesting similarities between ancient drilling techniques and contemporary ones, for example:

• In the ancient mine of Hotet, near the Abu Dahr Mountains in the southern part of the Eastern Desert, one will find evidence of gold mining in black morion veins. These same veins are known to be abundant sources of gold ore and are referred to as "uriferous quartz veins."

• The ancient Nile Valley miners drilled shafts with an angle of 45 degrees, which is the same angle used by geologists today. This specific procedure for extracting minerals has not changed significantly over the passage of time.

The Italian mathematician, Leonardo Fibonacci (ca. 1175-1204 A.C.E.,) is reputed to have been "the greatest mathematician of the Middle Ages." Fibonacci studied math in North Africa and learned, from the Arabs, the Hindu system of numbers (0, 1, 2, 3, 4, 5, 6, 7, 8, 9). He is credited with introducing this new numbering system into Western Europe. Prior to this time calculations were still being made by using the archaic Roman numerals and Greek letters.

In 1202 A.C.E., Fibonacci published *Liber Abaci* (Book of the Abacas) which discussed Hindu-Arabic numerals. It contained methods of arithmetic and mathematical applications for solving problems related to commerce.

There is also evidence to suggest that Fibonacci may have studied in Egypt, or at least was familiar with elements of the *Rhine Papyrus.* One of the math problems that Fibonacci used in his text stated: "Seven old women went to Rome; each woman had seven mules; each mule carried seven sacks; each sack contained seven loaves; and with each loaf there were seven knives; each knife was put up in seven sheaths."

*Map of the gold mine of King
Seti I, which was drawn on
papyrus, ca. 1300 B.C.E.*

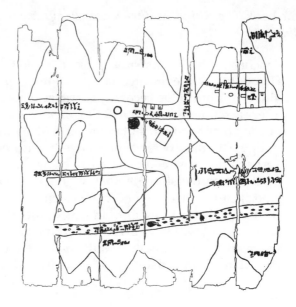

In close proximity to many of the ancient mines scientists have found numerous ovens which were built for melting ore and extracting metals. One site of particular significance is in the Abu Sawil area in Upper Egypt, which is located 180 miles south of Aswan. Recent investigations of Nile Valley metallurgy also appear to suggest the use of steel in the forging of weaponry. In the French edition of the December 1977 issue of *American Science*, two scientists announced their discovery of a steel object of successive layers which contained varying percentages of carbon. This object, believed to be the oldest of its kind, was identified as an Egyptian knife made sometime between 900 and 800 B.C.E.

An article in the *Egyptian Gazette* (July 15, 1990) referenced the Nile Valley influence on mineralogy:

> Ancient Egyptians made a lot of progress in the mining science[s]. They drilled some mines needing 400 workers, with [a] depth of more than 250 m [825 feet]....Ancient Egyptians also knew how [to] produce contouring maps. The oldest one is housed in the Toren Museum in Italy. It depicts one of the old gold mines in [the] Eastern Desert, and was discovered in the 19th century. This map refers to El-Fawkher mine and also to a series of gold mine[s] lying in the desert between Luxor and the Red Sea.

As with any mining project, problems were bound to arise during excavations. When the ancient miners encountered flooding, they used devices such as the *continuous screw* to pump water out of the mines. This device was in use hundreds of years before it had been "invented" by Archimedes. The ancient scientist Diodorus of Sicily verified the Nile Valley origins of this device when he stated that miners in ancient Kemet pumped water out of mines by using "screws that Archimedes of Syracuse invented during his trip to Egypt."

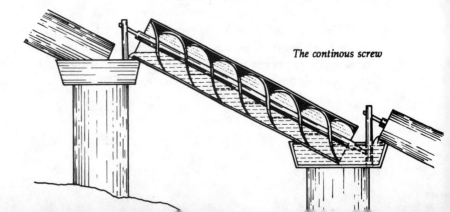

The continous screw

Shipbuilding

The ability of the people of Kemet, Nubia and Ethiopia to explore new worlds, transport goods and ferry huge monoliths for temple construction, was facilitated by their capacity to build and navigate a variety of seagoing vessels. Papyrus reed boats have been in use in the Nile Valley since the earliest dynasties, and the development of navigational skills allowed for the building of larger ships and travel to other lands. The first use of a sail on a ship has also been traced to the Nile Valley.

Earliest rendering of a boat found in Kemet. It is estimated to have been painted between 3200 and 2500 B.C.E.

The historical record of Kemet is replete with numerous examples of seafaring abilities. Seneferu, the first king of the Fourth Dynasty, was said to have sent a fleet of 40 ships to Lebanon, and by the Twelfth Dynasty, Ka-Kepra-Re Sen-Wosret I, also known to the Greeks as Kecrops, had crossed the Mediterranean Sea and founded the city of Athens in Greece. In the Twenty Fifth Dynasty, during the reign of Necho II, navigational technology had advanced to the point where sailors from Kemet successfully circumnavigated Africa and drew an extremely accurate map of the continent.

In 1970, the Norwegian-born ethnologist Thor Heyerdahl and a crew of seven, sailed a papyrus reed boat named Ra-II from the west coast of Africa to the Caribbean. Heyerdahl based the design of his boat on paintings found in Nile Valley monuments and he hired Africans to construct the ship. His aim was to prove that sailors from Kemet could have sailed in similar boats across the Atlantic Ocean to the "New World."

The most impressive ancient ship ever discovered was the 4,600 year-old-barge found buried near the Great Pyramid of Khufu at Giza in 1954. This 132-foot gondola-shaped vessel weighed an estimated 35 tons and was built almost entirely of Lebanese cedarwood. The entire craft was made of 1,224 pieces of wood, which were literally sewn together with ropes strung through slits on the inside of the hull. It was equipped with ten oars for rowing and two others which were attached to the stern and served as rudders.

In the fall of 1991, Egyptologists discovered a fleet of 12 royal ships, which were found at Abydos in an ancient burial ground 280 miles south of Cairo. These ships are 50 to 60 feet long and are estimated to be about 5,000 years old. They are believed to be the earliest boats found on Earth.

The world's oldest and best preserved wooden boat is currently on display in a museum next to the Great Pyramid at Giza.

Aeronautical Engineering

Nile Valley civilizations have been noted for a number of historical firsts including: writing, law, architecture and religion. But there now appears to be a new and unexpected field of study that can be added to the long list of "Nile Valley firsts," the experimentation with aeronautical engineering.

In 1898 scientists discovered a model of what was believed to be a bird. It was found in Saqqara, which is located 15 miles south of Cairo. This "Bird of Saqqara," as it was called, was made of sycamore wood in the fourth or third century B.C.E. and it was eventually placed among a collection of other bird models in the Cairo Museum, where it went unnoticed for 71 years.

In 1969, a physician by the name of Dr. Khalil Messiha, discovered the Bird of Saqqara as he was looking through a box of bird models in a storeroom of the museum. To his surprise the Saqqara bird was distinctly different from the other bird models. Upon seeing the model, he realized that it lacked the birdlike decorations of the other models; its wings were "on top" of its body instead of protruding from its side and it had a "vertical" tail as opposed to the traditional "horizontal" tail one would expect to see on a real bird or a model of one.

All of these peculiarities caused Dr. Messiha, who is also an artist and model aircraft amateur, to remark, "it was very much like some of the scale model planes which I used to make 20 years ago." Dr. Messiha was allowed to take the measurements of the "bird" in order to construct a accurate scale model. When the model was completed and thrown into the air, it actually glided several yards. Dr. Messiha's brother, Guirgus, who is a flight engineer, stated that the aerofoil shape of the body was intentionally designed to lessen drag, and that knowledge of this effect was not discovered by aeronautical engineers until relatively recently.

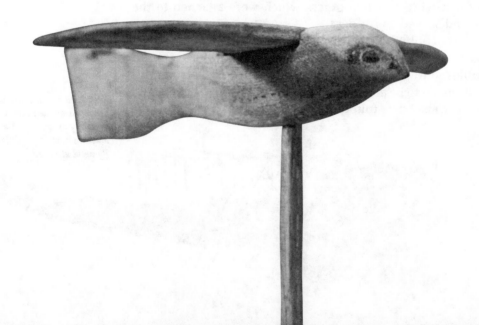

An official at the National Aeronautical and Space Administration (NASA) has taken a great interest in this discovery and his analysis of the model is as follows:

• The model is that of a *monoplane*, which has negative *dihedral angeled* wings, that provide for greater stability in flight.

• Its body has an *aerofoil shape*, which increases in thickness under the wing area and then tapers off as it extends to the tail section.

• It looks remarkably futuristic and bears a close resemblance to the American Hercules transport aircraft, which also has negative dihedral wings.

As a result of the renewed interest in the model by members of the International Aerospace Education Committee, the Cairo Museum relabeled this artifact the "Glider of Saqqara" and showcased it in a special "aeroplane" exhibition in 1972. Further research has revealed that the person who invented the glider was called "Pa-di-Imen," a name which means the "Gift of Amon." It is believed that Pa-di-Imen made several models before perfecting the one now on exhibit, and it is also felt that a full-scale model of the glider has yet to be discovered somewhere under the desert sands near Saqqara.

Part Two

The
Stolen
Legacy

Exploding The Myths
Volume 1

Chapter Four
The Europeanization of Kemet

Modern Attacks Against an Ancient History

The idea that the people of the Nile Valley were of African origin is certainly not a novel one. The belief that Kemet was populated and ruled by "Black Africans," since its earliest beginning until the end of the native dynasties, was widely held by the Kemites, and by the Greeks, who had frequent contact with them. Many of the questions concerning the ethnicity of the people of Kemet have been raised since the advent of the discipline of Egyptology in the early nineteenth century. Prior to that time, race was not an issue, and the color of the skin of Nile Valley dwellers was generally accepted to be of a dark hue.

In his publication, *The World and Africa*, W.E.B. Du Bois explained why Europeans began questioning the race and color of the Egyptians:

> There can be but one explanation for this vagary of nineteenth century science. It was due to the slave trade and Negro slavery. It was due to the fact that the rise and support of capitalism called for rationalization based upon degrading and discrediting the Negroid peoples. It is especially significant that the science of Egyptology arose and flourished at the very time that the cotton kingdom reached its greatest power on the foundation of American Negro slavery.

William Edward Burghadt Du Bois

In 1895, Du Bois became the first African American to receive a Ph.D. degree from Harvard. He was one of the founders of the NAACP and an early proponent of Pan-Africanism. In 1900, Du Bois assessed race relations in the United States and declared that "The problem of the twentieth century is the problem of the color line."

The suggestion that the history of ancient Egypt would be rewritten to support a racist ideology is more than a notion. In the late eighteenth century a Frenchman by the name of Count Constantine de Volney (1757-1820) wrote a wonderful history book entitled, Th*e Ruins of Empires*, which described his journeys in Egypt between 1783 and 1785. This book became a best-seller in France and the demand for it was so great that an English version was printed and an "American edition" became available in the mid 1790's.

Volney's descriptions of the ancient monuments were fair and objective. He described the appearance of the Sphinx as "typically Negro in all its features." To some, Volney's descriptions were too accurate, and they had to be "modified."

Count Constantine de Volney

For example, in deference to the American attitude regarding people of African descent, British editors decided to omit several lines of text from pages 15, 16 and 17 in the American edition of *Ruins of Empires*. One specific quotation described the ancient kingdoms of Ethiopia and the Egyptian city of Thebes. Another edited statement which described the people of Kemet read:

> There are a people, now forgotten, who discovered, while others were yet barbarians, the elements of the arts and sciences. A race of men, now ejected from society for their sable skin and frizzled hair, founded on the study of the laws of nature, those civil and religious systems which still govern the universe.

Volney discovered this glaring omission only after he had mastered the English language, and he forbade the future sale of his work until such time as it could be published in its entirety. This act of censorship was certainly not an isolated incident; it was representative of a clear and consistent pattern of covering up and denying African historical accomplishments. The gross misrepresentations of Nile Valley history have been referred to as a "stolen legacy," and have been perpetrated by many "learned scholars" for hundreds of years.

Two millennium prior to Volney's travels to the Nile Valley, other Europeans wrote about their experiences and observations. Like Volney, these travelers described people of color whom fifteenth century-Europeans would later enslave and classify as "Negroes." As early as the eighth century B.C.E., Homer, in *The Iliad*, stated that Zeus and all of the gods of Greece traveled to Africa to "feast with Ethiop's faultless men." Four hundred years later the historian Herodotus remarked:

Homer

> Almost all of the names of the gods came into Greece from Egypt. My inquiries prove that they were all derived from a foreign source, and my opinion is that Egypt furnished the greater number. The Egyptians were the first to introduce solemn assemblies, processions, and litanies to the gods, all of which the Greeks were taught to use. It seems to me a sufficient proof of this that in Egypt these practices have been established from remote antiquity, while in Greece they are only recently known.

Herodotus also stated that the Greek oracle, or prophet, was one of two Egyptian women who were allegedly kidnapped from Thebes (Waset) by Phoenician traders. One was taken to Libya (Oracle of Ammon) and the other was taken to Dodona, in Greece. Herodotus also described the Egyptians as "blackskinned" and having "wooly hair."

Four hundred years after the visit of Herodotus to Africa, a Sicilian writer named Diodorus recorded his observations of the Nile Valley inhabitants:

> The Ethiopians say that the Egyptians are one of their colonies which was brought into Egypt by Osiris. They even allege that this country was originally under water, but that the Nile, dragging much mud as it flowed from Ethiopia, had finally filled it in and made it a part of the continent....They add that from them, as from their authors and ancestors, the Egyptians get most of their laws. It is from them that the Egyptians have learned to honor kings as gods and bury them with such pomp; sculpture and writing were invented by the Ethiopians.

Zeus

Zeus was regarded as the king of the Greek gods and was worshiped by the Romans as Jupiter. Within Greek mythology it was said that Zeus regularly traveled to Africa to dine with "Ethiops faultless men."

Many classical scholars would have us believe that Greek civilization developed independent of any African influence and that Nile Valley civilization was the product of a "mixed" society. These same scholars have declared that the "eyewitness" accounts by the Greeks who consistently described the Egyptians and Ethiopians as "black skinned" and "wooly haired" were also erroneous. Even with all of the modern technological advances of today, it is physically impossible for someone living in the twentieth century A.C.E. to describe, with greater accuracy, events which were witnessed in the ninth, fifth or first century B.C.E.

It also seems highly unlikely that people would travel to a foreign land and create a culture, philosophy and religion which they didn't have at home. Traditionally, when people travel outside of their homeland, they generally return with newfound ideas, usually better or at least different than those they already possessed. By contrast, if a country is occupied by a foreign army which is more technologically advanced, that occupying army is likely to impose its technology and culture on the newly conquered occupants. Conversely, if an occupied nation has any technology, philosophy or theology superior to that of their conquerors, that knowledge will surely be claimed along with the new territories, or it will be summarily repressed. According to an age old dictum, "all's fair in love and war." Throughout the ages the losers in any conflict have been forced to give up their wealth, their women and their knowledge.

There currently exist volumes of evidence supporting the African origin of Nile Valley civilization and a Nile Valley presence in ancient Europe. Herodotus and other writers reported that Greece had once been conquered by a king named Sesostris, and Greek legends also indicated that the legendary founder of Athens was an Egyptian named Kekrops. Inscriptions recently found in the Egyptian city of Memphis attributed the conquest of Greece by land and sea to two Twelfth Dynasty kings, Senwosert I and Ammenemes II. In Kemet,

Senwosrt I

Senwosret was also known as *Kepre Kare Senwosret I*. His name was later changed by the Greeks to *Kekrops* and other Greek texts referred to him as *Sesostris*.

Herodotus was responsible for providing ancient Europeans with a first-hand account of his travels. He was given the moniker "father of history" by the Roman orator Cicero because he had written a number of books detailing his travels throughout the various parts of Greece, western Asia and North Africa. Many of the writings of Herodotus described the conquests of the Persian army, and he visited Kemet approximately 50 years after the Persian invasion.

The first Persian conquest of Kemet was in 525 B.C.E., and this was followed by a succession of other foreign invasions: the Greeks came in 332 B.C.E., the Romans in 30 B.C.E, the Arabs in 642 A.C.E, the French in 1798 and the English in 1881. The conquests of Egypt made it possible for many developing nations to wear the banner of civilization for the first time in their recorded history, for they now had access to the accumulated wisdom of more than 3,000 years of Nile Valley civilization. The conquests of Egypt After the Common Era also provided their invaders with profound discoveries in the areas of science, math and archeology.

During the early incursions into Kemet, the invading armies often retained elements of the indigenous culture. Foreign rulers often assumed African names, embraced Nile Valley theology and worshiped many of the gods of old, while their savants studied the arts and sciences in the numerous temples

The armies of the Nile Valley were considered the most formidable of their day. On one occasion the troops of King Taharqa ran a 30-mile race through the desert of Nubia. This competition was run in the evening in order to avoid the intense heat of the day and took five hours to complete. Taharqa followed his men on horseback and was so pleased with their performance that he rewarded both winners and losers of the contest.

that were to be found along the Nile. Many of the new ideas that were found in Kemet were infused into the culture of the invaders and dispersed throughout other newly conquered territories. Although Kemet no longer exerted any political influence in the world, her many accomplishments in the areas of science, religion and social behavior continued to influence civilizations for centuries to come.

The Greek invasion of Kemet was primarily responsible for the closing of many temples and consolidation of their curriculums in the newly formed city of Alexandria on the shores of the Mediterranean Sea. The Library of Alexandria was the nexus of a vast educational complex, which was said to contain more than 700,000 papyrus scrolls. It had a copy of every existing scroll known to the library administrators. Many were translated from Medu Netcher (hieroglyphic) into Greek.

A portion of the library was accidently destroyed by Julius Caesar during his conquest of Egypt, but it was later rebuilt by his successor Mark Antony around 40 B.C.E. In 391 A.C.E., the Christian emperor Theodosius decreed that "all that was ancient was pagan and therefore sinful," and the library was burned to the ground by a mob of Christian fanatics. As the knowledge of this ancient library faded from the memories of later generations, so, too, did the recollection of the Africans who had founded the earliest civilization in the ancient land that is now called Egypt.

The debate over the ethnicity of the ancient Egyptians has increased significantly within the last few years, primarily because of the growth of the African centered education movement, which has spawned the teaching of "politically correct" history in the United States and many parts of the world. Many classicists have decried this revision of history

These two photographs of
Queen Tiye represent the
attempt by some to disassociate
African people from Egyptian
history. Queen Tiye was the
wife of Amenhotep III and the
mother of Amenhotep IV
(Aknenaton). The photo above
is a popular image of her which
clearly illustrates her African
features.

The photo below appeared in
the February 4, 1990 issue of
the *New York Times* and was
used to illustrate an article
entitled, "Africa's Claim to
Egypt's History Grows More
Insistent." The caption
accompanying this photo read,
"Sculpture believed to be the
head of Queen Tiye of Egypt,
who lived in the 14th century
B.C. Revisionist historians
argue that she was descendent
of Black Africans."

as "Western civilization bashing" and "the newest academic sport." This topic has also been hotly debated in the press as some of the following newspaper headlines indicate: "Some Scholars Dispute 'Black Egypt' Theory" (*Washington Times*, May 26, 1990) or "Africa's Claim to Egypt's History Grows More Insistent" (*New York Times*, May 4, 1990) and "Goodbye Columbus, Hello Brave New Multicultural World" (*Sunday Times [London]* July 28, 1991). Many of those articles featured comments by "experts" who stated that any attempt to associate African people with ancient Egyptian history was nothing less than pure fantasy.

One consistent theme in many such articles is the use of photographs of statues with partially damaged faces or full faced images of personalities of questionable ethnicity. Take, for example, the September 23, 1991 issue of *Newsweek* which explored the validity of Afrocentrism. The magazine cover featured a "doctored" photograph of an unidentified queen wearing an Egyptian headdress and an earring in the shape of the African continent colored red, black and green. Not only was this cover an insult to a legitimate academic pursuit, but it also attempted to challenge the issue of Afrocentricity by posing the question, "Was Cleopatra Black?" The question of Cleopatra's ethnicity is irrelevant because it is generally agreed by all scholars that she was of mixed parentage.

The Egyptian queen Cleopatra VII was certainly not an African in the traditional sense of the word, but neither should she be considered European. At best she was a mulatto. Under no condition would she have passed for white in the United States. Had she lived in the Jim Crow era of the 1940's she most certainly would have been classified as black or Negro. Under the racist system of apartheid, which currently exists in the Union of South Africa, Cleopatra would surely be classified as colored.

If the editors of *Newsweek* were serious about exploring the "facts or fantasies" of Afrocentrism, they would not have selected the image of Cleopatra VII to question the validity of a black presence in the Nile Valley. They could have easily focused on the history of Kemet *before* it was conquered by foreigners and chosen from myriad images which would have supported the assertion of "black" rulership. One must question their intentions.

Cleopatra VII was born in 69 B.C.E., 1,322 years after Queen Tiye, 1,400 years after Queen Hatshepsut and more than 3,000 years after Aha, the first ruler of Upper and Lower Kemet. Why weren't any of these images used to question the ethnicity of the ancient Egyptians? Is it because they are too African in appearance and their very presence on the cover of *Newsweek* would have rendered the question of their ethnicity irrelevant?

All the queens who bore the name Cleopatra were descended

Ida Eisenhower

The picture above is of an orphaned mulatto woman named Ida Stover. This photo was taken on September 23, 1885, on the day she married a young German immigrant named David Jacob Eisenhower. Ida Eisenhower gave birth to six sons, one of whom was named Dwight David Eisenhower, who later became the 34th president of the United States.

Throughout his years of military service and tenure as president, no reference was ever made to Eisenhower's African roots. J.A. Rogers, in his publication *The Five Negro Presidents*, identified other presidents of the United States who were of African descent and opted to "pass for white" in order to advance their political careers.

Newsweek
September 23, 1991

One of the more interesting stories in the continuing attempt to Europeanize Kemet has been the debate over the ethnicity and image of Queen Nefertiti. The issue of Nefertiti's ethnicity is a legitimate debate because there are scholars who cite evidence stating she was the daughter of Artama, King of Mitanni, in western Asia. Other scholars have suggested she was of Kemetic origins because she was said to have been the daughter of "Ay," a man who became ruler of Kemet after the death of Tutankhamen. While scholars on both sides of this issue claim the validity of their evidence, the issue regarding the image of Nefertiti is one that might be more easily settled.

The representation of Nefertiti most people are familiar with is shown on page 145. There is, however, no evidence linking Nefertiti to this image. This unidentified and unfinished sculpture was discovered in an abandoned art studio, in the city of Armana by professors Hermann Rankee and Ludwig Borchardt, during the excavations of 1912-1913. It was not shown publicly until 1920, when it was prominently displayed in the Berlin Museum. This bust was assumed to have been an image of Queen Nefertiti because it was wearing the royal crown and was decorated with semi precious stones, which were also associated with royalty, but there is no physical evidence to support that assumption.

from the bloodline of the Greek soldiers who conquered Egypt in 332 B.C.E. under the command of Alexander of Macedonia. After his death in 323 B.C.E., a number of Alexander's generals fought for possession of his conquered territories. The general Ptolemy, who was already based in Alexandria, was successful in staving off all attempts to overthrow him and eventually proclaimed himself "King of Egypt," and married into the Egyptian royal family. The tradition of Greek generals and soldiers marrying the women of the nations that they conquered was a practice encouraged by Alexander. As a result of this practice, all of the descendents of the Ptolemies were the product of mixed marriages.

In Kemet, tradition dictated that the royal bloodline was always passed on through the lineage of the queen. This matrilineal system of determining rulership had been the basis of social organization in the Nile Valley for thousands of years and it continues in many parts of Africa today. By contrast, the line of succession in Greece and Rome has always been patrilineal, and there were no queens of note in Persian, Greek or Roman history. Female rulership in European culture is a relatively recent phenomena because females had no rights that males were obligated to respect.

During the Ptolemaic reign there were two females who ruled Egypt without a male coregent, Cleopatra Bernice (81-80 B.C.E.) and Bernice IV (58-55 B.C.E.). Ptolemy XII, who also referred to himself as "The New Osiris," was the father of the famous Cleopatra VII, who ascended the throne after her father's death in 51 B.C.E. Cleopatra VII was the first and last of her dynasty to speak Egyptian, and she was totally devoted to maintaining a policy of Egyptian nationalism until her death in 30 B.C.E. After Egypt fell to Rome, the Emperor Augustus claimed it as the "greatest prize of the new Roman Empire." Egypt was a bountiful source of grain which was "used to feed

There are a number of statues and carvings of Nefertiti (page 144), which were labeled and others that show her with her husband Akhenaton. These images differ dramatically from the *one* image which is now referred to as the "Berlin Bust of Nefertiti." Duplicates of this statue have been advertised as "The most beautiful woman who ever lived."

In an essay published in *Egypt Revisited*, Dr. Asa Hilliard commented on this curious anomaly: "Given the history of attempts in Germany, beginning in the mid 1700's, to degrade and to distort Kemetic history (Bernal, 1987), and given the racism permeating German culture at the time of the find of the bust, one must be very cautious with speculations by professors Ranke and Borchardt, and indeed the entire community of Egyptologists.

"To say that Nefertiti was a beautiful woman is one thing. To say that the 'Berlin Bust of Nefertiti' was the most beautiful image of a woman in Kemet, and perhaps the most beautiful image of a woman ever, is a bit much. Beauty is in the eye of the beholder. Was Queen Tiy [Tiye] not beautiful? Is this European image found in the midst of Africa felt to be beautiful mainly by comparison to African women?

"It is an irony of ironies that the world 'knows' an alien woman and an alien image as the most famous symbol of Africa's Grand Golden Age!"

the Roman legions as they continued their conquest of Africa and Asia Minor." The Roman Emperors maintained their control of Egypt until they were replaced by the Byzantine Emperor Constantine in 323 A.C.E.

Throughout the 655 years of Greco-Roman rulership in Egypt her foreign conquerors added nothing new, and often duplicated that which had been in existence thousands of years before their arrival in the Nile Valley. The Greco-Roman period is probably the least important era in the 3,000-year-old history of Kemet, but it contains the greatest amount of available information. The Temples of Dendera, Edfu and Kom Ombo were built during this period of foreign occupation, but they pale in comparison to those built a millennium or two earlier. They are, however, the best preserved temples in Egypt, not because they were better built, but because they were built later. The Greco-Roman period represented the end of Egypt's control as a dominating world power, and it is often cited because of its undeniably strong European presence.

This is not to suggest that the Greeks and Romans did not play an important role in helping modern man gain a better understanding of ancient Kemet. Without the discovery of the Rosetta Stone, (which was inscribed in 196 B.C.E. and contained several lines of text that were written in Greek) the hieroglyphics probably would not have been deciphered. But then again, if hundreds of thousands of authentic African texts had not been destroyed by foreign invaders, maybe the Medu Netcher would never have been lost, and there would not have been a need for a Rosetta Stone.

King Rameses II

Despite the existence of numerous images which supported an African origin of Nile Valley civilization, they were ignored by noted scholars who fabricated the myth of a "Great White Race."

The Myth of the Great White Race

James Henry Breasted (1865-1935), was an American archaeologist who was regarded as one of the world's foremost authorities on the archeology and history of Egypt and the Near East, which are collectively referred to as "the Orient." He was educated at Yale University and the University of Berlin and became professor of Egyptology and Oriental History at the University of Chicago in 1905, a position he retained for 30 years. The University of Chicago, one of the premier educational institutions in the world, was established in 1890 and received major endowments totaling $35 million from its co-founder John D. Rockefeller. In 1919, John D. Rockefeller, Jr. endowed Breasted with $1.5 million to create the Oriental Institute of the University of Chicago. Since its creation, the Oriental Institute has become the "world's leading center for the study of the history and civilizations of the Near East."

Breasted was highly respected by his peers and he was a prolific writer who authored more than 100 books on his archaeological findings. In 1916, he published a high school history textbook entitled *Ancient Times*, which contained two chapters on Egypt. Breasted was very specific about his depiction of the ancient Egyptians. He described them as "brown-skinned men...with dark hair" and compared them with the modern inhabitants of Egypt, whom he also described as "brown men."

Ancient Times was revised in 1935, the same year of Breasted's death, and in this new edition he praised the tremendous progress that had been made in the study of the ancient world during the past 18 years. Breasted acknowledged the invaluable assistance he received from a number of sources, including the Oriental Institute, Howard Carter (the discoverer of the tomb of Tutankhamen), George Reisner (Professor of Egyptology at Harvard) and John D, Rockefeller, Jr.

In his revised work, Breasted stated that the "history of civilization preceding the Greeks and Romans [had] been entirely rewritten." He also contrasted the grandeur and beauty of the civilization created by the Egyptians of the Pyramid Age and compared it with their contemporaries in Europe:

> We now realize how many more things the men of the Nile could make than the men of Europe, who were still living in the Stone Age towns at the very time the Egyptian tomb-chapels were built.

Breasted also compared the early Egyptian accomplishments in math with those later developed elsewhere in Europe:

> In *plane* geometry it is surprising to find that these

earliest known mathematicians already had rules for computing the area of a triangle, of a trapezium...a circle...[and] the calculation of the area of a hemisphere. It was a method <u>rediscovered</u> by the Greeks 1,600 years later....They also explain how to calculate the content of a frustum of a square pyramid, and even the cubical content of a hemisphere could be computed. <u>The formula for solving this problem was not discovered in Europe until 3,000 years later.</u>

The tone of his revised edition of *Ancient Times* began to shift dramatically in the fifth chapter when Breasted began to discuss *"The Quarter of the Globe where Civilization Grew Up and Developed."* He described three continental zones around the Mediterranean as, "a narrow belt along the northern end of Africa, the western part of Asia, and a large portion of Europe" where human life began and the ancient civilization which was to give rise to "Europe and America" developed.

Breasted referred to this region as the "Great Northwest Quadrant" and described its inhabitants as:

> ...members of a race of white men, who have been well called the Great White Race. The men of this race created the civilization which we have inherited. If we look outside of the Great Northwest Quadrant, we find in the neighboring territory only two other clearly distinguished races,-the Mongoloids on the east and the Negroes on the south. These peoples occupy an important place in the modern world, but they played no part in the rise of civilization.

After the creation of the Oriental Institute, Breasted's archaeological research led him to a number of interesting findings, such as the discovery of the "Earliest Known Reference of Negro Life" in Egypt, a relief found in a temple of Ramses II. This carving was dated to the thirteenth century B.C.E and

The 1935 edition of *Ancient Times* contained an illustration that Breasted referred to as *"The Earliest Known Representation of Negro Life."* He provided the following description: "Under a palm tree at the left a Negro woman sits stirring an earthen pot over a fire preparing food. Meanwhile a great commotion has arisen. A large group of defeated soldiers [on the right] fleeing before the wrath of the Egyptian king, have burst into camp. At the left, somewhat in advance of the main group, a wounded soldier is supported by two comrades who lead him to the arms of his wife and two children approaching from the left. In the palm tree beside them a monkey hops up and down and chatters frenziedly at the confusion, and an excited child rushes past to tell the cook of the misfortune which has befallen them. This relief is found in a temple of Rameses II, thus dating back to the Thirteenth Century B.C."

"The Earliest Known Representation of Negro Life"— according to James Breasted.

Racial Diagram of the "Great Northwest Quadrant"— according to James Breasted.

Breasted provided the following commentary on the "Great White Race" in Chapter 5 of *Ancient Times:* "The diagram is intended to show the three important geographical zones, numbered from north to south, I, II, and III, and to indicate in general the position of the subdivisions of the Great White Race on these geographical zones. At the bottom, below the twentieth degree of north latitude, the general position of the black race is noted; and similarly, at the right of the sixtieth degree of longitude, it places the Mongoloid, or yellow, race....A rough indication of the Mediterranean Sea is inserted to show that it separates the European of the Mediterranean type from those of North Africa. On the south of the Mediterranean the people of the Great White Race are darker-skinned than elsewhere."

portrayed "a large group of defeated soldiers fleeing before the wrath of the Egyptian king."

In an attempt to further disassociate the blacks in Africa from the whites in Egypt, Breasted also commented:

> On the *south* of the Northwest Quadrant lay the teeming black world of Africa, as it does today. It was separated from the Great White Race by the broad stretch of the Sahara Desert. The valley of the Nile was the only road leading across the Sahara from south to north. Sometimes the blacks on inner Africa did wander along this road into Egypt, but they came only in small groups. Thus cut off by the desert barrier and living by themselves, they remained uninfluenced by civilization from the north. The Negro peoples of Africa were therefore without any influence on the development of early civilization.

One would wonder what would cause Breasted to make such a dramatic flip-flop. In 1916 he stated that Egyptians were members of a "brown-skinned race" and in 1935 he reversed himself and said that they were now members of the "Great White Race." Did Breasted's research suddenly reveal the error of his previously published material, or were there other reasons for his radical and racial change of opinion?

In an interview, John G. Jackson, an historian often known for his candor, offered one plausible explanation for Breasted's sudden about-face on the issue of Egyptian ethnicity:

> A lot of them [white historians] have taken the position that the African is the low man on the totem pole and everybody had to be ahead of him. Some of these people are just plain lying because they have to have capital in order to operate. James Henry Breasted is a fine example. He published a high school textbook in 1916 called *Ancient Times*. It had two very fine chapters on Egypt and he plainly states in there that the ancient Egyptians were not white folks, but 'a brown-skinned race.' And then he needed money to establish the Oriental Institute and to do research in Egypt. John D. Rockefeller, Jr. gave him 1.5 million dollars, and then Breasted got out a new edition of his book and the Egyptians became 'members of the great white race.' In other words, in order to get Rockefeller's money he had to switch over the Egyptians to 'the great white race.'

Cheikh Anta Diop, author of *African Origin of Civilization*, also criticized Breasted's actions in a chapter entitled "Egyptian Race Seen by Anthropologists:"

> The dictatorial nature of Breasted's assertion is equalled only by the absence of any foundation, for the author gets caught in his own contradiction by claiming, on the one hand, that the Sahara has always separated Negroes from the Nile and, on the other hand, that this valley was their only road to the north. A glance at the map of Africa shows that one can go from any point on the continent to the Nile Valley without crossing a desert.

Breasted's views on the creation of Egyptian civilization by a "white race" were also shared by one his contemporaries, George Reisner. Reisner (1867-1942) was regarded as one of the world's finest excavators, and he directed the excavations of Harvard Camp at the Giza pyramids. He was also curator of Egyptian antiquities at the Boston Museum of Fine Arts and a tenured professor of Egyptology at Harvard University.

Reisner conducted some of the first excavations in Nubia as early as 1909. He claimed that Nubia was originally governed by a dynasty of "white" Libyans, and that all black dynasties were but an extension of them. Reisner and his associates also expressed the belief that, at best, the black-skinned Nubians were poor imitators of their lighter-skinned neighbors to the north.

In the beginning of the nineteenth century a curious paradox began to emerge in an attempt to explain the development of ancient civilizations outside of Europe in regions that were now occupied by Africans. This "scholarly" explanation required that one dismiss all logical thought and accept the myth that whites traveled outside of Europe into lands populated by blacks, where they developed great civilizations. These same whites would later return to Europe and create that which they never possessed. The reality, which was carefully avoided, was that Europeans only became civilized when they left Europe and made contact with Africans in northern Africa and the "Orient."

During the past 30 years, documentation has emerged which has proven the "Great White Race" theories of Breasted and Reisner to be totally invalid. In 1992 the research facilities with which both men were affiliated, the Oriental Institute and the Boston Museum of Fine Arts, belatedly created exhibits devoted exclusively to Nubian artifacts. Both exhibitions displayed evidence validating the presence of an indigenous African population in Nubia that preceded and influenced the indigenous African population in Egypt.

King Anlamani

In an interview published in the *Chicago Tribune* (January, 30, 1992), Timothy Kendall, associate curator of the Boston Museum of Fine Arts, provided a retrospective view of archaeological research during the early part of the twentieth century and described George Reisner as:

> A product of his times [who] didn't understand he was digging up an independent African kingdom as he moved up the Nile into Nubia.

Similarly, Bruce Williams, an archaeological specialist of Nubian culture with the Oriental Institute, also decried the role that racist ideologies played in distorting the perceptions of ancient Nile Valley history. Williams notes:

> Early archaeological expeditions were financed by turn-of-the-century big businessmen who endowed museums and for whom belief in the white man's superiority was virtually a religion.

In previous years, museums have only featured temporary Nubian exhibits, or they integrated them into less prominent positions in their Egyptian displays. Notable exceptions are the National Museum at Warsaw, which opened a permanent Nubian exhibition in 1972, and the British Museum, which opened an exhibit in 1991. The first permanent exhibit in North America, which was devoted solely to Nubian high culture, was opened in February, 1992, at the Royal Ontario Museum in Toronto, Canada.

Now that the issue of an African presence in the Nile Valley is being taken more seriously in academic circles, there is another important issue remaining to be resolved. It pertains to the "multiethnic" influence in the Nile Valley. This question was most eloquently addressed by Cheikh Diop in his publication *African Origin of Civilization*:

> It would be incorrect to say that civilization was born of racial mixture, for there is proof that it existed in Black lands well before any historical contact with Europeans. Ethnically homogeneous, the Negro peoples created all the elements of civilization by adapting to the favorable geographical conditions of their early homelands. From then on, their countries became magnets attracting the inhabitants of the ill-favored backward lands nearby, who tried to move there to improve their existence. Crossbreeding, resulting from this contact, was thus a consequence of the civilization already created by Blacks, rather than its cause. For the same reason, Europe in general—and Paris or London in particular—are gravitational poles where all the races in the world meet and mix every day. But 2,000 years hence, it will be inaccurate to explain European civilization of [1992] by the fact that the continent was then saturated by colonials each of whom contributed his share of genius. On the contrary, we can see that all the foreign elements, outdistanced, require a certain length of time to catch up, and for a long time can make no appreciable contribution to technical progress. It was the same in antiquity; all the elements of Egyptian civilization were in existence from the beginning. They remained as they were and at most, simply disintegrated on contact with the foreigner.

The many foreign invaders of the Nile Valley—Hyksos, Libyans, Assyrians, Persians, Greeks, Romans, Arabs, Turks, French and British—introduced no new concepts into Kemet. In every instance, they left Africa with a knowledge of science, mathematics, astronomy, religion, philosophy and architecture that was far greater than that which they possessed before their arrival.

King Taharqa presenting holy offerings

The Stolen Legacy

George Granville Monah James

Much has been written about the Greek theft and plagiarization of Nile Valley concepts, which have been referred to as the "stolen legacy." This term was popularized by the late George Granville Monah James, in his book entitled *Stolen Legacy*. Professor James was a learned man and held degrees and teaching certificates in theology, mathematics, Greek, Latin, logic, philosophy and social science. *Stolen Legacy* was written at a critical juncture in American history and was published in 1954, the same year as the Supreme Court's decision on *Brown vs the Board of Education*. James was a professor at Arkansas A. & M. and the University of Arkansas at Pine Bluff in 1954. He died under mysterious circumstances shortly after the publication of *Stolen Legacy*.

Dr. James was a brilliant scholar, whose thinking transcended the boundaries of traditional academic thought. He reexamined his views of African history and Greek civilization after reading the writings of C. H. Vail, Swinburne Clymer, E.A. Wallis Budge, Godfrey Higgins and others. According to a former colleague, the noted historian Dr. Yosef ben-Jochannan, these and other writings had a profound impact on James:

> When he read certain of those "Texts" that included the *Memphite Theology, Book of the Revolutions of Ra,* etc. and saw architectural and engineering layouts for pyramids, temples, tombs, mastabas, etc. along with their mathematical formula and calculations, he was compelled to rethink his original conclusion on the authenticity of a "Greek Philosophy"...Judaism and Judaeo-Christianity...

With respect for the accuracy of *Stolen Legacy*, which is subtitled, *The Greeks were not the authors of Greek Philosophy, but the people of North Africa commonly called the Egyptians,* Dr. ben-Jochannan further commented:

> *Stolen Legacy*...was thoroughly scrutinized by a large group of *African, Asian* and *European scholars* in the area of Egyptology, Paleontology, Linguistics, History, Theology, Philosophy, Science, Law, Metaphysics, Political Science...etc. in its original manuscript format; and *met the approval of most!*

The objectives of Stolen Legacy were clearly stated by Professor James. They were:

1. To prove that Greek philosophy was a misnomer

2. To demonstrate the African origin of the Mysteries Schools

Professor James lecturing to students at the University of Arkansas, Pine Bluff, ca. 1954.

3. To create a social reformation through the new philosophy of African redemption.

It was quite obvious to James that the evidence in support of the Greek theft of African philosophy was circumstantial at best. All of the accused, against whom charges had been leveled, had been deceased for more than a thousand years. But James was able to compile an impressive body of evidence to substantiate his thesis. Upon thorough investigation of the backgrounds of several Greek scholars, James discovered that they had several factors in common.

1. They were known to have studied in Kemet, or they were instructed by others who had studied there;

2. Those who had not studied under the priests of Kemet had access to the texts stored in the Library of Alexandria;

3. Upon returning to their native cities, many of the Greek scholars were exiled or condemned to death;

4. Many of the Greeks, as young students, disappeared from sight only to surface decades later as masters of various schools of thought foreign to their native lands.

At times *Stolen Legacy* reads like a mystery novel and the cast of characters often resemble suspects in a police manhunt. Professor James assumes the dual role of private investigator and prosecuting attorney. He meticulously links each of the accused to a specific crime and presents irrefutable evidence convincing the reader, who by now has assumed the persona of a grand juror, that each of the defendants should be indicted for the crimes with which they have been charged.

The following is a brief deposition of notable Greek scholars and the charges leveled against them in the commission of their crimes. They are grouped according to the schools with which they were affiliated. No names were changed to protect anyone, and all dates of birth are approximate and were recorded Before the Common Era.

The Pre-Socratic Ionian School

Thales (620-546) is credited with having taught that water is the source of all life and all things are full of God.

Anaximander (610-547) taught that the origin of all things emanates from an infinite source.

Anaximenes (?-528) espoused the view that all things originated from air.

Pythagoras (?-530) is credited with teaching knowledge of the *summum bonum*, or supreme good, and its relationship to the immortality and salvation of the soul. He also taught geometric sciences and the science of numbers. In addition, he believed in a universal fire which was the center of a solar system consisting of nine planets.

Professor James stated that all of these teachings were simply modifications of the Mystery System, the core curriculum which was taught in the temples of Kemet. Nile Valley philosophy taught a belief in the immortality of the soul, its relation to the Supreme Creative presence and a belief in the "Ennead" or family of Nine Netcherw which were created by the Supreme Netcher.

The Later Ionian School

Heraclitus (530-470) believed that fire was the governing element in the universe and he also taught a philosophy which stressed the "Union of Opposites."

Anaxagoras (500-430) taught that *Nous* or mind is the primary force in the universe and he also believed in the law of opposites.

Democritus (420-316) explained the properties of the atom and the drama of life and death.

(A)

(B)

Once again, James pinpoints the Nile Valley origin of these thoughts by showing the relationship between the "Union of Opposites," the African concepts of the male and female aspects of Netcherwy and the architectural representation for the same as expressed in the twin pillars and tekhenwy in the ancient temples. He also shows that the Greek idea of the atom was derived from the symbolic interpretation of the "Aton," which was described as the basic element in all life.

(A) Socrates prepares to drink the cup of poison, which was the sentence imposed upon him by the court of Athens. The students of Socrates react to his actions with great sorrow.

(B) Plato (left) lectures Aristotle on the higher aspects of life.

The Athenian School

Socrates (469-399) espoused the philosophical dictum of self knowledge, "Man, know thyself." He also echoed a belief in the concept of the supreme good, the harmony of the law of opposites and the salvation of the soul.

Plato (427-349) was a master of many philosophies such as the creation, Nous and the phenomenon of the universe.

Aristotle (384-322) appears as a multidisciplinarian who excelled in all the previously stated philosophies as well as matters dealing with metaphysics, astronomy and spirituality.

Professor James presented evidence which showed that the teachings of a supreme being existed in Kemet thousands of years before the development of a city or state in ancient Greece. Socrates' thoughts were not only foreign to his fellow countrymen but they also led to his being accused of "corrupting the minds of the youth" and introducing strange gods to the populous. For these actions Socrates was condemned to death and ordered to drink hemlock.

Socrates had a number of students under his tutelage at the time of his death. One of his most promising pupils was a 28-year-old named Plato. After the death of Socrates many of his

Athena

Athena was revered in Greek mythology. She was the goddess of warfare and wisdom. It was said that she sprang, full-grown and dressed in armor, from the forehead of Zeus, the king of the gods. She was also worshiped by the Greeks as the patroness of arts and crafts and her chief symbol was the owl. The Roman goddess Minerva was patterned after Athena who was originally patterned after the Kemetic Netcher Neith.

students fled for their own safety, including Plato who returned to Athens at the age of 40 and established an academy where he instructed students for two decades. Plato was the author of the "Timaeus," which recounted the fable of Atlantis which was told to Solon by an Egyptian priest.

Aristotle is described as a multitalented individual who excelled in subject areas for which he was never trained. For example, Socrates taught Plato and Plato taught Aristotle, but there is no evidence to show that either Socrates or Plato was versed in physics, economics, metaphysics or politics. James maintains that Aristotle was the personal tutor of Alexander of Macedonia for 13 years, and was rewarded by his former student after his conquest of Egypt, by being given free access to the accumulated wisdom that was contained within the Library of Alexandria.

The issue of Aristotle's authorship of a variety of works was of extreme interest to Professor James. Aristotle is credited with writing hundreds of books on more than 30 unrelated subjects. Citing two of several lists of Aristotle's writings, James shows that they differ in number, style, subject matter and date. For example, the list of Hermippus (200 B.C.E) contains 400 books and the list of Ptolemus (200 A.C.E.), contains 1,000 books. Professor James asks the reader to consider one simple question, "If Aristotle in 200 B.C. had only 400 books, by what miracle did they increase to 1,000 in the second century A. D.?"

Ancient Greece is described by many as the birthplace of Western or European civilization, and it has held that distinction for the last 2,500 years. Many of the social, political, architectural and philosophical expressions of world culture have been traced to a common origin in Greece, despite their earlier appearance on the continent of Africa. Professor James begs us to consider the fact that it was impossible for the Greeks to teach or claim that which they did not originate. Whether this legacy is referred to as "stolen," "borrowed" or "inherited," it still represents a body of knowledge which was not indigenous to Greece. The consequences of this cover-up, whether intentional or otherwise, will continue to have a profound effect upon future generations until this issue is honestly and fairly addressed.

There are many classicists who have held fast to the belief that the civilization of ancient Greece was not an extension of African or Egyptian civilization. Mary Lefkowitz, humanities professor at Wellesley College, attempts to address this issue in an article entitled "Not Out of Africa: The origins of Greece and the Illusions of Afrocentrists," which appeared in the February 10, 1992 issue of *The New Republic*. Ms Lefkowitz emphatically states that there is a "distinction between influence and origins," a distinction which she says is often lost in the debates on

Afrocentrism. Dr. Lefkowitz further declared that:

> ...to show influence is not to show origin. One people or culture may introduce its ideas or its symbols or its artifacts to another people or culture, but the differences between the peoples and cultures may remain....The evidence of Egyptian *influence* on certain aspects of Greek culture is plain and undeniable, though surely it must be pointed out that other Mediterranean civilizations also had important influences on Greek (and Egyptian) culture, so that the picture of whom came first, and who took or loaned what to whom, is anything but clear. But the evidence of Egyptian *origins* for Greek culture is another thing entirely.

The key words in Dr. Lefkowitz's defense of the proprietorship of Greek knowledge are "influence" and "origins." These two words must be carefully examined in order to understand why the Greeks are so fervently defended by the promoters of Eurocentric ideology.

The *Webster's New Twentieth Century Dictionary* gives us the following definitions of *influence* and *origin*:

Influence [from *influens*, to flow in] *the power of persons or things to affect others, seen only in its effects.*

Origin [from *oriri*, to rise]
1. *a coming into existence or use; beginning.*
2. *parentage; birth; lineage.*
3. *that in which something has its beginning; source; root; cause.*

The key words in the definition of **influence** are; *affect* and *effect*. To <u>affect</u> is to imitate or assume the character of. To <u>effect</u> is the power or ability to produce consequences or results. Simply stated, **influence** is the power of persons to cause others to <u>imitate</u> aspects of their character in such a manner that it can be <u>witnessed</u> in the actions or creations of the imitators.

The central issue surrounding the question of Greek "origin" or "influence" of specific concepts can be determined by analyzing their admiration for the culture of Kemet. The early Greek writers frequently praised the cultural supremacy of the people of Kemet in areas which included, but were not limited to religion, philosophy, architecture, astronomy, medicine, science and mathematics. Issues of race did not concern the first Greeks who came to Kemet seeking higher knowledge. But as Greece became more politically aggressive, under the rulership of Alexander of Macedonia, she became more nationalistic. True to the historical doctrine, "to the victor go the

The New Republic
February 10, 1992

This publication followed in the tradition of the September 23, 1991 issue of *Newsweek* magazine and attempted to lampoon the Afrocentric movement by portraying on its cover a bust of a Greek philosopher wearing a Malcolm X cap.

ORIGIN or INFLUENCE
A Comparison Between Two Kemetic and Greek Myths

A. The Netcher Anpu adjusts the balance on the scale which is to weigh the soul of a person against the symbol of the Netcher Maat. Djhuiti is on hand to record the event.

B. A judgement scene from a Greek vase shows Hermes (the Greek version of Djhuiti/Thoth) weighing the fate of two warriors as Zeus looks on. The female figure on the right is believed to be Athena, the Greek goddess of war.

C. The Kemetic Netcher who is referred to as "Turn Face" prepares to transport the soul of the deceased across a river through the underworld.

D. The Greeks had a feisty boatman named Charon whose job was to transport souls across the river in the underworld. But unlike his Kemetic counterpart Turn Face, Charon refused to transport those souls that were unable to pay for his services.

spoils" the Greeks, like any other military force, claimed ownership over all they plundered. And their conquest of Kemet was no exception.

If the question of the African "origin" or "influence" of civilization is much more difficult to answer today than 2,000 years ago, it is primarily because of the role racism has played in the theft and manipulation of African

a mountainous region in southwestern Europe and originally included parts of Bosnia (formerly Yugoslavia), Bulgaria and Greece. After 1100 B.C.E. the Macedonians came under the influence of the Greeks, who were later conquered by Phillip of Macedonia in 338 B.C.E. So envious was Alexander of his father's conquests that he was reputed to have commented, "My father will get ahead of me in everything, and will leave nothing great for me to do." Alexander was 13 when he began his tutelage under Aristotle, and over the years he developed a great love and appreciation for Greek culture. Alexander was 20 when he became king of Macedonia, after the assassination of his father.

Alexander's love for Greece was secondary to his lust for power. During an insurrection in the Greek city of Thebes, Alexander's forces sold over 30,000 people into slavery and burned every building in the city—with the exception of the temples and the house of the poet Pindar. After that battle, Alexander turned his attention to Persia, where he defeated the army of Darius III in 333 B.C.E., then murdered and enslaved thousands of people. He went on to "liberate" Egypt one year later.

Martin Bernal gives a plausible explanation as to why Alexander spared the home of Pindar during the destruction of Thebes:

> Early in the 5th Century B.C., the poet Pindar wrote a Hymn to Amon which opened 'Ammon King of Olympos.' This cult of the Libyan variant of the Egyptian Amon was attached to Pindar's native town of Thebes.

Alexander consolidated his rulership of Egypt in the newly created city of Alexandria, which was located on a strip of land between Lake Mareotis and the Mediterranean Sea. During the construction of the city, Alexander made the long and arduous journey to the oracle of Amon (later renamed Zeus-Ammon), where he was told by the African mystic that he was the son of God. Martin Bernal's *Black Athena* provides additional information on the importance of this oracle in the life of Alexander:

> Alexander the Great clearly considered himself to be a son of Ammon. After his conquest of Egypt, he set out into the desert to consult the god's great oracle at the Libyan oasis of Siwa. The oracle told Alexander that he was the god's son, which explains why from then on Alexander's coins portray him as a horned Ammon.

Alexander's willingness to save the home of the poet Pindar from destruction during the burning of Thebes says some-

Silver coin issued ca. 300, B.C.E. which portrays Alexander wearing the horns of Ammon.

The royal seal of Augustus was designed in the form of a sphinx and was affixed to all personal and private correspondence. Augustus also ordered his artisans to design signet rings bearing the likeness of himself and Alexander, son of Ammon.

thing about his respect for the cult of Ammon, which thrived in that city. After his conquest of Egypt, Alexander sought the advice of the oracle of Amon; and, thereafter, declared that Ammon, not Phillip, was his true father. Alexander's empire extended from Greece to India, with Babylon as its capital. After his death in Babylon on June 13, 323 B.C.E., Alexander's body was taken to Memphis, Egypt, and he was buried in a golden coffin in the city of Alexandria. His desire to be buried in Egypt, as opposed to Macedonia, Persia or Greece and his profound affinity for Egyptian religion, say a great deal about that nation's influence over the man historians refer to as Alexander the Great.

The Library of Alexandria

In 295 B.C.E., King Ptolemy I, the successor to Alexander, issued a proclamation declaring that "all the books of the world" and the "writings of all nations" be placed within one repository in the city of Alexandria, Egypt. The Latin politician Winterious, a student of Aristotle, was given the task of overseeing the administration of a vast educational complex, which consisted of the Mouseion (a research center), the Temple of Serapis, and the famed Library of Alexandria. It has been acknowledged by Western scholars that this facility "established the foundations for the systematic study of mathematics, physics, biology, astronomy, literature, geography and medicine." It is because of this heritage that many scientific, legal and religious terms retain their original Latin names, even though it is now considered a dead language.

The creation of this new center of learning was due in part to Alexander's conquering of Egypt and the closing of the numerous temples and universities that were situated along the Nile River. Hundreds of thousands of papyrus scrolls were taken to Alexandria, where they were translated, catalogued into ten subject areas, arranged alphabetically by author and stored in the ten research halls designated for specific fields of study. More than half a million books were amassed during a period of two generations, and that number increased to more than 700,000 books over succeeding years. The library also contained an observatory, dissecting rooms, botanical gardens, a zoo and lecture halls.

In addition to the texts that were taken from Kemet, the Ptolemies allocated tremendous sums of money for their librarians and purchased books from various parts of the known world. Commercial ships that docked in the thriving seaport of Alexandria were often searched by the military and their books were confiscated. Agents were dispatched from Alexandria to various countries where they often purchased and acquired numerous books through various nefarious means.

The Library of Alexandria was said to have contained a copy of every scroll known to man. During its day it was regarded as the most prestigious library in existence.

Egyptian historian Mostafa El-Abbadi, author of *The Life and Fate of the Ancient Library of Alexandria*, stated that not all of the acquisitions were obtained honorably. For example, Ptolemy III gave the city of Athens a substantial amount of silver as collateral for the safe return of the original manuscripts of Aeschylus, Euripides and Sophocles, which were to be copied in Alexandria. After the library's dictationist read the contents of the manuscripts to the scribes, who made several copies of each, Ptolemy III returned the facsimiles and kept the originals in Alexandria, much to the displeasure of the outraged Athenians.

For more than 600 years, this site was the command center for the world's scientific and cultural development. Euclid, the reputed "Father of Mathematics" studied in Alexandria and later wrote *The Principles of Mathematics*, which was to have a profound impact, 2,000 years later, on a 12-year-old boy named Albert Einstein. Heron invented gear trains and steam engines, and authored the first book on robotics called *Automata*. Apollonius was a mathematician who demonstrated the forms of the conic sections. Hipparchus was an astronomer who mapped the constellations and estimated the intensity of stars. Galen was a dominate figure in the medical field; his books on healing and anatomy were used until the European Renaissance. The library was also a center for religious research. It was where Hellenized Jewish scholars produced the first Greek translation of the Old Testament, the *Septuagint*.

Erasthothenes, an Egyptian mathematical scientist and archaeologist was one of the most famous alumni of this renowned educational center. He rediscovered the formula for measuring the circumference of the Earth after stumbling upon an ancient document taken from Syene in Upper Egypt. Erasthothenes was a master of many disciplines. In addition to his fame as an astronomer, philosopher, historian, poet and theater critic, he was also head librarian of the Library of Alexandria. There is no doubt that access to the accumulated wisdom of Nile Valley scholarship helped to create the foundation upon which scholars such as Erasthothenes, Galen, Euclid, Dionysius and hundreds of others stood.

The last great scholar affiliated with the famed University of Alexandria was Hypatia. Hypatia was a true scientist in her own right, having gained notoriety in the fields of mathematics, physics, astronomy and philosophy. She was born in Alexandria in 370 A.C.E., some 400 years after Egypt had been conquered by the Roman army. Her father was the famed Egyptian mathematician Theon, and Hypatia enjoyed many privileges unheard of for women in Classical Greek society.

Hypatia was 21 years old when the University and its library was ordered destroyed by the Christian emperor Theodosius, who viewed the teachings of science, mathematics and philosophy as antithetical to the new religion. Despite the threat of personal danger, Hypatia continued to teach and publish because of her close friendship with the Roman governor. These actions angered Cyril, the Archbishop of Alexandria, and in 415 A.C.E. his monks encouraged an angry mob to attack Hypatia as she was riding through town. She was pulled from her chariot and dragged into a church where she was stripped naked and the flesh was scraped from her body with oyster shells. Her corpse was burned along with all of her writings and Archbishop Cyril was made a saint.

The destruction of the Library and University of Alexandria extinguished the flame of knowledge that had been passed on to the Greeks and Romans by the inhabitants of the Nile Valley. With this glorious light of Egypt now extinguished, the nations of Europe would stumble in darkness for more than a thousand years before knowledge was brought to them during the Moorish conquests.

On February 12, 1990, Hosni Mubarak, the president of Egypt, was joined by international dignitaries in Aswan, Upper Egypt, to launch a fundraising effort for the revival of the 2,000-year-old Library of Alexandria. It is expected to open in 1995 with 200,000 volumes and expand to five million volumes by the end of the century. The new building was designed by a team of Norwegian architects and will be constructed in the shape of a partially submerged disc, which is said to represent the rising sun. The estimated cost of the structure is $80 million. "The purpose of its recreation is to rekindle the light of scholarship [and] to resemble its old prototype, a public library for research in the humanities and sciences, with particular interest to stimulate the cultural development of Egypt and that of the whole of the Mediterranean area, Africa and the Arab world."

Horus Magazine
Spring 1990

Hypatia being dragged from her chariot.

The Roman Conquest of Egypt

Cleopatra VII was the last of the Ptolemys to rule Egypt. Her struggle to retain control over her country has been the subject of numerous plays, novels and songs. She became queen of Egypt at the age of 17, but was later stripped of power by her brother and coregent Ptolemy Dionysos. After a period of self-exile in Syria, Cleopatra was returned to power by the Roman general Pompey, who later died in a struggle for power against Julius Caesar. Caesar, who had come to Egypt in pursuit of Pompey, met and fell in love with Cleopatra, and secured her position on the Egyptian throne.

Cleopatra gave birth to a son by Caesar and eventually moved to Rome with him, where they lived until Caesar's assassination in 44 B.C.E. After returning to Egypt, she eventually met and fell in love with Marc Antony, one of Caesar's successors. Antony plotted with Cleopatra and utilized the wealth of Egypt to assist him in securing the throne in Rome. These actions angered the Roman emperor Octavian, who declared war on Egypt and defeated the combined forces of Cleopatra and Antony in the Battle of Actium in 31 B.C.E. After the death of Cleopatra VII in 30 B.C.E., the legacy of Egypt was claimed by Rome, which had then become the mightiest nation on Earth.

Julius Caesar

Julius Caesar briefly forsaked his empire in Rome for the love of Cleopatra VII. Their son, Caesarion, was born in Egypt and was delivered by a physician via the surgical procedure which now bears his name, the "Caesarean Section."

Greco-Roman Architecture

The Roman conquest of Egypt was similar, in many respects, to that of the Greeks. In both instances the wealth and knowledge of the land was appropriated by the new occupants and dispersed throughout their vast empire. Greece and Macedonia had already become a part of the Roman Empire around 146 B.C.E., and the Romans borrowed the architecture, philosophy, culture and art of the Greeks, which they spread throughout their ever-expanding empire. Since the Greeks had conquered the Egyptians almost a century earlier, the Romans, while assimilating Greek culture, were also assimilating the Egyptian culture, which the Greeks had appropriated earlier. Three excellent examples can be found in the similarities between Greek and Roman architecture, mythology, and their close resemblance to those first developed in Egypt/Kemet, and the evolution of the alphabet from Kemetic to Greek to Roman.

Colonnade halls were an integral part of Nile Valley temple architecture, and they first appeared in Kemet around 2600 B.C.E., almost 2,000 years before the development of the first Greek city-state. During this same time, Romulus and Remus, the legendary founders of Rome, were still being nursed by a wolf, who served as their surrogate mother.

It has been suggested by the mathematical scientist Livio Setcchini that the column represents the map of Egypt. The

Romulus and Remus were twin brothers and the legendary founders of Rome. They were abandoned as children and raised in the wild by a female wolf. Romulus slew his brother Remus and later named the city of Rome for himself. According to Roman law, only men were allowed to live in the city and women were frequently kidnapped from nearby tribes to provide pleasure for the Roman subjects.

Romulus, Remus and the she-wolf

shaft is Upper Egypt (the south) and the capital is Lower Egypt (the north). According to Setcchini the symbolic proportion of the geographic and geometric ratios in the Egyptian columns were duplicated by the Greeks:

> This explains why, among the Greeks, who learned the use of the columns from the Egyptians, for the Doric order, the most conservative of the Greek orders, there was a rule that the shaft should be six units high and the capital one unit high. In the Greek orders the base of the column preserves the arrangement on three horizontal lines, which are the symbol of the tropic of Cancer....The column basically represents the three meridians of Egypt and through its curvature suggests the extension of the system of meridians to the east and west of Egypt. But, since the column is circular, the structure of the column was related to the problem of presenting the map of Egypt as part of a cylindrical projection of the surface of the earth....The elaborate numerical rules for the proportions of Greek columns...can be explained when one considers the two interrelated problems of describing mathematically the curvature of the earth and of projecting a curved surface on a flat map. The theory of conic sections, which is considered their highest achievement of Greek mathematics, may have been developed in order to solve these problems.

Columns consist of three primary components, a *capital* and a *shaft* which usually rests on a *base*. Above the columns is a horizontal beam of stones called an "entablature" which supports the roof. These two elements, the "column" and "entablature," comprised in classical architecture what was referred to as an "order." Three orders evolved in Greece and two in Rome. They have had a profound influence on later architectural styles.

The "Doric order" was the first, and most simplistic, of the three Greek orders. Normally, the Doric is the only order that does not have a base. The second order developed by the Greeks was the "Ionic." Its capital is carved with decorations that symbolized spiral scrolls. The "Corinthian order" is the last of the three Greek orders. It is similar to the Ionic order but its capital is elaborately decorated with carvings of leaves that represented the acanthus plant.

Roman columns were practically identical to the Greek columns and had only minimum modifications. The "Tuscan order" resembled the Doric order but it has a base and the shaft is unfluted. The "Composite order" was essentially a combination of the Greek Ionic and Corinthian orders. Its capital was comprised of the carved scroll of the Ionic order and the acanthus leaf decoration of the Corinthian.

A. Temple of Saqqara

B. Temple of Phile

C. Temple of Luxor

D. The Ramesseum

The architectural styles of columns in Kemet varied greatly throughout the millennium.

A. Engaged columns of the Saqqara Temple complex, ca. 2700 B.C.E.

B. Flowering capitals of the Temple of Phile, ca. 325 B.C.E.

C. The open courtyard of the Southern Ipet (Luxor Temple) contains columns which represent bundled papyrus plants, ca. 1380 B.C.E.

D. The columns in the Ramasseum contain a variety of styles. Shown are the lotus columns and statue columns of the Netcher Ausar, ca. 1225 B.C.E..

In Greco-Roman architecture, columns in the shape of men were called *atlantes* by the Greeks and *telamones* by the Romans. Female figures so used were called *caryatides*.

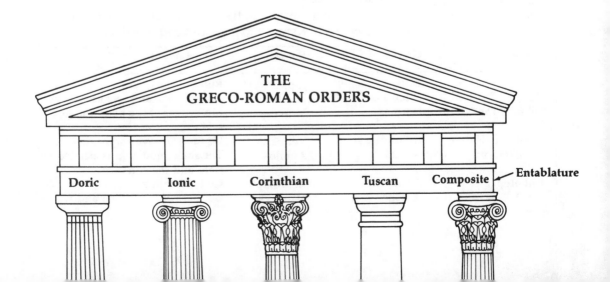

THE GRECO-ROMAN ORDERS

Doric   Ionic   Corinthian   Tuscan   Composite   ← Entablature

1.   2.   3.

1. Djhuiti, the Netcher of science, writing, measurement, divine articulation of speech and medicine holds in his hand two staffs with entwined snakes. One serpent wears the crown of Upper Kemet, the other wears the crown of Lower Kemet. Djhuiti was referred to as *Thoth* by the Greeks.

2. Hermes was the Greek equivalent of Djhuiti. He is shown carrying a staff which has two entwined snakes. It was called "the Staff of Hermes." In Greek mythology he was associated with wisdom, and the "Hermetic sciences" were named in his honor.

3. Mercury is the Greek version of Hermes and Djhuiti and he is similar in all aspects. The staff that Mercury carries is called the "caduceus" and it has been adopted as the universal symbol of medicine.

Greco-Roman Mythology

Just as certain architectural stylings, which originated in Kemet, greatly influenced the Greeks and Romans, the same can be said for the Nile Valley concepts of the Netcherw whom the Greeks and Romans referred to as gods. The *Pyramid Texts* in Kemet (3,200-2,250 B.C.E.) described a family of nine Netcherw, which became known as the Great Ennead. This term is derived from the Greek word *ennea* which means *nine*. The basic sources of Greek mythology, all of their primary characters and themes, were contained in three classical works. Hesiod's *Theogony* and Homer's *Iliad* and *Odyssey* which were all written in the eighth century B.C.E.

During the third century B.C.E., the Romans began to closely identify with divinities of Greece. Rome's classical literature of religious and moral teachings was written in the latter years of the first century B.C.E. by the poet Virgil. This great work was called the *Aeneid*, and it consisted of 12 books. Virgil based the first six books on the *Odyssey* and the last six books were modeled after the *Iliad*. Virgil wrote the *Aeneid* to establish the divinity of the Roman empire, which he closely associated with that of Greece.

The following table lists similarities between some of the Netcherw of Kemet and gods and goddess of Greece and Rome.

Kemet	Greece	Rome	Divine Aspects
Amon	Zeus	Jupiter	Ruler of the gods
Bes	Dionysus	Bacchus	God of wine and reckless behavior
Djhuiti/Thoth	Hermes	Mercury	Messenger of the gods and god of science
Het-Heru/Hathor	Aphrodite	Venus	Goddess of love and beauty
Heru/Horus	Apollo	Apollo	The son of god also associated with light and the sun
Imhotep	Asclepius	Aesculapius	God of healing
Neith	Athena	Minerva	Goddess of crafts, war and wisdom

The Alphabet

One of the most significant contributions to have emerged from Rome is the 26-letter Roman alphabet. But as one might suspect, this alphabet was a modified version of the system which was derived from the Greeks. In fact, the word *alphabet* is derived from *alpha* and *beta*, the first two letters of the Greek alphabet. The words *alpha* and *beta* were derived from the Semetic words *aleph* and *beth*, which were derivatives of characters that were first developed in Kemet. The following is an abbreviated chronology of the evolution of the alphabet as referenced in the 1986 edition of the *World Book Encyclopedia*.

Medu Netcher, the oldest form of writing, was developed in the upper regions of the Nile Valley, and by 3,000 B.C.E. it was being used in ancient Kemet. These early signs specified the consonants in syllables and no vowels were written. The Semites developed their alphabet around 1,500 B.C.E. and they also wrote without vowels. In an attempt to stress the originality of the Semetic alphabet, the *World Book Encyclopedia* states:

> ...historians can find no instances where the Semites borrowed the characters from Egyptian writing. They invented their own set of characters to stand for the consonants in their language.

However, upon examination one will find every character in the Semetic alphabet is identical to those that came from Kemet. In fact, even the meanings are the same.

The next significant writing system emerged around 1,000 B.C.E. and it was developed by a people who, like the Semites, also lived along the coast of the Mediterranean Sea. They were called Phoenicians, and their alphabet was similar to the ones developed by the Kemetic people and the Semites. The Phoenician alphabet contained only consonants and lacked vowels. While the characters of the Phoenician alphabet were markedly different from the Semetic and Kemetic, their meanings were similar in many respects.

The Greeks developed their alphabet from the Phoenicians, and began using a modified version of it around 800 B.C.E. The Phoenician alphabet contained more consonants than the Greeks could effectively use in their language; they began using the extra characters for vowel sounds. The Greeks also modified the shapes of the Phoenician characters. Some were inverted and others were stylistically altered. Some characters were added, while others were eliminated. Eventually, the Greeks formed an alphabet that was comprised of 24 letters.

The Roman alphabet, as it exists today, was perfected about 114 A.C.E. The Romans learned their alphabet from the Etruscans who migrated into Italy from the eastern region of the Mediterranean and brought the Greek alphabet with them. The early Roman alphabet consisted of 20 letters, and six others were added over time.

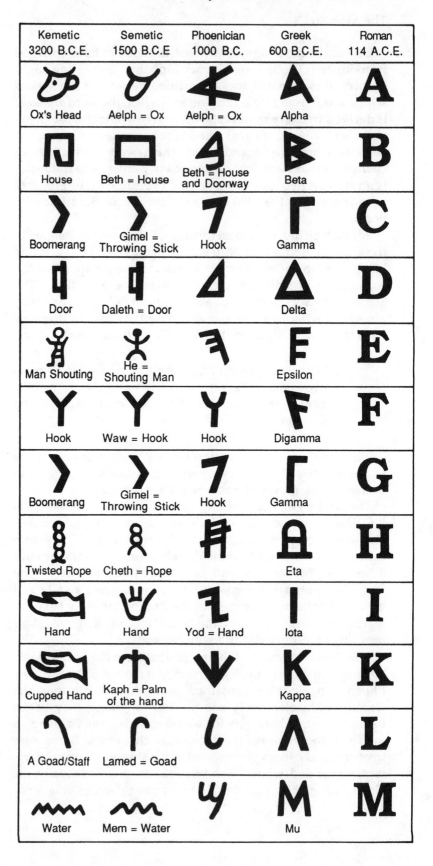

Kemetic 3200 B.C.E.	Semetic 1500 B.C.E	Phoenician 1000 B.C.	Greek 600 B.C.E.	Roman 114 A.C.E.
Ox's Head	Aelph = Ox	Aelph = Ox	Alpha	A
House	Beth = House	Beth = House and Doorway	Beta	B
Boomerang	Gimel = Throwing Stick	Hook	Gamma	C
Door	Daleth = Door		Delta	D
Man Shouting	He = Shouting Man		Epsilon	E
Hook	Waw = Hook	Hook	Digamma	F
Boomerang	Gimel = Throwing Stick	Hook	Gamma	G
Twisted Rope	Cheth = Rope		Eta	H
Hand	Hand	Yod = Hand	Iota	I
Cupped Hand	Kaph = Palm of the hand		Kappa	K
A Goad/Staff	Lamed = Goad			L
Water	Mem = Water		Mu	M

Kemetic 3200 B.C.E.	Semetic 1500 B.C.E	Phoenician 1000 B.C.	Greek 600 B.C.E.	Roman 114 A.C.E.
Snake	Nun = Fish		Nu	N
Eye	Ayin = Eye		Omicron	O
Mouth	Pe = Mouth		Pi	P
Qoph = Monkey	Qoph	Qoph	Koppa	Q
Head	Resh = Head		Rho	R
Tusk	Shin = Tooth		Sigma	S
Check Mark	Taw = Mark		Tau	T
Hook	Waw = Hook	Hook	Upsilon	V
Fish	Samekh/Fish	Fish	Chi	X
Hook	Waw = Hook	Hook	Upsilon	Y
Arrow	Zayin = Weapon	Weapon		Z

The letter *V* evolved to become the letter *U* around 500 A.C.E. *VV* was also written as *UU* and later became known as *"double U"* around 1000 A.C.E. The last letter to be added to the contemporary alphabet was the letter *J*. It evolved from the letter *I* around 1600 A.C.E.

Napoleon's Scientific and Artistic Commission published their findings on Egypt in a 21-volume publication entitled *Description de L'Egypte*. This illustration is from the Frontispiece.

Chapter Five
The Rape of Egypt

One of the most important lessons history teaches us is that no civilization lasts forever. Of the many civilizations that have developed in the Nile Valley, only a very few are known to us today. The once grand nation of Kemet is now less than a shadow of its former self. Internal conflicts of the fourth and third millennium B.C.E. made Kemet susceptible to conquests by the Persians, who were later conquered by the Greeks, who in turn were conquered by the Romans. Finally, the division of Rome into an Eastern and Western Empire contributed mightily to its inevitable decline.

As the Western Roman Empire grew increasingly weaker, the Vandals, Visigoths and other Germanic tribes ransacked the nation and finally overthrew it around 476 A.C.E. The Eastern Roman Empire survived as the Byzantine Empire until it was overthrown by the Turks in 1453. Even though the Roman Empire was now politically extinct, Rome's cultural heritage continued to have a profound impact upon the world. The Roman Catholic Church became a major influence on other cultures as did the Latin language and the Roman legal and political systems.

When the nations of Greece and Rome fell, they were still able to control their land, history, language and culture. Conversely, when Kemet fell, she was renamed "Egypt" and her history, culture, language and religion were violated in a manner unlike any nation before or since. Throughout the past 1,600 years, Egypt has been raped by wave after wave of foreign invaders, who have robbed her temples, desecrated her tombs and destroyed innumerable artifacts, all in the name of history, science and distorted perceptions of God.

The Islamic Occupation

In 640 A.C.E., the Islamic Army attacked the Byzantine Empire and seized control of Syria, Palestine and Egypt. The Arab military was led by General 'Amr when the city of Alexandria fell. After their conquest of Egypt, the Arabs expressed little interest in preserving its historical past. The great kings and queens of old had been forgotten, and the mighty temples they had built were now lying in ruins after

Justinian, the Byzantine emperor, was responsible for closing the last Egyptian temple, on the Island of Phile, in the year 527 A.C.E.

centuries of neglect. The ability to read the Medu Netcher had been lost for almost 250 years, and the Netcherw, or gods, of the ancient Kemites, who had been worshiped by both the Greeks and Romans, and regarded as pagan by the Byzantines and Coptics, were now looked upon with even greater disdain by the Muslims.

It has been said that General 'Amr played a major role in the final destruction of the Library and University of Alexandria. He ordered his army to demolish the last remnants of these educational institutions, and when scholars begged him to spare them 'Amr declared, "If the library contains what is not in the Koran, it is false. If it contains what is already in the Koran, then it is superfluous. Burn it." In other instances, the temples that were not burned were dismantled block by block and the stones were used to build new structures in Cairo and various other cities. Temples that were not destroyed at the hands of men succumbed to the ravages of nature and time. Many temples were literally buried under tons of sand and silt to the point where only their roofs were exposed. These roofs were later used as the floors for the homes that the villagers built on top of them.

A number of the advances that the early Arabs made in mathematics and astronomy have now been attributed to their conquest of Egypt. Muslim scholars sought out the writings of Euclid, Galen, Plato, Aristotle, Ptolemy and other Greek teachings, and had them translated into Arabic. Quite often, Coptic monasteries were raided for the valuable books kept in their libraries, and the famed caliph, Harun Al-Rashid, regularly paid scribes their weight in gold for each manuscript they translated.

Arabian astronomers making astronomical observations.

By 763 A.C.E., the "Arab Scientific Renaissance" was well under way and the Arabs were making phenomenal strides in the fields of advanced mathematics, astronomy and medicine. They later developed many scientific instruments, which helped to establish the basis for many modern scientific methods. In a recent article in the Autumn, 1991 issue of *Horus* magazine, a publication of EgyptAir Airlines, the author referenced the impact that Greek writings had upon early Arab culture:

This *astrolab* is believed to have been made in France during the fourteenth century. Its design was influenced by Moorish technology.

> The introduction of paper to Baghdad in 751 AD ensured that books and libraries flourished, and popularized scholarly pursuits. If the Greek manuscripts had not been translated, preserved and been accessible, then few of the 16th century renaissance discoveries would have been possible.

Beginning in 813 A.C.E., a major center for learning was created in Baghdad and a number of universities were established by the new caliph, Abdullah Al Mamun, the son of the former ruler Harun Al-Rashid. Al Mamun was responsible for the translation into Arabic of the astronomical works of Ptolemy. He once claimed that Aristotle appeared to him in a vision and directed him to commission scholars to produce a number of scientific maps of the Earth and the heavens. The study of these great works helped the Arabs to become the most scientifically literate people of their day.

Unfortunately, Al Mamun's love for science did not extend into the area of archaeological preservation, for he was responsible for violating one of the greatest monuments in the world - The Great Pyramid. In 820, Al Mamun led an army of stone masons, engineers and architects on an assault of the Great Pyramid in an attempt to find the treasures that were purported to be hidden inside. Al Mamun's men tunneled more than 100 feet through solid masonry before entering into the descending passageway. The Arabs searched in vain for treasure and in a fit of rage they destroyed sections of the walls and floors looking for secret passageways, but they found none.

It has been rumored that Al Mamun had a quantity of gold spirited inside the Great Pyramid in an attempt to appease his disgruntled men. When this gold was later discovered, the amount just happened to have equalled the total wages due each man. This coincidence Al Mamun attributed to the infinite wisdom of Allah. Over the next 500 years the Arabs removed more than 22 acres of the 100-inch limestone which once covered the outer surface of the pyramid. These stones were used to build several mosques, palaces and two bridges in and around the city of Cairo.

As Islam became more firmly entrenched in Egypt, restric-

Al Mamun's men searching for treasure inside of the Great Pyramid.

The Mosque of Sultan Hasan was built in Cairo in 1356 with the limestone blocks which were removed from the Great Pyramid.

tions were placed on Christians and other tourists. A Catholic monk named Bernard the Wise and several companions bribed their way into Cairo in 870 in an attempt to see the pyramids, which they believed to have been the granaries built by Joseph during the Hebrew enslavement in Egypt. But in 1757, Egypt was invaded by the Turks and became a province of the Turkish Empire. The Turks guaranteed the safety of French and Spanish travelers and other non-Muslims and made Egypt more accessible to outsiders.

Grave robbers searching for buried treasure.

The Incredible Edible Mummy

Two hundred years before West Africans were enslaved and sold in the West, the bodies of their Nile Valley ancestors were being marketed and distributed throughout Europe. Illiterate Arab villagers often used mummy cases for firewood and sold the corpses for medicinal purposes. Since the twelfth century, "mummy" had been prescribed as medicine for a variety of illnesses ranging from epilepsy to ulcers. The word mummy, derived from the Persian word *Mummia* (*mumija* in Arabic), and is a term which means pitch or bitumen. Bitumen was one of the substances used by the people of Kemet in the ancient embalming process. Bitumen was similar in appearance to pissasphalt, which had long been regarded as a cure for nausea, cuts, bruises and a variety of other ailments. During the times when pissasphalt was in short supply, mummies were used as a convenient substitute. Before long, businesses were established in Cairo and Alexandria where "mummified human flesh" was being packaged and exported throughout Western Europe.

Other Mummy Facts. In the mid nineteenth century mummy bandages were often used by manufacturers to make paper. Because the bandages were heavily soaked with resins that could not be bleached out, the paper produced from them was brown in color. As the result of a paper shortage during the Civil War, Augustus Stanwood of Maine used mummy wrappings to produce paper in his mill. Stanwood's brown paper was often used to wrap meats and groceries until his mill was identified as the source of a cholera epidemic, which was spread by his workers handling infected mummy bandages. It was Stanwood's use of mummy wrappings for paper that eventually led to the use of brown paper bags nationwide.

In Mark Twain's book *Innocents Abroad* he noted, in a humorous context, that mummy was used as fuel for the trains that ran throughout Egypt. Twain commented: "the fuel they use for the locomotive is composed of mummies three thousand years old, purchased by the ton or by the graveyard...sometimes one hears the profane engineer call out pettishly, 'Damn these plebeians, they don't burn worth a cent-pass out a king!'"

One ambitious man, John Sanderson, spent a year in Egypt (1585-1586) and purchased more than 600 pounds of mummified flesh, which he exported to England and sold for a substantial profit. It was not uncommon for some individuals to create artificial mummy by slicing the flesh off of recently deceased corpses and packing it in asphalt for several months, in an attempt to duplicate the real thing. During the European Renaissance, many artists added powdered mummy to their paints with the hope that it would prevent their pictures from cracking with age. As recently as 20 years ago, it was reported that ground mummy could be purchased for $40 an ounce at a pharmacy in New York City.

Napoleon's Invasion of Egypt

In the late eighteenth century, the French began to view Egypt as a site of military significance because of its prime location on the Mediterranean Sea. By 1797, General Napoleon Bonaparte had conquered Italy and began to set his sights on plans that would extend the French Empire into India. In April of 1798, Napoleon was authorized by the French government to conquer Malta and Egypt, and he was also given a directive to build a canal across the Isthmus of Suez which would connect the Mediterranean and Red seas. This idea was proposed because it would shorten the distance from France to India by some 4,000 miles, and would pave the way for easier access to India and eventual worldwide domination.

On May 19, 1798, Napoleon set sail from Toulon, in southern France, to Egypt, with a fleet of 328 ships and 35,000 soldiers. They were also accompanied by an elite corps of 175 scholars, who were members of the Scientific and Artistic Commission that was "selected by Napoleon to provide a cultural and technological background for his ambitious plans for the colonization of the Nile Valley." These "savants," as the commission members were called, brought with them copies of practically every book ever written on Egypt and numerous supplies which included some of the most technically sophisticated scientific and measuring instruments of their day.

On the evening of July 1, 1798, Napoleon's fleet landed at Abukir Bay near the city of Alexandria, where they finalized plans for attack. At that time, Egypt was under the control of foreign mercenaries called Mamelukes who ruled the land for the Turkish Empire. The Mamelukes had an enormous army, but their weapons were no match for the superior firepower of the French cannons and rifles. By noon of July 2, the city of Alexandria belonged to Napoleon. By July 3, the members of the Scientific and Artistic Commission went ashore and began their research.

Napoleon Bonaparte

As Napoleon prepared to leave France for Egypt, his West Indian-born mulatto wife, Josephine, instructed her husband to bring her something back from Egypt. Napoleon complied with her request and presented her with this statue upon his return in 1799. The sculpture was later sold to an Englishman in the nineteenth century and then bought by the late publishing magnet William Randolph Hearst in the 1920s. It was later placed on exhibit in the Brooklyn Museum in New York.

On July 12, 1798, Napoleon and an army of 25,000 men marched to the Giza Plateau in preparation for the great "Battle of the Pyramids." It was at this site that Napoleon informed his men, "Soldiers, remember that from the top of these monuments forty centuries are looking down upon you!" Within two hours the battle was over. More than 2,000 Mamelukes were killed and Napoleon was said to have lost only 20 men. By July 21, Napoleon's forces conquered Cairo and shortly thereafter the commission arrived and established an "Institute of Egypt," which was housed in one of five palaces "appropriated" for their special use.

Napoleon suffered his first defeat in Africa at the hands of the British admiral Lord Nelson, who had amassed a fleet of ships and followed Napoleon to Egypt. Nelson demolished the French navy in the "Battle of the Nile" on August 1, 1798, and established a blockade that cut Napoleon's supply lines from France and Malta. During the course of the following year, the British developed alliances with the Turks and the Russians and continued to pose a serious threat to Napoleon's plans for world conquest.

On August 12, 1799, three days before his 30th birthday, Napoleon toured the Great Pyramid and asked to be left alone inside of the King's Chamber to contemplate his future, as Alexander of Macedonia had reportedly done before him. Upon exiting the chamber hours later, Napoleon was described as "pale and impressed." He later hinted that he had received a glimpse of his destiny, but he refused to discuss with anyone the details of his experience. Ten days after this event, on August 22, Napoleon left Egypt and returned to France. He crossed the Mediterranean in a small boat to avoid the British blockade and he arrived in Paris on October 16. Napoleon orchestrated a coup d'etat on November 9, 1799, and was named the First Consul the following day. By 1804, Napoleon had crowned himself Emperor of France.

Napoleon inside of the King's Chamber of the Great Pyramid.

Zodiac of Dendera

After Napoleon fled Egypt for France, the British navy maintained their blockade of Alexandria and the Turks continued to engage the French troops in minor skirmishes. Despite these and many other persistent problems, the members of the Scientific and Artistic Commission continued their research throughout Egypt, where they remained for a total of three years. The savants followed the French army as they pressed their way into Upper Egypt to the very boarders of the city of Aswan. Whenever the French came under attack, the troops would form their famous fighting squares, which were ten soldiers deep, and give their aggravating directive "savants and asses to the center." The savants were not looked upon favorably by Napoleon's Army, and they were not provided with weapons or rations. The soldiers believed that the savants role was to look for hidden treasure and civilize the barbaric Egyptians.

During their excursions in Egypt, the savants saw many objects that are no longer in existence, such as the Temple of Armant, which was dismantled when its stones were used to build a sugar factory. In 1799, a General by the name of Desaix discovered the marvelous Temple of Dendera which contained a wondrous circular zodiac in the ceiling of a room that was believed to have been used as an observatory. The zodiac was dynamited from the ceiling by Desaix's men and shipped to France, where it was later sold to Louis XVIII for 150,000 francs. It is now prominently displayed in the Louvre Museum.

The Rosetta Stone was stolen from the French in 1801 and presented to the Society of Antiquarians in London in 1802. The Society promptly circulated copies of it throughout the non-French-speaking world. In July of 1802, King George III ordered that the Rosetta Stone be housed in the British Museum. It has remained on display in London since that time. The stone is made of fine-grained black basalt and is about the size of a small gravestone marker.

A portion of the top and a section of the lower right side are missing. It is 3 feet 9 inches wide, 2 feet 4 and one half inches high and 11 inches thick and weighs three quarters of a ton. The British allowed the stone to be exhibited in the Louvre in 1973, but to date neither the French nor British have consented to have any of their stolen artifacts exhibited in Egypt.

One of the most significant discoveries made during the French occupation of Egypt was that of a black basalt tablet with carved inscriptions. This stone was found, half buried in the soil, by a member of Captain Pierre Bouchard's engineering corps in 1799 as they were digging fortifications at Fort Rachid near the town of Rosetta. Realizing the possible importance of this stone, Bouchard shipped it to the Egyptian Institute in Cairo. Copies and casts of this stone were made and immediately shipped to France for further investigation.

The "Rosetta Stone," as it was later called, was inscribed with three translations of a text divided into three columns, Medu Netcher at the top, Demotic (a late cursive form of Medu Netcher) in the middle, and Greek at the bottom. The Demotic was the best preserved, the Greek portion was partially damaged, and two thirds of the Medu Netcher had been destroyed. Despite its condition, this stone provided the modern world with the first key to deciphering the long forgotten language of Kemet—the Medu Netcher. The Greek inscription was easily translated, and found to contain a decree written in 196 B.C.E. to commemorate the crowning of Ptolemy V. Segments of the Demotic text were decoded over the following years, but the Medu Netcher would remain undecipherable for almost a quarter of a century.

While Napoleon was back in France suffering from delusions of grandeur, his enemies, the British, Turks and the Mamelukes, were rapidly seizing control of Egypt. On August 30, 1801, the French troops surrendered to the British and began to negotiate terms for their safe return to their homeland. One of the major stipulations imposed by the British was that they would inherit all of the Egyptian artifacts discovered by the Scientific and Artistic Commission. The French scholars vehemently refused, and at one point in the negotiations they threatened to destroy all of their findings rather than give them to the British. A compromise was eventually reached with the commission, but the British insisted they must have possession of the Rosetta Stone.

During the negotiations with the British, the Rosetta Stone was being kept in the home of the French general Menou in Alexandria. One evening, under cover of darkness, a British colonel named Thomas Turner assembled a team of men who raided Menou's house and seized the prized tablet. With the Rosetta Stone now in the possession of the British, the savants were permitted to return to France with their notes, drawings and selected artifacts. Upon their arrival in France, the members of the commission were instructed by Napoleon to produce a monumental work which was to document "the sites, buildings, inscriptions, life, language and manners of the ancient and modern Egyptians."

During the course of the next 25 years, a legion of artists, engravers and typographers produced a 19-volume masterpiece entitled *Description de l'Egypte*. This state-published

Jean Francois Champollion

"The Egyptians of old thought like men a hundred feet tall. We in Europe are but Lilliputians."

Champollion

document helped turn France's military defeat in Egypt into a major archaeological and political triumph, which formally legitimized the study of Egyptology. The *Description de l'Egypte* shattered the myth of the cultural supremacy of the Homeric Greeks and established Egypt as the forerunner of all ancient civilizations. So impressed were the Americans with this academic achievement that they elected Napoleon Bonaparte and the famed French artist Vivant Denon as honorary members to the newly formed American Academy of Arts.

Demotic (Gr. *demotikos*, "popular"), or *encohorial* (Gr. *enkhorios*, "native") as some of the the earliest decipheres called it, is a very rapid form of hieratic that made its first appearance about the time of the Ethiopian Dynasty (700 B.C.E.-300 A.C.E.). It was the language people used in every day activities.

While the world was now savoring the visual delights of ancient Egypt which the *Description* now provided them, they were still unable to read the ancient language. However, 23 years after the discovery of the Rosetta Stone, a young Frenchman named Jean Francois Champollion, succeeded where others had failed and deciphered the hieroglyphic alphabet in 1822. With the French now basking in international glory, the government financed a 17-month expedition to Egypt in 1828, which allowed Champollion to conduct primary research on the history and language of ancient Egypt. Champollion was further rewarded for his scholarship by being appointed the first professor of Egyptology at the College de France in 1831. His career ended abruptly when he died a year later at the age of 42.

Champollion was responsible for bringing to France innumerable artifacts from his tour in Egypt, including a tekhen. He secured from Mohammed Ali, in exchange for a clock which never worked, one of the two tekhenwy that stood in front of the Temple of Luxor. The tekhen was transported to Paris in 1830 and erected in the Place de la Concorde on October 25, 1836, in the presence of King Louis Philippe and 200,000 spectators.

The leap of the Mameluke

The Mamelukes, a dynasty of slaves, ruled Egypt more than 600 years. Most of them were white, having been slaves brought from Russia and Armenia, but many were Negroes from the Sudan there being no color-line. Mohammed Ali in 1811 put an end to their power by the following strategy: he summoned them all to Cairo upon the pretext of consulting them concerning an invasion of Arabia. After a hospitable reception they were invited to parade in the courtyard of the citadel. The walls closed behind them and immediately the army of Mohammed Ali opened a fire of musketry upon the defenseless men but the Mamelukes met death in a manner worthy of their past deeds of valor. Only one escaped to tell the manner of his companions death. He spurred his horse, and without dismounting, horse and rider leaped over the walls, making a leap which has never been outdone in all history. He released himself from his dying steed, and escaped into the desert, a hero.

J. A. Rogers
Your History

The Khedives and British Occupation of Egypt

France and England had been at odds with each other for a number of years, for both sought to control and dominate the world and each saw the other as the major obstacle to their success. The British roused the French out of Egypt in 1801, and finally defeated Napoleon's forces at the Battle of Waterloo in 1815. While the French and the British were bitter enemies, they frequently forgot their differences when it came to matters regarding the acquisition of Egyptian antiquities.

As European nations were forming national museums to ensure the survival of their own heritage, they were also taking a profound interest in the culture of other lands. One of the first national museums created was the British Museum, which was established by an act of Parliament in 1756 and formally opened in 1762. As the interest in Egyptian antiquities grew, so did the collection in the Egyptian Gallery of the British Museum.

The British expressed little desire in annexing Egypt and making it a part of their Empire, and they chose to allow the Turks to control the territory. In 1805 a Macedonian-born mercenary named Mohammed Ali, who had risen to power while serving in the Turkish army in Egypt, became the new ruler of Egypt. Mohammed Ali was a cold and calculating despot whose primary interest was in consolidating his power and selling the riches of Egypt to the highest bidder.

On May 1, 1811, Mohammed Ali annihilated his primary adversary, the Mamelukes, after extending an invitation to them to attend a great feast in his honor. As a contingent of 420 Mamelukes arrived at the Citadel of Mohammed Ali, they were diverted into a small street, ambushed and murdered in a barrage of rifle and cannon fire. Under Mohammed Ali's rule, Egypt was stripped of thousands of artifacts by tourists, collectors and various fortune hunters. Members of the British diplomatic corps were extremely successful in buying and smuggling numerous treasures out of Egypt, which eventually wound up in the British Museum or in private collections.

In 1816, Henry Salt was appointed the British consul general of Egypt and he was simultaneously hired by the trustees of the British Museum. Salt was charged by William Hamilton, the undersecretary of state at the Foreign Office, with the responsibility of "finding another Rosetta Stone...whatever the expense of the undertaking." During this same period, the French, also looking for Egyptian artifacts, were giving the British stiff competition. Salt reached an understanding with his major rival and French counterpart, Bernardino Drovetti. Together they agreed to divide the Nile Valley into "spheres of influence" for their respective nations.

Salt and Drovetti were also quite successful at eliminating most of their competitors - by hook or crook. Howard Carter, the British discoverer of the tomb of Tutankhamen, described this era in the early nineteenth century as:

> ...the great days of excavating. Anything to which a fancy was taken, from a scarab to an obelisk, was just appropriated, and if there was a difference with a brother excavator, one laid for him with a gun.

Giovanni Belzoni

As a means of insuring the trustees of the British Museum that they would have access to the finest discoveries ancient Egypt had to offer, Salt secured the services of Giovanni Battista Belzoni, the man who would later be referred to as "the greatest plunderer of them all." Belzoni was an Italian-born soldier of fortune who had made a living as a circus strongman before entering the field of archaeology. He was a commanding figure who stood over six feet six inches in height and his immense strength, knowledge of hydraulics and commanding personality were the primary skills that led to his enormous success. Within a period of three years, Belzoni excavated the Temple of Abu Simbel, gained entry into the Second Pyramid at Giza, discovered the royal tomb of Seti I (father of Rameses II), recovered a statue of Amenhotep III, an obelisk from Philae Temple and a host of numerous other artifacts.

In a written account of his exploits as a tomb robber, Belzoni openly described his reason for living:

> My purpose was to rob the Egyptians of their papyri; of which I found a few hidden in their breasts, under their arms, in the space above the knees, or on the legs, and covered by the numerous folds of cloth.

Mohammed Ali was a converted Christian from Macedonia who exploited Egypt for his own personal interest. It is said that he had a harem of 500 women, with 200 in Alexandria and 300 in Cairo.

Belzoni also commented on some of the difficulties he encountered while plundering the tombs for papyri:

> [I] sought a resting place, found one, and contrived to sit; but when my weight bore on the body of an Egyptian, it crushed like a bandbox. I naturally had recourse to my hands to sustain my weight, but they found no better support; so that I sunk altogether among the broken mummies, with a crash of bones, rags, and wooden cases, which raised such a dust as kept me motionless for a quarter of an hour, waiting till it subsided again.

Belzoni retired to London in 1820 where he penned his memoirs and gained instant notoriety among all quarters of the city. On May 1, 1821, Belzoni exhibited his findings in the Egyptian Hall in Piccadilly, where he drew more than 1,900

Mohammed Ali

Some of the items stolen by Belzoni.

visitors on the first day. One of the main attractions of the opening was the unwrapping of the mummy of a young man who was advertised as being "perfect in every part." Some of the leading doctors in London were invited to witness this macabre striptease show.

A. Statue of Sekhmet taken from the Temple of Mut.

B. Wooden statue of the Ka of Rameses I, taken from his tomb.

C. Partially damaged head of Rameses II (once thought to be "Young Memnon") which was found in the city of Luxor.

D. Sculpture of Seti II holding a small shrine. This object was stolen from Luxor.

E. Magnificent head of Amonhotep III, which was taken from the city of Karnak.

F. Kneeling figure of Pa-Ser, the governor of Nubia during the reign of Rameses II. This figure was stolen from the Temple of Rameses II at Abu-Simbel.

G. One of a pair of Tekhenwy which formerly stood at the entrance of the first pylon of Phile Temple. Belzoni sold it to William Banks for 1,000 sterling pounds. It currently stands on the grounds of the Kingston Lacy House in Dorset, England.

The Egyptian Hall

Howard Carter (left) and Lord Carnarvon standing in the entrance of the burial chamber of King Tutankhamen.

Of all the finds in Egypt, the discovery of the tomb of the young King Tutankhamen in 1922 by the British Egyptologist Howard Carter ranks as the most significant. This was the first —and only—tomb of an Egyptian king which was discovered intact. Carter's expedition was financed by a fellow countryman named Lord Carnarvon who gave the contents of the tomb to the Cairo Museum. However, it was discovered more than 60 years later that both Carnarvon and Carter had secretly transported items out of the tomb which they kept in private collections. These actions are not surprising as they reflect the moral consciousness of the men who profited in the robbing of ancient graves. Regarding these activities Howard Carter once commented:

> One can imagine the plotting beforehand, the secret rendezvous on the cliff by night, the bribing or drugging of the cemetery guards, and then the desperate burrowing in the dark, the scramble through a small hole into the burial chamber, the hectic search by glimmering light for treasure that was portable, and the return home at dawn laden with booty.

In February of 1988, the Earl of Carnarvon uncovered a cache of Egyptian antiquities that had been hidden in several secret compartments in the family's home at Highclere Castle, in Hampshire, England, for more than 60 years.

More than 300 objects were discovered when a 75-year-old retired family butler, who was assisting the Earl of Carnarvon with compiling an inventory of the castle's contents, mentioned that the task was almost complete, "except for the Egyptian stuff."

The butler then led the way to two hidden cupboards, an unused document room and a housekeeper's drawer where the artifacts were found. The items were stolen by Carter and Carnarvon during several archaeological digs. They are considered to be of great scholarly value.

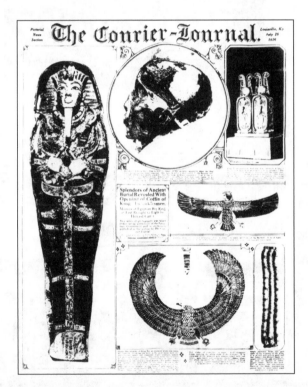

Chapter Six
The Nile Valley Presence in Europe

...if the parallels between the mythological history of Isis and Horus and the history of Mary and the Child be considered, it is difficult to see how [Europeans] could possibly avoid perceiving in the teaching of Christianity reflections of the best and most spiritual doctrines of the Egyptian religion.

Sir E.A. Wallis Budge
The Gods of Egypt

The discoveries of Egyptian antiquities in the eighteenth and nineteenth centuries fueled the passions of Europeans in every nation of the continent. The collections amassed in the Louvre and British Museums "created a surge of nationalistic lust for the precious and exotic" artifacts of the Nile Valley. Egypt was systematically raped and pillaged for more than a century before academicians developed an archaeological methodology for excavations. By then, countless monuments had been destroyed, thousands of papyri and mummies were burned and some of the finest statuary in the world had been spirited away in private collections.

This second wave of the European invasion into Egypt was similar in many respects to the invasions by the Persians, Greeks and Romans more than 2,000 years earlier. In both instances, the mystique of ancient Egypt held the European mind in a trance, and created within them an insatiable desire to recreate the spirit of the Nile Valley within their homelands. One of the elements most often duplicated in Europe was that of the African concept of God. The Netcherw of the Nile Valley evolved to become the gods of the Greeks and Romans. The names of the African Holy Royal Family of Ausar, Aset and Heru were changed by the Greeks to Osiris, Isis and Horus. They were later referred to as the "Father, Son and Holy Ghost" in early Christiandom.

An image depicting the Weighing of the Soul was carved on the west tympanum of Autun Cathedral in France. It details the souls of men being weighed on the scales of judgement (Maat) while devils and angels manipulate the scales. The saved souls cling to the hem of the angels' garments for safety while the souls of those condemned to damnation are seized by devils and cast into the pit of hell.

The Weighing of the Soul

In Roman times the worship of Isis was widespread on all the main lines of communication in Europe, usually in ports and important market towns on rivers. With the advent of Christianity many chapels of Isis were taken over, and the representations of the goddess with the infant Horus in her arms became pictures of the Virgin Mary carrying the Holy Child. As Isis was dark-skinned, they became famous Black Virgins. Notre Dame in Paris was built on the remains of a Temple of Isis; the original name of the city was *Para Isidos,* the Grove of Isis. There are Black Virgins near Marseille, near Barcelona, at Czestochowa in Poland, and in numerous other cities in Europe.

Egerton Sykes
Everyman's Dictionary of Non-Classical Mythology

Isis and Horus

The worship of Isis and Horus as the Black Madonna and Child was widespread throughout southern Europe until the convening of the Nicean Council in 332 A.C.E. After that meeting, the images of the African-born Aset and Heru became European in appearance and their names were changed to Mary and Jesus. Despite this action, many churches in Europe continued to secretly worship the "Black Madonna and Child." There are shrines of the Black Madonna in Italy, Spain and Russia, and currently whenever Pope John Paul II visits the shrine of Czestochowa in his native Poland, he often prays at the feet of the Black Madonna.

It has also been suggested by Diop that Paris, France was also the site of a temple that was formally dedicated to Isis. He suggests that the term "Parisii" could mean "Temple of Isis," because there was a city of that name in Kemet. Diop states:

> The worship of Isis was evidently quite widespread in France, especially in the Parisian basin: temples of Isis, in Western parlance, were everywhere. But it would be more exact to say "Houses of Isis," for in Egyptian these so-called temples were called *Per*, the exact meaning of which in ancient Egyptian, as in present-day Wolof, is: the enclosure surrounding the house. The name "Paris" could have resulted from the juxtaposition of Per-Isis, a word that designated certain cities in Egypt, as Hubac observes (quoting Maspero). According, the root of the name of France's capital could be derived basically from Wolof. This would indicate to what extent the situation has been reversed.

Throughout his numerous writings Diop referenced the many linguistic similarities between Medu Netcher and Wolof, the language spoken in his native land of Senegal.

One of the finest examples of Gothic architecture is the famed Cathedral of Notre Dame, which stands on the small island of the Île de la Cite, on the Seine River in the center of Paris. This cathedral is dedicated to *Notre Dame,* the French expression for *Our Lady,* the Virgin Mary. The construction of this building occurred between 1163 and 1250 A.C.E., but it was built on the site of two ancient temples, the earliest of which was originally called Per-Isis and was dedicated to Isis.

E.A. Wallis Budge, former keeper of Egyptian and Assyrian antiquities at the British Museum, described the similarities between Isis and Mary in Volume 2 of his book, *The Gods of the Egyptians.* Budge declared:

> ...it is clear that the early Christians bestowed some of [Isis'] attributes upon the Virgin Mary. There is little doubt that in her character of the loving and protecting mother she appealed strongly to the imagination of all the Eastern peoples among whom her cult came, and

that the pictures and sculptures wherein she is represented in the act of suckling her child Horus formed the foundation for the Christian figures and paintings of the Madonna and Child. Several of the incidents of the wonderings of the Virgin with the Child in Egypt as recorded in the Apocryphal Gospels reflect scenes in the life of Isis as described in the texts found on the Metternich Stelle, and many of the attributes of Isis, the Godmother, the mother of Horus...are identical with those of Mary the Mother of Christ. The writers of the Apocryphal Gospels intended to pay additional honour to Mary the Virgin by ascribing to her the attributes which up to the time of the advent of Christianity they had regarded as the peculiar property of Isis.

The *Metternich Stelle*, referenced here by Budge, was discovered in Alexandria in 1828 and was given to Prince Metternich by Mohammed Ali. It was translated into German in 1877.

There are a host of other images from Kemet which have also made their way into religious iconography. The paintings and carvings of the winged Netcher Maat served as the prototype for the Christian concept of the angel. Maat represented the principals of truth, justice, righteousness and reciprocity and her symbol of the "scale of justice" was used to weigh the souls on their day of judgement. In some religious paintings of the Middle Ages, images of the angel of God can be seen holding the scale of Maat.

One of the more prominent images from the Nile Valley to appear throughout Europe was that which represented the resurrection of the African Netcher Ausar. This powerful symbol was called a *tekhen* in Kemet, but it was later renamed by the Greeks who called it an *obelisk*. Currently, obelisks can be found in Paris, London, Istanbul, Igel and numerous other cities throughout Europe. The very first obelisk erected in Rome was in 10 B.C.E. to commemorate Augustus' conquest of Egypt. A second obelisk was removed from Alexandria and erected in Rome in the spring of 357 A.C.E., after the establishment of Christianity.

There are now a total of 13 obelisks in Rome. The most famous obelisk in Italy stands in the center of St. Peter's Square at the Vatican (the Piazza di San Pietro). Very few people realize that on Easter Sunday as the Pope stands on his balcony overlooking the multitudes and delivers his sermon praising the resurrection of the son of God, Jesus the Christ, he faces a 6,000-year-old symbol that represents the resurrection of the Nile Valley Netcher Ausar.

Mary and Jesus

The Tekhen in St. Peter's Square

Tekhen of Rameses II in Paris

Tekhen of Thutmose III in London

St. Peter's Square, the Vatican

Notre Dame, Paris, as viewed from the southeast

The erection of the tekhen of Thutmose III in London during the nineteenth century.

The Development of European Secret Societies

One of the most enduring aspects of Nile Valley civilization was the proliferation of its scientific and philosophical thought which became known outside of Kemet as the "Mystery Schools" or the "Hermetic Sciences." From the earliest of times, the masses of Europeans were poor and ignorant, while only the most fortunate men, noblemen, lords, scribes and various religious leaders were provided with an education. Of this group, an even smaller number knew how to adequately read or write. The dogma of Christianity was readily available for the masses of people, while the educated elite studied the ancient teachings, which were also called *gnosis* or "true knowledge."

The newly emerging schools of Hermetic, Neo-Platonic and Gnostic thought in Europe were loosely based on the Nile Valley principles of education, which were designed to awaken within an individual "knowledge of self." This knowledge led to an awareness of the powers of God which exist within man, as expressed in the myths of Ausar and Heru. This philosophy was in direct conflict with Christianity, which taught that man was conceived in sin and that salvation could only be gained through Jesus the Christ, the Pope or other accepted intermediaries. One example of the clash between these opposing ideologies can be found by studying the symbolism incorporated in the story of St. Patrick and the Druids of Ireland.

Peter Tompkins in his wonderful book, *Secrets of the Great Pyramid*, provided a clue to this mystery in a brief overview of the Druids:

> Druid in Old Irish meant "he who knows." Julius Caesar, our earliest source on the subject, considered the Druids highly educated and well organized. In *De Bello Gallico* he commented: 'It is especially the object of the Druids to inculcate this—that souls do not perish, but after death pass into other bodies, and they consider that by this belief more than anything else men may be led to cast away the fear of death, and to become courageous. They discuss many points concerning the heavenly bodies and their motion, the extent of the universe and the world, the nature of things, the influence and ability of the immortal gods; and they instruct the youth in these things.'

The Druids were also known to dress in a style similar to the priestly kings of Kemet. Their heads were often adorned with a ureaus, which was the symbol of the cobra that was worn on the crown of the pharaoh. Because of this symbolic imagery, the Druids were often referred to by outsiders as the "snake people." Their presence and ideology were viewed as a direct threat to the development of Christianity in Ireland. In 432

Djhuiti was known to Europeans as *Hermes Trismegistus* (thrice great, philosopher, priest and king). He was regarded as the god of wisdom, science, medicine, magic, measurement, mathematics, and he is said to have authored innumerable books on these and other subjects. Masons regard him as the author of all Masonic initiatory rituals.

Hermes is said to have been the author of 42 books which contained the wisdom of ancient Egypt. According to Manly P. Hall, "the Romans—and later the Christians—realized that until these books were eliminated they could never bring the Egyptians into subjugation."

Books on the *Hermetic sciences* were said to contain information regarding the Egyptian's understanding of immortality, which was based on the knowledge that "the body is the tomb of the soul."

During the Greco-Roman occupation of Egypt, the soldiers formed a secret body for specialized scholarship and training in the "Hermetic sciences." They became known as "Druids" and later moved from Egypt into Greece and Rome before establishing a "school" in Ireland.

Hermes Trismegistus

A.C.E., Pope Celestine I sent a former British slave named Patrick into the region to convert the population.

In the name of Christianity, Patrick's army slew thousands of Irishmen, and he is said to have founded more than 300 churches and baptized more than 120,000 persons. Patrick also introduced the Roman alphabet and Latin literature into Ireland. He was rewarded by the Vatican with sainthood and today, millions of people throughout the world celebrate *Saint Patrick's Day* on his feast day, March 17. To the average person, who dresses in green, wears shamrocks and marches in parades this day commemorates the myth of the man who drove the "snakes" out of Ireland. What most people fail to realize is that the snakes St. Patrick drove into the sea were not the snakes that crawled on the ground, but the "snake people" who walked on two feet and were once known as Druids.

In 1517, the Reformation, a religious and political movement in opposition to the Roman Catholic Church, began spreading throughout Europe. Participants in the movement were called *Protestants,* which is derived from the Latin word *protestans,* which means *one who protests.* This term first came into use in 1529 at a special assembly in Speyer, Germany. Many Protestants were also interested in ancient Egypt and the Hemetic sciences. In the seventeenth century, an organization called the Rosicrucians emerged in Germany, France and England. They advocated a "true" religion which was reserved for the enlightened elite. This organization was similar in many respects to many newly emerging organizations that attempted to pattern themselves after the "Mystery Schools" of the Nile Valley.

One of the greatest European scholars to emerge in the seventeenth century was the English scientist and mathematician Sir Isaac Newton. Newton is credited with inventing integral and differential calculus, introducing the laws of gravity and developing profound theories on light and color. He was identified by the Rosicrucians as one of their most learned members. Newton fervently believed that Egypt was the fountain of knowledge in the ancient world as referenced in his writings *Principia Mathematica:*

> The Egyptians were the earliest observers of the heavens....For from them it was...that the Greeks, a people more addicted to the study of philology than of nature, derived their first as well as their soundest notions of philosophy; and in the Vestal ceremonies we can recognize the spirit of the Egyptians, who concealed mysteries that were above the capacity on the common heard under the veil of religious rites and hieroglyphic symbols.

The Christian church was the major civilizing force during

Martin Luther (1483-1546) was the leader of the religious movement known as the Reformation. Its creation led to the development of Protestantism. Luther also authored a German translation of the Bible, which is still regarded as a brilliant literary accomplishment by biblical scholars.

Martin Luther nailing his thesis to the door of Wittenburg Church, 1517.

medieval Europe, for it was a source of leadership, social development and education. The era of cathedral building occurred between 1000 and 1500 and these structures served as the center around which the common people lived their lives. The walls of the cathedrals were lined with paintings and stained glass windows, which portrayed scenes from the Bible and the lives of numerous saints. These buildings served as a visual talking book and provided within their artwork a source of knowledge for the many illiterate worshippers who could neither read nor write.

Cathedral design and architecture was patterned after the ancient temples of the Nile Valley, which were always oriented to celestial bodies. In every instance, the cathedral was shaped like a cross. The entrance faced west. The alter is in the east in a semicircular area known as the apse. Behind it is an isle called an ambulatory, which leads to several chapels. In the front of each cathedral were two steeples which represented the twin obelisks that often stood in front of the Egyptian temples of old. The great rose-window of the cathedral is a design which represents the solar disk of the Netcher Amen.

The British astronomer Sir Norman J. Lockyer, author of *Dawn of Astronomy*, elaborated on the similarities between Egyptian temple orientation and European cathedrals. He stated emphatically that:

The west facade of St. Etienne, Caen, France

All our churches are more or less oriented, which is a remnant of old sun worship. Any church that is properly built today will have its axis pointing to the rising sun on the saints' day—i.e., a church dedicated to St. John ought not to be parallel to a church dedicated to St. Peter. It is true that there are sometimes local conditions which prevent this; but if the architect knows his business properly he is unhappy unless he can carry out this old-world tradition. But it may be suggested that in our churches the door is always to the west and the alter is always to the east. This is perfectly true, but it is a modern practice. Certainly in the early centuries the churches were all oriented to the sun, so that the light fell on the alter through the eastern doors at sunrise.

Below- aerial view of St. Sernin, Toulouse, France

Left - Plan of St. Sernin
1. Entrance
2. Altar
3. Ambulatory

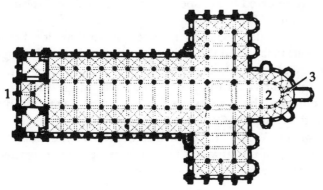

Eighteenth century French Freemasons exacted oaths from their initiates at swordpoint, while other candidates (under shrouds at left) awaited their turn. Masonic lodges were often meeting places for the aristocratic intellectuals in Germany, France and Great Britain.

It is uncertain whether Napoleon was a Mason. There is, however, no doubt that he was deeply involved in Masonic affairs, that there were many members of the craft in the higher ranks of his army and that Masonry 'flourished exceedingly' under his rule. It is also clear that he took his imperial symbol of the bee from Egypt and probably through Masonic sources. His initial behavior in Egypt also indicates this influence: he tried, for instance, to transcend Christianity and appear as a champion of Islam and Judaism and he dutifully went into the Great Pyramid and had a mystical experience.

Martin Bernal
Black Athena, Vol. 1

Lockyer also described the architectural peculiarities of St. Peter's Cathedral in the Vatican:

> ...So exactly due east west was the Basilica that, on the vernal equinox, the great doors of the porch of the quadriporticus were thrown open at sunrise, and also the eastern doors of the church itself, and as the sun rose, its rays passed through the inner doors, and penetrating straight through the nave, illuminated the High Alter.

The men responsible for constructing the cathedrals in medieval Europe were members of secret societies who were called "operative masons." These men had a particular affinity to ancient Egypt, which they viewed as the birthplace of Masonry. Most cathedral building came to an end after the Reformation and the Wars of Religion, but elements of Masonry survived in Britain among members of the ruling class who were referred to as "speculative masons," and their order was renamed "Freemasonry."

There also exists a number of similarities between the Rosicrucians and the Freemasons. They both made special use of measurements and proportions of buildings. This knowledge, derived from Nile Valley teachings, was designed to represent the universe and man's particular relationship to it, and symbolize God, who was commonly referred to as the "Master Architect." Both organizations believed in the divine destiny of enlightened men to serve as world leaders and to create a more righteous life on Earth.

Chapter Seven
The Nile Valley Presence in America

The Nile Valley, Masonry and The Founding Fathers

The history of the United States stands as a glorious example of what man can achieve when freed of the burden of religious persecution and allowed to pursue true enlightenment. The United States was the first nation in the modern world established on the principles of reason and understanding, as opposed to warfare. The true spirit of America is rooted in the fundamental principle called democracy—freedom of speech, freedom of assembly, freedom of religion, etc. For this reason alone, America has served as the model form of government for Europe and the rest of the world.

We must, of course, understand that the democratic concepts espoused by America's Founding Fathers applied only to "free white men of means," and not Africans, native Americans, women and the poor. A careful study of the events which led to the creation of the United States of America reveals an attempt by white males of European ancestry to recreate in the new world the spiritual essence that once existed in the Nile Valley.

America's Founding Fathers were eighteenth century *deists* who were profoundly influenced by the philosophical ideologies of the secret societies in France, Germany and England. The United States of America is the only nation that has printed on its currency the words, "In God We Trust." This is not a reference to the God of the Bible. As deists, the Founding Fathers did not believe in the fall of man. They believed in the existence of God, but they also felt that the creator exercised no control over the lives of people after the creation of the world.

The Founding Fathers believed that man could *know* God through reason and the refinement of the intellect. This was the quintessential spirit of democracy. They believed that every mind was capable of enlightenment. It was, therefore, unnecessary to have an authorized figure of the church to dictate revelation. A mind that was "cleansed of secondary and merely temporal concerns, beholds with the radiance of a cleansed mirror a reflection of the rational mind of God." This was the reason for the Founding Fathers insistence on the separation between church and state.

George Washington's Masonic apron was presented to him by General Lafayette in 1784. It contained numerous symbols which were associated with the French Masonic lodge.

Members of the St. Andrew's Masonic Lodge dressed as Mohawk Indians dumping "Consignments of a few Shiploads of Tea" into the Boston Harbor.

The Green Dragon Tavern, ca. 1773

The Green Dragon Tavern in Boston served as a meeting place for the members of St. Andrew's Masonic Lodge. Freemason John Johnson wrote that the Green Dragon Tavern was the location "where we met to Plan the Consignment of a few Shiploads of Tea. Dec 16 1773." The lodge records indicated that the meeting set for December 16, 1773 was adjourned "on account of the few Brethren present."

Throughout the years, historians have glorified the American Revolution and its struggle for independence; but an issue which must be closely examined is how an army of ill-equipped and improperly trained "minutemen" defeated the mightiest military force in the world. There is no question that European secret societies and Freemasonry helped to determine the outcome of the war. They influenced many individuals and events relating to the American Revolution and the development of the United States, as the following list indicates.

The Boston Tea Party was a raid by American colonists on three British ships docked in Boston Harbor on December 16, 1773. Approximately 40-50 men, disguised as Indians, threw 340 chests of tea into the harbor to protest British policies on imported tea. This was one of a series of events which led to the Revolutionary War. The plans for the Boston Tea Party were discussed by masons at a meeting of the Green Dragon Tavern, which also doubled as their Masonic lodge. Daniel Webster once described this site as "the headquarters of the Revolution."

The Revolutionary War against England was declared on April 19, 1775, and George Washington was named commander-in-chief of the army on June 15. George Washington had been initiated in a Masonic lodge in Fredericksburg, Virginia, on November 4, 1752. There were 33 generals, assorted officers and numerous enlisted men who were members of the Masonic order and who fought under the command of Washington during the war. Masonic lodges were also established on the military bases so that the "Craft" could be practiced on a continual basis. According to Marquis de Lafayette, General Washington:

> Never willingly gave independent command to officers who were not Freemasons. Nearly all the members of his official family, as well as most other officers who shared his inmost confidence, were brethren of the mystic tie.

Marquis de Lafayette

Lafayette was a French Freemason who came to the United States in 1777 and brought with him weapons, mercenaries and funds to help finance the war against the British. He was given the position of major general in the army and he was a member of Washington's staff. Lafayette fought in major battles of the Revolutionary War and helped to negotiate the "Treaty of Paris," which was signed in 1783, formally ending the war with Britain. He was later rewarded by Congress with $200,000 and given land in Louisiana and Florida. Lafayette Park, which is located across Pennsylvania Avenue in front of the White House, was also named in his honor.

Lafayette was not the only Frenchman to be honored by the newly formed government of the United States. In 1799, the town of Louisville, Kentucky, was named in honor of King Louis XVI, in gratitude for France's assistance during the American Revolutionary War.

The Declaration of Independence, which was adopted by the Second Continental Congress on July 4, 1776, led to the establishment of the United States of America. The Declaration was written by Thomas Jefferson and was a sweeping indictment of King George, the British Parliament and its people. This document embodied the true democratic spirit of America and the principles for which the Founding Fathers fought. Fifty of the 56 signers of The Declaration were active members in various Masonic organizations.

It has been suggested by William A. Brown, former curator and overseer of the library and archives of the George Washington Masonic Memorial in Alexandria, Virginia, that the Declaration of Independence was a Masonic document. Brown stated that the sentence structure and structure of The Declaration is unmistakable proof of its Masonic nature. While not saying that the text was written in a "secret code" or embodied a "hidden agenda," Brown did comment:

> We're just accustomed to using certain words and phrases which tell us that this was definitely written by a Mason. Anyone could see a pattern here. That's what I mean by Masonic document.

The *Declaration of the Rights of Man* was a document adopted by the French National Assembly on August 27, 1789, during the French Revolution. It set forth the principles of human liberty and personal rights. It declared that all people were free and equal in "liberty, property, security and resistance to oppression." The writers of the declaration were greatly influenced by the United States Declaration of Independence and the Bill of Rights.

George Washington saying good-bye to his officers and Masonic brothers at Fraunces Tavern in New York City on December 4, 1783. The tavern was owned by Samuel Fraunces, a Mason who allowed his brethren to meet there on regular occasions.

The Constitution of the United States was signed on September 17, 1787, and 13 of the 40 signers of the document were Freemasons. Throughout the early development of the United States, four of her first five presidents have been Freemasons, and of the 41 men who have been elected president, 16 have been documented as members of "the Craft" and four others were questionable.

It can be said that a number of factors contributed to the Colonists' defeat of the British. The rebels had the "home field advantage" and fought with guerrilla warfare tactics. There was also the great distance created by the Atlantic Ocean, which separated America from Britain; and while King George was fighting the colonists, he was also engaged in separate conflicts with the Spanish and the Germans. All of these factors helped to determine the final outcome of the war. Many Masons also strongly believed that it was the Masonic rituals and initiations which helped to create the mental and emotional bond among the troops, which aided them during their darkest days of the war.

The Nile Valley Origins of the Great Seal of the United States

We have already discussed, in previous chapters, the role that the Nile Valley played in the development of religious thought and secret societies in Europe, and we have also briefly surveyed the role of Masonry in the American Revolutionary War and the establishment of the United States. Let us now investigate the relationships between the Nile Valley and the Great Seal of the United States.

The first great seals appeared in seventh century-Europe and were used exclusively by royalty. The term "great seal" emerged in the thirteenth century. It was used to make a distinction between the "privy," or lesser seals, which were used by royalty for personal or business affairs. Over the years, great seals have come to represent the heart and soul of

The reverse and obverse of the Great Seal on the back of the dollar bill.

a nation. The United States, following in the tradition of its British ancestors, decided to create a great seal for her new nation, and thus incorporated into its design elements of masonry, numerology and Egyptian symbolism.

A committee was formed to create a great seal on July 4, 1776. Its members consisted of Benjamin Franklin, Thomas Jefferson and John Adams. A Frenchman named Pierre Du Simitiere was hired as a consultant, and he is credited with introducing the shield, E Pluribus Unum, the Roman numerals MDCCLXXVI (1776) and the eye within the triangle. The final design submitted by the committee was rejected, and a second committee was formed in January of 1777. Francis Hopkinson served as the design consultant for this group, and he proposed the pyramid, an olive branch and a radiant constellation of thirteen stars. No favorable action was taken on these designs and a third committee was formed five years later.

The third and final committee met on May 4, 1782, and Secretary of Congress Charles Thompson appointed William Barton as chief artistic consultant. These two men borrowed and modified the ideas from the two previous committees and finalized the designs that ultimately graced the obverse and reverse of the official Great Seal. Slight modifications were made on the front, or obverse, of the Great Seal in 1885 when a new die was cut, and the emblem has remained unchanged since.

The reverse of the Great Seal was not used publicly until 1934 when Henry Wallace, secretary of agriculture and former vice-president, submitted a proposal recommending that both sides of the Great Seal be used on a coin. While researching his suggestion, Wallace saw a similarity between the Latin phrase *Novus Ordo Seclorum* (new order of ages) and the *New Deal* (new deal of the ages), which was then in 1933 being implemented by President Roosevelt. Roosevelt was so impressed with the correlation that he decided to use both sides of the Great Seal on the dollar bill instead of a coin. Wallace and Roosevelt were both Masons, and shared a fond appreciation and understanding of the symbolic significance of the pyramid and the eye above it on the Great Seal's reverse.

The words "In God We Trust" have appeared on United States currency since 1864 with the exception of a period between 1907 to 1908 when President Theodore Roosevelt ordered the motto eliminated.

Roosevelt felt money and God simply didn't mix and that coins were an inappropriate place for the deity's name. Roosevelt was condemned by clergymen and politicians alike and was called a blasphemer by others. In the spring of 1908, Congress approved legislation requiring that the motto be placed on the currency. In 1955, Congress made it mandatory that all United States currency carry the motto "In God We Trust." To date, America is the only nation to require such a stipulation.

The Obverse   *Emblem of Heru*

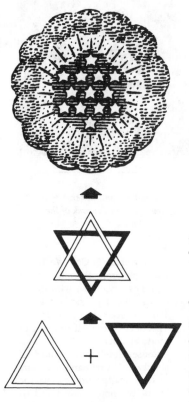

The state of Israel has adopted as its national emblem the cabalistic* symbol of two overlapping triangles. These two triangles should be seen as inscribed in a circle: they represent the poles, the tropics and the ecliptic, besides having the added meaning of the male and female elements coming together to generate the cosmos. The Founding Fathers adopted as the seal of the United States a pyramid: they wanted to convey the notion that a perfect society had been organized, and in order to convey it they adopted a symbol which, through the tradition transmitted by Masonic societies, goes back to the Egyptian idea of Maat.

Peter Tompkins
Secrets of the Great Pyramid

* The cabala is regarded as a Hebrew underground religion or philosophy.

The official dies for the Great Seal are on permanent exhibition in the Department of State Building, in Washington D.C. The conventional description of the Seal is as follows:

The Obverse bears the design used on official documents. The American eagle, with an escutcheon, or shield, on its breast, symbolizes self-reliance. The 13 vertical stripes on the escutcheon came from the flag of 1777. The chief above the stripes in 1782 symbolized Congress, but since 1789, it has represented all branches of the United States government. The eagle holds an olive branch of 13 leaves and 13 olives in its right talon, and 13 arrows in its left. It faces the olive branch to symbolize a desire for peace, but it is always prepared for war. In its beak is a scroll inscribed *E pluribus unum*, which translates as *One* (nation) *out of many* (states). Above the eagle's head is the 13-star "new constellation" of the 1777 flag, enclosed in a glory, or golden radiance, breaking through a cloud.

The Reverse of the seal contains a pyramid of 13 courses of stone which represent the Union, and it has the date of 1776 written in Roman numerals on its base. Above the pyramid is the Eye of Providence enclosed in a pyramid. The motto *Annuit coeptis*, meaning *He* (God) *has favored our undertaking*, is written above the pyramid. The words at the bottom, *Novus ordo seclorum*, means the *New order of the ages*, which began in the year 1776.

Manley P. Hall, noted expert on Masonic lore, has described the reverse of the Great Seal as the signature of an exalted body of men who helped establish the United States for "a peculiar and particular purpose known only to the initiated few." Hall referred to the unfinished pyramid as "a trestle board setting forth symbolically the task to the accomplishment of which the U. S. Government was dedicated from the day of its inception."

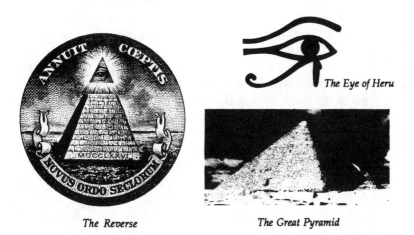

The Reverse　　　　　　　*The Eye of Heru*

The Great Pyramid

In India the triangle pointing down is a special emblem of Vishnu, representing the female and the triangle pointing up is an emblem of Mahadeva or Siva, representing the male. When combined they are called the United Symbols of Vishnu and Siva, the Sherkun or Six-Points. This is the well-known 'Star of David.' It is still used in all Oriental countries and, in Masonry, is a symbol of the Royal Arch Degree.

An equilateral triangle was also used as a symbol of the deity, its three sides representing his three-fold power....An eye within a triangle is a Masonic symbol of the Great Architect....Early Christians used a similar device as a symbol of the Holy Spirit.

Ernest Busenbark
Symbols, Sex and the Stars

The pyramid and the eye above it (which represents the eye of Heru—the son of God) clearly establishes an Egyptian link with the reverse of the Great Seal. The obverse of this seal is strikingly similar to the Nile Valley image of Heru, and the differences represent the cultural nuances which were unique to the United States. Above the eagle's head are 13 stars which are arranged in the form of the *Magen David*, which is also called the Seal of Solomon. This is an ancient symbol that predates Judaism and represents two pyramids. The two pyramids symbolize the two pillars of Solomon, which play a significant role in ritualistic masonry. They have been described by one Masonic historian, Dr. John A. Weisse in his 1880 publication *The Obelisk and Freemasonry*, as "an imitation of two obelisks at the entrance of Egyptian Temples (as) are the two towers on Gothic cathedrals and two steeples on churches."

Even the repetition of the number thirteen on the Great Seal was of significant symbolic importance to the Founding Fathers. Joseph Campbell, author of *The Power of Myths*, commented on its meaning in an interview with Bill Moyers. Campbell stated:

> The number thirteen is the number of transformation and rebirth. At the Last Supper there were twelve apostles and one Christ, who was going to die and be reborn. Thirteen is the number of going out of the field of the bounds of twelve into the transcendent....These men were very conscious of the number thirteen as the number of resurrection and rebirth and new life, and they played it up all the way through.

The Nile Valley Influence on American Architecture

There are a number of cities and monuments in the United States that were influenced by Nile Valley architecture and symbolism. Probably one of the most easily recognizable symbols can be found in the nation's capital, Washington, D.C. Of all of the monuments that could have been built to honor George Washington, one has to wonder why an obelisk was selected. It is not a structure indigenous to the United States, nor does it represent the cultures of France, Germany, Britain or any other European nation. The obelisk's relationship to Egypt, Egypt's relationship to Masonry and Masonry's relationship to George Washington and the Founding Fathers provides the only logical reason for the selection of the obelisk as a fitting memorial to George Washington.

The Washington Monument was completed on December 6, 1888. On that day, a Masonic ceremony was performed to formally dedicate the memorial to George Washington. This structure is 555 feet 5/8 inches and is the tallest obelisk in the world. Current architectural restrictions in the District of Columbia forbid the construction of any building taller than 13 stories. This unique height regulation has been in effect since 1894, when objection was made to the height of the newly completed Cairo apartments and hotel in Northwest Washington.

One will also find an obelisk on Bunker Hill in Charlestown, Massachusetts. This memorial was built in honor of the soldiers who died fighting in the American Revolutionary War. The literature describing this monument falsely attributes the origin of the obelisk to the Greeks. The obelisk, or tekhen, has been used for hundreds of years, in countries throughout the world, as a gravemarker for the dead, particularly veterans who happen to have also been Masons. This structure is one of the oldest symbols to represent the process of spiritual resurrection, and it was originally associated with the Kemetic Netcher Ausar, who became known to the Western world as the Egyptian god Osiris.

The city of Washington, D.C. also has a number of architectural and symbolic elements which can be directly linked with a Nile Valley counterpart. For example:

The Washington Meridian. Sixteenth Street is the north-south axis of the city and is the site of its prime meridian. Two hundred years ago there was a stonemarker on 16th Street which marked the meridian for the city; it was at an elevation called Meridian Hill. This specific site was determined by Benjamin Banneker, surveyor for the Federal city, who plotted the exact position of the sun at high noon on the spring equinox in March of 1791. Meridian lines are used to measure longitude, which is the distance east or west of a line passing through the prime meridian, which is located on 0 degree longitude. In

The Washington Monument

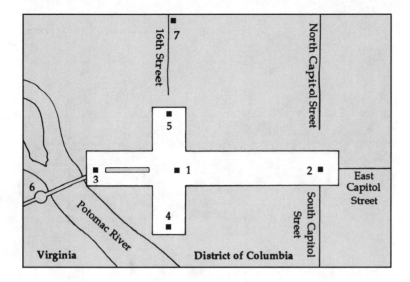

1. Washington Monument

2. The Capital
3. Lincoln Memorial
4. Jefferson Memorial
5. The White House
6. Arlington Cemetery
7. Meridian Hill

1791, the prime meridian was oriented to the Great Pyramid of Giza in Egypt, and all meridians of longitude were numbered east or west of this site. In 1884, an international conference of astronomers met in Washington, D.C., and determined that the line passing through Great Britain's Greenwich Observatory would become the <u>new</u> prime meridian of the Earth. This location is currently used to measure all time zones in the world.

In 1790, a permanent site was chosen for the capital of the new nation. One hundred square miles of rural land from the Maryland and Virginia banks of the Potomac River were ceded for the creation of the new Federal City. George Washington was responsible for determining that the new city would be diamond shaped (ten-miles on each side) and tipped so as to include as much of the port city of *Alexandria* as possible.

The square shape of the city and the horizontal, vertical, perpendicular and diagonal streets, along with its many circles, represent just a portion of the Masonic symbolism which went into its creation.

Pierre Charles L'Enfant, a French architect, engineer and fellow Mason was hired by Washington to design the city. Regarding the task that lay before him, L'Enfant stated, "I see the Capital City as something more than a place to live and work...I see it as a symbol...I think we should plan now with the realization that a great nation is going to arise on this continent...Right now we have a place which no nation has ever given itself...How can America plan for less than greatness?"

The Potomac River. In Kemet, the east and west banks of the Nile River held a specific symbolic meaning. The sun rose on the east bank, which symbolized life, and the sun set on the west bank, which symbolized death. In the ancient city of Waset (now called Luxor and Karnak), temples, palaces and homes (activities pertaining to life) were built on the eastern bank of the river. The tombs for the royalty of Kemet (the Valley of the Kings, Queens and Nobles) were built on the western bank of the Nile, which represented the afterlife. One will find a similar relationship in the original design for Washington, D.C., where the Potomac River divided the city into an eastern and western bank.

Eventually, the land west of the Potomac was not incorporated into the District and was given back to the state of Virginia. But the symbolism of Kemet is still present in the current design. Directly behind the Lincoln Memorial is a bridge which spans the Potomac River and leads up the "Avenue of Heroes" to the gates of Arlington Cemetery on the *west* bank. This cemetery is where the presidents and nobles of this country are buried—it is the American equivalent of the Valley of the Kings.

The Mall. West central Washington has a long, narrow park like area, the location of some of the city's leading attractions. It is called the Mall. Shaped like a cross, this area has four monuments located at each of its primary points. The Capitol is located in the east, the Lincoln Memorial in the west, the Jefferson Memorial is found in the south and the White House

The Tekhenw and their reflection in the Sacred Lake at Karnak

The Washington Monument and its reflection

in the north. The Washington Monument stands in the approximate center of the horizontal and vertical axis of the cross and was to be aligned to the prime meridian on 16th Street.

There is an interesting similarity between the mirrored image of the Washington Monument in the Reflecting Pool and reflection of the tekhenw of Queen Hatshepsut and Thutmuse I in the Sacred Lake of the Temple of Karnak. Upon seeing the resemblance between such structures, one can't help but marvel at the influence artisans of the Nile Valley have had on artists and architects over the years. The Lincoln Memorial, which is at the opposite end of the Reflecting Pool, provides us with an excellent example of such a comparison.

The Lincoln Memorial is a temple-like monument, sur-rounded by 36 Doric columns. There is a column for each state of the Union at the time of Lincoln's death. Inside the memorial is a statue of Lincoln seated in a chair, which is strikingly similar to images of Rameses II seated at his temple in Abu Simbel. What is most fascinating about the Lincoln Memorial is an alternate design which was given brief consideration prior to the construction of the existing monument. In 1912, the famous architect, John Russel Pope, proposed a design to memorialize Lincoln that was to have been built to the pro-portions of the Great Pyramid of Khufu at Giza. Pope's design was viewed as "lacking in originality," and a more traditional Greek-styled memorial was built in 1922.

Washington, D.C. is not the only American city with an affinity to Nile Valley architecture and symbolism. In the early nineteenth century, Andrew Jackson founded the city of Mem-phis, Tennessee, along the banks of the Mississippi River

John Russell Pope's design for the Lincoln Memorial, 1912

The Greek Temple design of the Lincoln Memorial

Rameses II at Abu-Simbel, ca. 1250 B.C.E.

Abraham Lincoln in the Memorial

Memphis Pyramid

San Francisco Pyramid

because it reminded him of the Nile River. Jackson, who was a Mason and the 7th president of the United States, named the city in honor of the Nile Valley city of Memphis, the first capital of Kemet. Memphis, Tennessee, currently has a sister city relationship with Memphis, Egypt.

The newest landmark in Memphis, Tennessee, is a $62 million, 32-story glass-covered pyramid, which is five-sixths the size of the Great Pyramid at Giza. It also has a large statue of Ramses II at the front entrance. Plans are currently underway to build an elaborate Egyptian theme park featuring holographic pharaohs and a boat ride through a spiritual netherworld. There have been suggestions that the body of Elvis Presley be enshrined inside this pyramid as a fitting memorial to "the King."

Approximately 150 miles north of Memphis, where the Mississippi river caresses the southern gulf coastal plane of the state of Illinois, there is an area called "Little Egypt." The local inhabitants named this region because they saw a similarity with the land between the Mississippi and Ohio rivers and the Nile Delta in Egypt. At the southern most tip of Illinois is the city of "Cairo" and 20 miles to the north, in the county of "Alexander," is the city of "Thebes." Also located within this region is the city of "Karnak" and two Kemetic-named bodies of water, "Lake Egypt" and "Lake Rameses."

Developers in Las Vegas, Nevada, have recently announced plans for the construction of a new hotel/casino complex called the "Luxor." It will consist of a 30-story pyramid-shaped building with more than 2,500 guest rooms. The $300 million project will feature a "museum" containing replicas of early Egyptian artifacts and a full-scale replica of King Tut's tomb. The interior of the hotel will have a waterway called the "River Nile" and boats will be used to transport guests from the registration desk to the elevator lobbies.

There are numerous examples of Nile Valley architecture and symbolism throughout the United States. This topic will be explored in greater detail in the the second volume of our *Exploding the Myths* series.

Mrs. Matthew Stirling poses alongside the first Olmec Head unearthed.

The Nile Valley Presence in Mesoamerica

The question of an African presence in early American civilization was first raised in 1858 when a gigantic head with African features was discovered in the village of Tres Zapotes, Mexico. A brief description of this head appeared in the bulletin of the *Mexican Society of Geography and Statistics* in 1869. It was authored by Jose Meglar and it read:

> In 1862 I was in the region of San Andres Tuxtla, a town in the state of Veracruz, in Mexico. During my excursions, I learned that a Colossal Head had been unearthed a few years before....On my arrival at the hacienda I asked the owner [of the property where the head was discovered] to take me to look at it. We went, and I was struck with surprise: as a work of art, it is without exaggeration a magnificent sculpture...what astonished me was the Ethiopic type represented. I reflected that there had undoubtedly been Negroes in this country, and that this had been in the first epoch of the world.

Contemporary scholars reacted to Melgar's discovery with great skepticism, and a serious investigation was not undertaken until many years later. Matthew Stirling, a researcher with financial backing from the Smithsonian Institution and the National Geographic Society, led an archaeological team to Tres Zapotes in 1939 and excavated the gigantic head that Melgar had described 77 years earlier. The head was carved from a single block of basalt and its measurements were astounding. It was described as being eight feet high, 18 feet in circumference and it weighed more than ten tons. Stirling's description of the head echoed the sentiments of Meglar. He stated:

> ...It presented an awe inspiring spectacle. Despite its great size, the workmanship is delicate and sure, its proportions perfect. Unique in character among aboriginal American sculptures, it is remarkable for its realistic treatment. The features are bold and amazingly Negroid in character.

After achieving tremendous success in Tres Zapotes, Stirling later set out for La Venta in the Mexican state of Tabasco, where scholars had earlier reported finding gigantic heads. La Venta turned out to be a veritable gold mine. Stirling found four additional heads—all African in appearance and similar in detail to the head found in Tres Zapotes. In addition to facial similarities, all of the heads wore helmets, some even wore earplugs, and others had cornrows. Historians have identified these statues as belonging to the Olmec civilization. The word *Olmec* is derived from the Aztec root *ollin*, which means "rubber," thus Olmec may be translated as "the rubber people," or the people from the land where rubber is produced.

Years of research and excavations have proven that La Venta was the center of the Olmec civilization. It was the home of the Olmec priests/kings and their most sacred site. The four heads found at La Venta had originally been incorporated into a ceremonial platform which was oriented on a north-south axis, as was a pyramid that was also discovered in the same area. This was the first pyramid to have been found in ancient America.

La Venta also yielded evidence that allowed for the dating of the Olmec statues. At the location where the heads were found, nine samples of wood charcoal were taken from the remains of the ceremonial court. Five of these samples were believed to have been incorporated into the platform which once held the heads and they were radiocarbon dated. The dates attributed to the samples ranged from 1160 to 580 B.C.E.- more than 3,000 years ago. To date, a total of 16 heads have been identified, two in Tres Zapotes, four in La Venta, six at San Lorenzo in the state of Veracruz and four others have been found at other sites. The heads vary in weight from ten to 40 tons and the largest is nine feet, four inches high.

There were a number of skulls and skeletons found in graves at various Olmec sites. A careful study of them lent great support to the theory that there was a significant African presence within the Olmec population. In September, 1974, at the 41st Congress of Americanists in Mexico, Dr. Andrzej Wiercinski, one of the world's leading skull experts, announced that African skulls had been found at Olmec sites in Cerro de

Two Olmec heads in the Jalapa Museum of Anthropology

las Measa, Monte Alban and Talatilco.

Wiercinski's evidence noted that at the pre-Classic cemetery of Talatilco, 13.5 percent of the skeletons examined were found to be African, as compared to the 4.5 percent African skeletons found in the cemetery at Cerro de las Measa, which dated from the later Classic period. Graves from the pre-Classic period showed native American female skeletons buried alongside skeletons of African males, but the couples found buried at the later Classic sites were found to be racially similar. This skeletal evidence indicated that an African element intermixed with the indigenous population at an early date (the pre-Classic period) and had been significantly absorbed into the native group by the Classic period.

This skeletal information suggests that an African element appeared during the early years of the Olmec civilization, and was genetically absorbed into the general population over the years. The skeletal evidence suggests that there probably were not more than 500 Africans in the Olmec world. A significant number of their skeletons were found buried in royal graves. The stone heads and skeletal remains prove that there was an African presence in ancient America. The question begging an answer is, "From what part of Africa did these people come?" Upon examination of all the evidence, the obvious answer is "the Nile Valley."

One of the first clues linking the Olmec heads to the Nile Valley was the helmets, which are identical in every detail to those worn by Nubian soldiers in Africa between 948 and 680 B.C.E. Dr. Ivan Van Sertima, noted author of *They Came*

Before Columbus: The African Presence In America, described the similarity between the Olmec and Nubian helmets:

> If we examine some of these helmets we will find they are uncannily similar to leather helmets worn by the Egyptian-Nubian military in the era of the Ramessides (Egyptian kings) and in the first millennium B.C. They completely cover the head and the back of the neck, and they have tie-ons attached to the crest and falling in front of the ears. The details on some of them, although almost 3,000 years old, have become a little obscured, but there is one in particular, now in the Jalapa Museum, which can be examined for comparative purposes. It has the circular earplug and incised decorative paralleled lines found on other colossal Nubian heads in the Egyptian seaport of Tanis.

The Nubian people that Van Sertima referenced played a major role at the beginning and the ending of civilization in Kemet, and history has proven them to be the true custodians of Nile Valley traditions. The Nubian kingdom of Ta Seti gave rise to the culture in the north around 3400 B.C.E., and the Nubian rulers of the Twenty Fifth Dynasty (750-675 B.C.E.)

Most convincing of the presence of Africans in the New World is, of course, the famous colossal stone head of Tres Zapotes No. 2, not only on account of its purely negroid features, but even more so by its typically Ethiopian braided pigtails, endings in rings and tassels. This head first appears in recent times in *Nile Valley Civilizations,* edited by Van Sertima. It has been seldom displayed among the other Olmec heads.

Alexander von Wuthenau
African Presence in Early America

Rear of Tres Zapotes Head

brought political stability to Kemet during the last centuries of native rule. The Nubians were responsible for initiating numerous building projects, such as temple construction, pyramid building and mummification, during the same time frame that Africans began appearing in the Americas (1160-580 B.C.E.).

Africans had been sailing ships up and down the Nile and throughout the Mediterranean Sea for countless years. The pharaoh Necho II (ca. 600 B.C.E.) directed a fleet of ships that circumnavigated the continent of Africa. In 1970 Thor Heyerdhal sailed an Egyptian-designed papyrus reed boat named Ra II from North Africa to the West Indies, in a successful attempt to prove that the ancient Egyptians had the capacity to sail similar boats to America. Van Sertima and others have shown the existence of numerous currents and trade winds, off the coast of West Africa, which circulate to and from the Americas. The reality exists that Africans had the capacity to travel to the New World regardless of whether they intentionally set out to travel there.

Ivan Van Sertima

Currently there are numerous examples supporting a Nile Valley presence in Mesoamerica, although we do not know exactly when they arrived and under what conditions. The similarities between the Olmec civilization and the Nubian/Kemetic culture are too plentiful to be viewed as circumstantial. There existed among both groups identical traits that were shared between members of the royal and priestly class. The examples are as follows:

1. All kings in Kemet wore a double crown, which signified that the pharaoh ruled over Upper and Lower Egypt;

There is an image of an Olmec dignitary at Cerro de la Piedre who is shown wearing a double crown, and he is offering an object, which has Egyptian symbols on it, to a person with a distinct African appearance.

2. All kings in Kemet were portrayed with an artificial beard which was attached to their face;

Most Olmec sculptures are beardless, but on the few sculptures where beards are portrayed, they appear to be attached to the face. The men who wore false beards were portrayed in very distinguished and authoritarian poses, and the beard appeared to be an indication of high rank.

3. The royal flail of the pharaohs was a symbol of authority, and it was often shown resting on the shoulder of the king;

An Olmec painting found at Oxtotitlan portrays a man sitting on a throne holding a flail in a manner similar to Kemetic royalty.

Mexican Priest   *Egyptian Priest*

4. Purple was a sacred color among the Egyptians, and it was worn only on special occasions and by people associated with royalty and the priesthood;

One of the Olmec heads found at San Lorenzo was found to have been originally painted with a purple dye that was identical in intensity to the shade used in the Nile Valley.

5. The sacred boat of the king appears among both cultures and is similar in appearance, function and name.

The Indian scholar Rafique Jairazbhoy, in a publication entitled *Ancient Americans and Chinese in America*, documents a similarity between a Kemetic priest, holding a snake-like instrument, performing the Opening of the Mouth Ceremony on a person seated before him. We find the identical image in Mexico, and in both instances, the person performing the sacred ceremony is wearing a leopard skin garment with a tail hanging between his legs. In both cultures priests wore leopard skin clothing.

The technological similarities between the Olmecs and the Kemiu/Nubians are even more fascinating. The first American-made pyramid at La Venta was constructed along a north-south axis, which is the same orientation as the pyramids in Egypt and in Sudan. Incidentally, the world's first pyramid, the Step Pyramid of Saqqara, evolved from the mastabas or burial mounds which first appeared in Nubia. What is most fascinating is that the Olmecs, and succeeding civilizations, continued to build elaborate pyramids hundreds of years after they ceased being built in the Nile Valley. It certainly appears as though pyramid-building was introduced into the Olmec culture, where it continued to evolve over the years.

The Pyramid of the Sun

1. The first pyramid in the Americas was located at a ceremonial site which contained four colossal African-looking stone heads. This pyramid had a total volume of three and a half million cubic feet and it was the first structure in America oriented to a north-south axis. The pyramids in Mexico and the Nile Valley were both used as temples and tombs.

2. The Pyramid of the Sun at Teotihuacan has a base practically identical to the Great Pyramid at Giza. It is the tallest pyramid in the Western world and it is oriented to the setting sun of the summer solstice. It was also used as an observatory and a geodetic marker.

3. The Pyramid of Kukulkan at Chichen Itza is so perfectly oriented to the spring and fall equinoxes that a marvelous phenomenon appears twice a year. At the time of the equinox, the interplay between sunlight and shadows forms triangular patterns, creating the image of a serpent slithering down the northern staircase of the pyramid.

4. The Pyramid of the Niches at El Tajin is similar in design to Imhotep's Step Pyramid. Both were formed by six boxlike steps. Within the El Tajin pyramid, there are 365 tiny windows which are built into each of the six divisions of the pyramid. It is believed that each window was dedicated to one day of the year.

Some of the pyramids in Mesoamerica, particularly the one at La Venta, were constructed by a means totally foreign to the native population, and has yet to be fully explained. The La Venta pyramid was built of stone blocks which varied in weight from two to 50 tons, and were transported from quarries that were 60 to 80 miles away. One scholar, R. F. Heizer, noted a number of "startling similarities" between the "heavy trans-

The Pyramid of Kukulkan

Alexander von Wuthenau

portation techniques" that were used by the people of the Nile Valley and the ancient Americans.

Another strong argument in favor of a pre-Columbian, African presence in the Americas has been articulated for more than 30 years by the German-born art historian and former diplomat, Alexander von Wuthenau. Von Wuthenau has amassed an extraordinary collection of terra cotta sculpture which vividly portrays Africoid men and women as chiefs, priests, dancers, drummers and in a variety of other situations. Terra cotta is a form of clay ranging in color from buff brown to various shades of red. The beauty of terra cotta is that it allowed the artist to depict the eyes, nose and lips of the subject with great detail, and through this medium the artist was also able to show the variances of skin color and hair texture among his subjects. Regarding the terra cotta sculptures, Dr. Van Sertima comments:

> With respect to coloration, the clay chosen or the oxide dyes used to evoke the blackness or dark brownness of the skin is particularly striking because they are reserved for the types with the non-native noses, lips, hair textures, etc. These were deliberate choices of artists dealing with human models.

Unlike the Olmec heads, of which 16 have been discovered, there are thousands of African images in terra cotta which were made between 1500 B.C.E and 1500 A.C.E. Von Wuthenau's most recent publication is entitled *Unexplained Faces in Ancient America*, and despite criticism of his research by some scholars and associates, he has been given constant support by members of the Mexican government, including former president Portillo. Von Wuthenau recently expressed his reasoning for continuing his research:

> After thirty-five years of intense study concerning the human images forged by pre-Columbian artists, I dare to put these artists on the historical witness stand. In these times of racial unrest, a cool evaluation of historical truth and the reacknowledgment of ethnic roots—behind and below the ancient population of the Americas—should have a sobering and healing effect on many a confused mind.

Many health care practitioners believe that overcoming denial is the first step towards healing a confused mind. There must exist within the world a yet-unnamed disorder which impairs vision and allows people to actually believe that African-looking images are not what they appear to be. This disease has already reached epidemic proportions among researchers of Nile Valley history and it is now affecting researchers of Meso American history. For example, Michael Coe, Harvard-educated and chairman of the Department of Anthropology at Yale. He is recognized as America's leading historian on Mexico, and says that the Olmec heads have broad noses and thick lips because the tools used to cut them were too blunt to make sharper noses and thinner lips. Coe reasons that this was done because the sculptors did not want to create "protruding or thin facial features that might break off."

What logic did Coe use to justify this line of reasoning? He simply stated, "I hope nobody, a thousand years from now, thinks that people had two noses and three eyes in our time just because Picasso painted people that way." Terra cotta sculptures of African images found in pre-Columbian America are displayed in the Museum of Anthropology in Mexico City and in the Diego Revera Museum. They can also be found in the private collections of Josue Saenz and Alexander von Wuthenau. When this same Michael Coe, one of America's foremost archaeologists, was asked if he knew of these clay sculptures that corroborate the ethnicity of the Olmec heads, he admitted that he had never heard of them.

One of the most extensive collections of Olmec heads can be found in the Mexican city of Jalapa, at the Jalapa Museum of Anthropology. Upon entering the museum one can see overhead a declaration, carved in stone, which attests to the significant contributions of the Olmec people. It reads:

Attention Mexicans:

This is the root of your history, its cradle and its altar. Listen to the most silent voices of the most ancient culture in Mexico, the mother of the civilization of our continent. The Olmecs converted rain into harvest, the sun into a calendar, stone into sculpture, cotton into cloth, pilgrimage into commerce, mountains into thrones, jaguars into religion and men into gods.

This incredible sculpture, with distinctive African features, was said to have been carved around 1100 B.C.E. It was discovered in Tres Zapotes and is now on display in San Andre's Tuxtla, Veracruz, Mexico.

Part Three

The African Renaissance

Exploding The Myths
Volume 1

Chapter Eight
The World's Best-Kept Secret

In the past I have frequently stated that "the history of African Americans is the best-kept secret on the planet." Over the years, as a result of studies and travels, I have expanded that statement and can now say with certainty that "the history of Africans worldwide, is the world's best-kept secret." A secret is described as "something known only to a certain person or persons and purposely kept from the knowledge of others." Most people of African descent know little or nothing of their recent history, let alone their ancestral history, which includes major accomplishments in every endeavor known to man.

I have met math teachers who knew nothing about the African contributions to math; ministers who could not properly place African people in the Bible; physicians who had never heard of Imhotep; and students from Southern Africa who knew nothing about Nile Valley history. One factor that all of these people had in common was that they had been educated by the very people who had written them out of their own history.

Carter G. Woodson, in one of his most significant works, *The Mis-education of the Negro*, reminded his audience:

> Philosophers have long conceded...that every man has two educations: 'that which is given to him, and the other that which he gives himself. Of the two kinds the latter is by far the more desirable. Indeed all that is most worthy in man he must work out and conquer for himself. It is that which constitutes our real and best nourishment. What we are merely taught seldom nourishes the mind like that which we teach ourselves.'

We live in a world where we are constantly bombarded with information. How that information is presented to us, its accuracy and how it is perceived, determines our perception of reality. Learning to develop critical thinking skills is the first lesson one must master in pursuit of the "other education"

Carter G. Woodson

When you control a man's thinking you do not have to worry about his actions. You do not have to tell him to stand here or go yonder. He will find his 'proper place' and will stay in it. You do not need to send him to the back door. He will go without being told. In fact, if there is no back door, he will cut one for his special benefit. His education makes it necessary.

Carter G. Woodson
Mis-education of the Negro

that Dr. Woodson referenced. Critical thinking skills allow people to become aware of hierarchal levels of thought, which gives them the capacity to assume greater control over their lives. The three essential levels of cognitive thought are:

The Literal: where one learns to accept all information at face value and never looks beneath the surface for additional details.

The Inferential: where one learns to *infer* or "read between the lines," and sees the hidden or dual meaning in information that is presented.

The Evaluative: where one learns to make an intelligent decision based upon the comparison of various sources of information, particularly those drawn from one's own personal experiences.

The objective of critical thinking is to learn how not to take all information literally, to read between the lines for deeper understanding and then evaluate that information by comparing it with other sources of knowledge. This process expands one's mind and opens up new vistas for learning. It is the means by which one may be resurrected from mental death and experience a profound rebirth of consciousness.

Who Defaced Her-em-akhet?

If one understands the evaluative method of thinking and applies that knowledge to the evolution of the names associated with the statue we now call the Sphinx, one will understand how inappropriate the term is. To the Greeks, the *Sphinx* was a monster who strangled innocent passersby. To the Arabs, it represented *Abu Hol*, the great Father of Terror. To the Africans, who created the statue, it represented *Her-em-akhet*, the physical symbol of the spiritual concept of the power of God manifested in man.

Many stories have been written concerning the "Riddle of the Sphinx," but one of the most perplexing riddles to date is, "who defaced Her-em-akhet, when and why?" A number of people have attributed this dastardly deed to Napoleon Bonaparte. I am aware of no written evidence which actually links Napoleon to the shooting off of the nose and lips of Her-em-akhet, although rumors have persisted for more than 150 years. I have now come to realize that it is through Napoleon's desire to document the history of Egypt that his culpability can be proven.

In 1981, I was informed by a representative of the Egyptian Embassy in Washington, D.C., that they had petitioned the British government for the return of certain sections of the head of the Sphinx. To date, the British Museum has acknowl-

This profile of Her-em-akhet, in contrast with a profile of Khafre, the reputed builder of the Sphinx, bears little resemblance, even though historians maintain that they are one and the same. A new body of scientific evidence indicates that the statue of Her-em-akhet is not 4,500 years old, as most archaeologist suggest, but perhaps 7,000 to 9,000 years old.

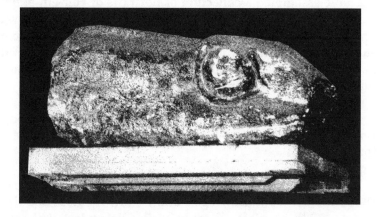

The ureaus from the crown of Her-em-akhet and a portion of its beard are currently on exhibit at the Cairo Museum. The beard was constructed during the reign of King Thutmose IV (1401-1391 B.C.E.) The copy of the ureaus and fragmentary portion of beard, are casts from the originals which are now in the British Museum.

In correspondence with the British Museum concerning the beard, they never volunteered the fact that they were in possession of the ureaus. One must ask the logical question, "how many more artifacts do they have of which the public is also unaware?"

edged having possession of only the beard. In response to a letter of investigation, I was informed by a representative from the Director's Office of the British Museum that:

> The British Museum does not possess the entire beard of the Sphinx. It has a fragment only - about one-thirtieth of the whole beard....The British Museum's fragment was presented to the Museum in 1818....A few years ago it was decided in Egypt to carry out considerable structural repairs and conservation of the Sphinx, and someone suggested that the fragment of the beard in the British Museum should be returned for incorporation in any reconstruction. The British Museum is not allowed by law to return objects, but we were prepared to cooperate in so far as we could. Negotiations, therefore, led to the proposal that we should make a long-term loan of the fragment to Egypt for the planned reconstruction.

In response to a direct inquiry regarding Napoleon's involvement with the destruction of Her-em-akhet, the museum official stated that, "The head of the Sphinx was damaged long before Napoleon reached Egypt." I was then provided with copies of prints to support that assertion. One of the documents sent to me was a copy of page 36 from the April, 1991 issue of *National Geographic*. This copy referenced an article written by the American archaeologist Mark Lehner, who is directing the reconstruction of the Sphinx. Lehner commented:

> I sought clues from history and archaeology for the computer reconstruction of the Sphinx. An early 15th-Century Arab historian reported that the face had been disfigured in that time. Yet to this day the damage is wrongly attributed to Napoleon's troops. Scholars accompanying the French invasion of 1798 recorded the monolith and the antiquities, opening Egypt to European scholarship.

Mark Lehner's statement concerning the "early 15th-century Arab historian [who] reported that the face [of the Sphinx] had been disfigured in that time" references the writings of the Arab historian El Makrizi who died in 1436 A.C.E. El Makrizi's comments regarding the event are as follows: "In our time there was a man whose name was Saim-el-Dahr, one of the Sufis. This man wished to remedy religious matters, and he went to the pyramids and disfigured the face of Abul-Hol [the Arabic name of Her-em-akhet], which has remained in this state from that time to the present. From the time of the disfigurement the sand has invaded the cultivated lands of Giza and the people attribute this to the disfigurement of Abul-Hol."

Nowhere in this statement does El Makrizi mention what portion of the face was disfigured or the extent of the damage. It seems reasonable, had the nose been broken, it would have been mentioned.

Computer generated image of the Sphinx, which is to be used as a model for facial reconstruction.

I have assembled a collection of portraits of Her-em-akhet that were drawn over a period of 100 years, from 1698 to 1798. These illustrations are the only evidence currently available showing the deterioration of the statue over the years. Careful observation reveals that the greatest destruction took place during Napoleon's occupation of Egypt.

Illustration 1 is dated 1698, and it shows a poorly proportioned, almost European-looking face. The nose and lips are intact.

Illustration 2 is dated 1743, and it is similar in appearance to Illustration 1. Both drawings 1 and 2 show the nose and lips intact. This physical evidence contradicts Mark Lehner's statement concerning the "early 15th-Century Arab historian" who "reported that the face had been disfigured in his time."

Illustration 3 is dated 1755, and shows the first evidence of damage. We can, therefore, assume that the nose was "partially damaged" sometime between 1743 and 1755. We can also see in this picture that the bridge of the nose and the lips are still in place.

Illustration 4 was drawn by the famous artist Vivant Denon who, along with Napoleon, was elected to the American Academy of Arts for his research in Egypt. Denon's drawing is one of the most beautiful and popular portraits of Her-em-akhet in existence. This profile clearly shows the prognathism and generous lips of the statue, which are further indications of its Africanness. The men standing on its head are the savants who are taking its measurements. This illustration shows the same amount of facial damage as Illustration 3. Illustrations 4 through 6 were drawn by artists who accompanied Napoleon to Egypt between 1798 and 1801. These renderings are far superior to those that preceded them; they are more accurate and they provide greater detail.

Illustration 5 indicates more extensive damage to the bridge of the nose than drawings 3 or 4.

Illustration 6 is the *piece de resistance*. This rendering clearly shows much more extensive damage to the face than in any of the previous drawings. The nose has been totally gouged from the bridge down. In drawings 3 thru 5 one can still see the nostrils, but in this illustration not only are the nostrils gone, so is the upper lip which was so pronounced in drawing 4.

Illustration 1

Illustration 2

Illustration 3

Illustration 4

Illustration 5

Illustration 6

Stelle of Akhenaton, Nefertiti and their daughter making offerings to Aton.

Many images of Akhnaton and Nefertiti show them making offerings to the sun Netcher Aton. The rays of light emanating from the sun disk all end in hands which symbolize Aton blessing all that he touches. The hands closest to the nostrils of the king and queen are holding ankhs to their noses, which represent their being supplied with the most precious gift of all—the breath of life.

There are several reasons why there are so many disfigured statues in Egypt today. Some of the statuary was destroyed by racial and/or religious zealots. Others might had been disfigured by time and the elements. There is also a great deal of evidence to show that many statues were destroyed by the Egyptians themselves for political reasons. It was not uncommon for a king to destroy the images of his predecessor and remove their names from temples and statues. In some instances, noses were chiseled off in an attempt to condemn someone to eternal damnation in the afterlife.

The nose is that part of the body which is expressly designed to bring air into the body, and breath is the method by which one may receive spirit. Spirit is derived from the word *spirae*, which means *to breathe*. In the ancient times it was believed that destroying the nose of a statue would destroy the lifeforce or *Ba* of that person.

We know for certain that the last three drawings were made between the time the savants arrived in Egypt on July 1, 1798, and the time they left Egypt in September of 1801. While it is evident that there was partial damage to the nose of Her-em-akhet by the year 1755, we can say with certainty that the greatest disfiguration occurred during the three years that Napoleon's troops were in Egypt.

This body of evidence is circumstantial, but it gives credence to the old adage that *a picture is worth a thousand words*. Until there is reason to believe otherwise, Napoleon must bare some responsibility for the damage done to Her-em-akhet. Others may try to defend him and place the blame on the shoulders of someone else, but in the final analysis, the nose knows.

Reclaiming African History Through Symbolic Interpretation

Arnold Toynbee was a world-renowned historian whose 12-volume work, *A Study of History*, divided world history into various civilizations and traced their rise, decline and fall. Regarding people of African descent, Toynbee stated:

> When we classify mankind by color, the only one of the primary races...which has not made a creative contribution to any of our twenty-one civilizations is the black race...

With minds such as Toynbee's, and those who have preceded and followed him in directing the educational institutions of the world, there is little wonder why Egypt has been removed from Africa and placed in the "Middle East." These actions have contributed mightily to the inability of people to think of Africa and Africans in a favorable light.

While the people and history of Africa were being appropriated, their religion, philosophy, science and symbols were stripped of all traces of their Africanness, modified to suit a new cultural orientation and then reintroduced into society as "original creations." When Kemet was conquered by foreigners, it was not uncommon to find the images of African personalities modified to reflect the appearance of the new rulers of the nation.

A small statue of a Sphinx on display in the British Museum actually states that the "face of the statue was reworked" during the Roman occupation of Egypt. A visit to the catacombs of Alexandria, Egypt, reveals numerous images of African Netcherw with European faces. The constant manipulation of African images reflect a psychological need that the foreigners had to project themselves into a history and culture that was not their own.

A great percentage of the statues of Egyptian figures (above) who appear to be distinctly African in appearance are missing noses. This is in stark contract the the numerous statues of distinctly European looking figures (below), which have their noses intact.

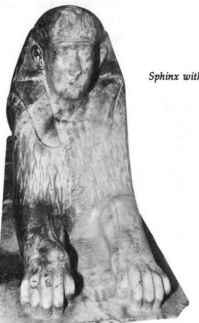

Sphinx with "reworked" nose

Roman emperor with pharaonic headdress

Rameses II at the Temple of Nefertari in Abu Simbel

The interesting fact about "cultural thievery" is that it has continued throughout the ages. The manipulation of the image of Rameses II provides an excellent example. Rameses II was the king of Kemet during the Nineteenth Dynasty; he ruled from approximately 1292 to 1225 B.C.E. Rameses II is regarded as one of the most prolific builders in Kemet. He completed the Great Hall of the Temple of Amon-Re at the Ipet-Isut (Karnak Temple), and he constructed the outer pylon and the Great Court of the Southern Ipet (Luxor Temple). Rameses also took credit for many of the buildings of his predecessors, often replacing their names with his. One of Rameses's most impressive creations was his marvelous temple at Abu Simbel, which was built near the border of Kemet and Nubia. Rameses also had a number of wives and is said to have fathered more than 140 children.

There have been numerous depictions of Rameses II throughout the past 40 years, and few have portrayed him as an African. Probably one of the most well-known portrayals was Yul Brynner in the 1956 film, *The Ten Commandments*. In that motion picture, all of the Egyptians—Rameses, Moses and the well publicized "cast of thousands"—were played by Europeans. Only the slaves and Nubians were portrayed as African.

In May of 1966, *National Geographic* featured a story on the international project to save the temples of Abu Simbel from destruction. That issue contained a series of illustrations portraying the design, construction and dedication of the Temple of Rameses as it may have appeared more than 3,000 years ago. In the illustrations, every Egyptian was portrayed as an European and the servants were presented as Africans. Similarly, in a 1983 characterization of Rameses in a *Ripley's Believe it or Not* comic strip, he was depicted as European and his foes as African.

There are symbols which originated in the Nile Valley that have since become indelibly linked to corporate identities of multimillion-dollar enterprises. Yet one would never associate Africans with these images because of the successful manipulation of African images and history.

In 1983, Schmid Products Company produced this ad for *Ramses Condoms*, which is antithetical to Rameses' proclivity to produce heirs to the throne. It has been stated that Rameses II sired more than 80 sons.

The Caduceus is currently used as a symbol representing a variety of disciplines in the medical profession. General practitioners, dentists, ophthalmologists and veterinarians all use various modifications of the caduceus as logos. This symbol has been associated with the Roman god Mercury and his Greek predecessor Hermes. At one time it was referred to as the "Staff of Hermes." Both Mercury and Hermes evolved from the Nile Valley Netcher Djhuiti, who was also associated with medicine. There are a number of carvings in Egypt where one can see Djhuiti holding a staff with a cobra intertwined around it. This emblem can also be found adorning the walls of many ancient temples. The winged sun disc, a symbol of Heru, was later combined with the serpentine staff and became the symbol now referred to as the caduceus.

The Rx abbreviation for prescriptions was derived from the Latin *"recipe"* which means *"to take."* The Rx symbol was first introduced by the Roman physician Galen who used this sign when writing prescriptions for his patients. The Rx sign is but a stylized version of the "Utchat Eye," which is a distinctly African symbol that represents several complex themes. The right eye is a symbol for the sun and is called the "Eye of Heru." The left eye (which the Rx represents) is a symbol for the moon and is called the "Eye of Djhuiti." As an amulet, this symbol placed the wearer under the protection of Djhuiti and brought *good health, happiness and protection from harm.* These expressions of good fortune are embodied in the word "utchat" which meant *whole* or *sound of mind and body,* that is, health or freedom from disease.

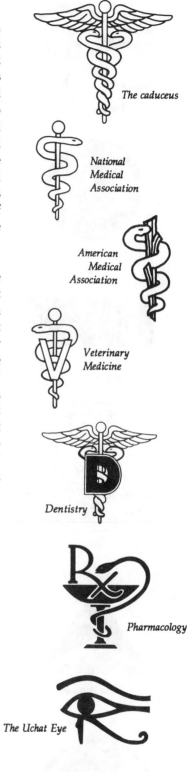

The caduceus

National Medical Association

American Medical Association

Veterinary Medicine

Dentistry

Pharmacology

The Uchat Eye

A doorway in the Temple of Kalabsha in Aswan was inscribed with a winged sun disk overhead and cobras intertwined on staffs on either side. The cobra on the left of the entrance wears the crown of Upper Kemet and the cobra on the right wears the crown of Lower Kemet. These three elements were later combined to form the caduceus.

The Eye of Heru

C B S

GENERAL SERVICES
ADMINISTRATION

Delta Airlines

Hollywood Pictures

The Eye of Heru is also known as the Eye of Ra. Both symbols represent Netcherw associated with the sun and express the divine omnipotence of the creator. When used as an amulet, it places the wearer under the protection of God, and when incorporated into a logo it has been used to represent the omnipotent objectives of that particular company. The Columbia Broadcasting System (CBS) has used a modified version of the Eye of Heru on their television stations for years. As recently as 1991, an eye was used in an equilateral triangle as a backdrop during their station identification breaks. For the last several years in some areas, the CBS local news broadcasts have been referred to as "Eyewitness News." According to CBS, Inc., since 1952, the CBS Television Network has been the world's largest advertising medium in terms of dollar value of advertising. CBS also owns W. B. Saunders Co., which is the world's largest medical publisher.

As the television industry expanded, more channels were added to the VHF band, and later the UHF channels were created. This was soon followed by the introduction of cable television, which can carry up to 60 channels. With the rapid expansion of cable TV, it was not too surprising to find that one of the early giants in cable TV, Home Box Office (HBO), followed CBS's lead and incorporated an "eye" into its logo.

Symbols of pyramids and sphinxes have been used in thousands of corporate logos and designs throughout the world. Their use is an indication of the great admiration that artists and business persons have for the power and knowledge which existed in the Nile Valley as recently as 3,000 years ago. If Arnold Toynbee were still alive it would behoove him to revise his comments concerning the civilizations of mankind to correctly read:

> When we classify mankind by color, the only one of the primary races...which *has* made a creative contribution to *all* of our twenty-one civilizations is the *African* race...

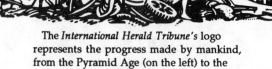

The *International Herald Tribune*'s logo represents the progress made by mankind, from the Pyramid Age (on the left) to the Industrial Age (on the right).

Symbols from the Nile Valley have long been used to represent activities associated with life and death in the Western world. The stelle between the paws of Her-em-akhet was placed there by Thutmose IV (1401-1391 B.C.E.) to record his excavation of the statue. As tombstones, these structures continue to be used to record historically significant events in a person's life. The presence of tekhenw in cemeteries also underscores the psychological need that many cultures have to surround themselves with African symbols while simultaneously denying their African origins.

The crown of Queen Meryt Amon was duplicated for the movie *Cleopatra*, but the hairstyles worn by these ancient Africans were deemed unsuitable for Elizabeth Taylor to wear during filming.

Hair pick used by Africans during the New Kingdom, ca. 1550 B.C.E.

The Politics of Hair and the Nile Valley

In my first publication, *From the Browder File: 22 Essays on the African American Experience,* included is an essay entitled "The Politics of Hair." It examined the many hairstyles worn by African Americans during a 60-year period, and associated them with gains and losses in the arena of political and civil rights. This essay pointed out that in the 60's, when African Americans began wearing African dress and hairstyles, they began developing an African consciousness. This directly correlated to their desire to struggle for and achieve civil rights. By the mid-70's, when the cultural emphasis declined, there was a corresponding decline in political activity and an erosion of civil rights and legislation.

Hairstyles often relate to consciousness. In the late 1980's two African American females were fired from their jobs at two different Washington, D.C. hotels for refusing to change their cornrowed hairstyles to a more "professional" style. These women subsequently sued their employers, and not only won a handsome settlement, but they also won the right to express their ethnicity in the workplace. The media has played a major role in influencing perceptions of style, consciousness and culture. Many people mistakenly believe Bo Derrick was responsible for the creation of cornrows. She may have popularized the hairstyle in the movie *10,* but it had existed thousands of years earlier in Africa and among Africans in the Americas.

Hollywood has been greatly responsible for creating incorrect perceptions of Africa, primarily because most people are too lazy to study African history on their own. Take a minute and visualize an image of Cleopatra. If you are over 35, chances are a picture of Elizabeth Taylor popped into your mind. In 1963, Taylor starred in a multimillion-dollar production of *Cleopatra,* which forever ingrained her image in the minds of millions of people as an accurate one.

Many people cannot imagine the Egyptians wearing "African hairstyles," but they certainly did and very seldom are these images portrayed on the screens or in print. There are hundreds of mummies, statues, wigs and drawings which clearly illustrate the texture and hairstyles of African people who lived in the Nile Valley in ancient times. These images are often suppressed or replaced with inaccurate ones that create a false historical perspective of a truly African characteristic.

Profile of a sphinx
(Note that hair is worn in plaits similar to those of Tutankhamen on following page.)

Kemetic Princess, ca. 1350 B.C.E.

Front and rear of Gold Mask of Tutankhamen, ca. 1330 B.C.E.

Kemetic Queen, ca. 1000 B.C.E.

Front and rear of statue of Amenemhet III, ca. 1890 B.C.E.

Eritrean woman, ca. 1900 A.C.E.

Contemporary African American woman examining wigs worn by priests of the Twenty-first Dynasty, ca. 1070 B.C.E.

Chapter Nine
How To Free Your African Mind

Mental bondage is invisible violence. Formal physical slavery has ended in the United States. Mental slavery continues to this present day. This slavery affects the minds of all people and, in one way, it is worse than physical slavery alone. That is, the person who is in mental bondage will be "self-contained." Not only will that person fail to challenge beliefs and patterns of thought which control him, he will defend and protect those beliefs and patterns of thought virtually with his last dying effort.

Asa G.Hilliard, III
from the Introduction to the
1976 reprint of *Stolen Legacy*

Asa G. Hilliard, III

The world mourned the passing of Asa Grant Hilliard, III who made his transition on August 13, 2007 in Cairo, Egypt. Dr. Hilliard will be remembered for his numerous accomplishments as an Educator, Historian, Psychologist, Author, Lecturer and Pan-Africanist.

While Asa's sudden passing has left an incredible void within the academic community, his work will be carried on by his colleagues and those he inspired.

Persons interested in helping preserve the legacy of Dr. Hillard, through the continued publication and distribution of his books and DVD's, may make financial contributions to the **Per Maat Foundation**, P.O. Box 357171, Gainesville, Florida 32635.

The Man in the Mirror: The Psychological Effects of Mental Slavery

Mental slavery is a condition effecting people regardless of their race, nationality or economic status. The perceptions of reality that you have in your mind will either free you or keep you enslaved. One has to ask the question, "What has been the cumulative effect of the manipulation of the history of African people?" This question is of particular importance to people of African descent. What has happened to the minds of generations of African Americans who grew up believing that straight hair was "good hair" and that light skin was "fair skin?" What has happened to the minds of millions of people who grew up hearing that "your skin is too dark, your nose is too wide, your lips are too thick and your hair is too nappy"?

What happens to a people who grow up believing that the image of the man or woman who stares back at them in the mirror is inferior and incapable of correct thoughts or actions? Over a period of years, these people would become mentally enslaved to thoughts of inferiority, and if given the opportunity to change the physical appearance of the image that stares back at them in the mirror, they probably would. If given the opportunity today, millions of African Americans would gladly pay a plastic surgeon to do to them what Napoleon allegedly did to the Sphinx, that is, change their noses and lips in an attempt to become something other than what God created.

Many people mistakenly believe that money will bring them happiness, but money without consciousness will usually lead to self-destruction of some form or another. Take for example entertainers who serve as larger-than-life role models for most youth and many adults. They have money and fame, but most lack a sense of security and cultural identity. A survey of a select group of African American entertainers will show that as their popularity increased they "crossed over" commercially and physically. As these entertainers crossed over you could see a profound change in their hair, their noses and their lips.

CHANGING FACES IN THE ENTERTAINMENT INDUSTRY
(Before and After Cosmetic Surgery)

Pattie La Belle   *George Benson*

Stephanie Mills   *Michael Jackson*

No person in the entertainment industry has ever undergone a "makeover" as dramatic as Michael Jackson. Analyzing his career, one can see that the most radical changes took place after the release of the *Thriller* album in 1983. This album became the largest selling record in the history of the music industry and made the name Michael Jackson a household word. The tremendous success of the *Thriller* album (more than 42 million have been sold to date) sent shock waves throughout the show business industry. Show business has been described by some executives as "five percent show and ninety-five percent business." Entertainers (like their athletic counterparts in the sports arena or historical counterparts on the plantations) are commodities to be marketed in a manner similar to Apple Computers, Toyotas or Nike sneakers.

The challenge faced by those responsible for marketing Michael Jackson after the enormous success of the *Thriller* album was formidable. How is one to market the world's most popular entertainer when the image of African Americans is the most consistently negatively portrayed image in the world? A simple solution for a complex problem was found almost immediately. As we can now see, it was much easier to change the image of one African American than to change the image of all of them. Thus, the new Michael Jackson was remade in a manner similar to Frankenstein, except that his body parts were all artificial. Jackson was given a new nose, mouth, chin, hair, eyes and skin. In one of his tunes Michael declares to the world that it doesn't matter if you are black or white, and he certainly speaks from experience because he has been both.

The music video industry was spawned by the success of the Michael Jackson videos that emerged from his *Thriller* album. Since that time, music videos have become an important component of both cable and commercial television, as well as the record industry. In fact, oftentimes it is the images in the video that often sell the record and they usually have little or nothing to do with the lyrics. Sex and violence are used as tools to promote record sales. Females are portrayed as sex objects and males are "looking to get paid." The youths and adults who spend hours weekly viewing these images begin to internalize them as acceptable modes of behavior.

Many of the problems we see in the African American communities throughout the country can be traced to negative self-images instilled in us from birth and perpetuated by the media to which we expose ourselves. Television is the most powerful form of mass communication in the world. It stimulates emotion while simultaneously diminishing thought and creativity. Television programming presents a quick fix to complex problems while exploiting the fears and manipulating the desires of the viewer. The more one watches television (educational programing excluded), the more detached one becomes from reality. It is as addictive as alcohol, cigarettes and crack.

Michael Jackson's video *Black or White* received rave reviews primarily because of its high tech special effects, but many criticized it because of its excessive violence and scenes of simulated masturbation. Jermaine Jackson was also highly critical of his brother's ever-changing skin color and addressed this issue in a song entitled *Word to the Badd*. The lyrics stated:

*Once you were made
You changed your shade.
Was your color wrong?
Could not turn back
It's a known fact.
You were too far gone.*

Congressman John Conyers (D-Michigan) visited four Asian nations in 1989, as part of a Congressional fact-finding mission, and expressed his outrage at the number of racially offensive images that he had seen while traveling abroad. Conyers stated that one of the most disturbing instances of racial stereotyping was on an item called "Darkie Toothpaste."

This product, which is manufactured by the Colgate company, is distributed "exclusively" throughout the Far East. It featured an "Al Jolson type, black-face minstrel with big teeth." When news of this event came to the attention of the American media, the manufacturer agreed to modify the name and package design of the product. The original design is shown above and the "new" design is below

A recent television survey, conducted by Nielson Media Research, disclosed that African American households nationwide watch 48 percent more television than all other households. This figure averages out to 69 hours and 48 minutes per week for African Americans, as opposed to a national average of 47 hours and six minutes. African American women, and children between the ages of two and 17, watch more television than any other segment of the American population. African American children and teens were said to watch more television than any other group of children surveyed. The group who watches the least amount of television is also the group who has the highest level of academic achievement; they are the Asian American population.

To many, television is viewed as simply a means of entertainment, but anytime a people spend more time being entertained than working, those people, and their offspring, will become a burden to society. Most of the roles played by African Americans on television are limited to situation comedies. Very few, if any, have been regularly featured in dramas or as characters representing integrity and substance and decent family values. These are not images foreign to the African American experience, they are plentiful; but they are seldom presented for the general public to see. Other ethnic groups understand the power of television and they exercise a sense of cultural responsibility by seeing to it that their group is represented in a balanced perspective.

On the whole, African Americans are so starved for images that they will accept a negative image of themselves over none at all. The popularity of *In Living Color* attests to this fact. Civil rights organizations have been fighting for years to destroy the stereotypes aired weekly on *In Living Color*. In all my years of television viewing I have never seen females referred to as "bitches" and "whores" as often as they are on that one program. Does this behavior become more palatable because it is black folk talking about black folk? I don't think so. The African American community should be outraged and writing letters to the Fox Television Network demanding immediate changes. But I doubt seriously this will happen. We accept negative images because that is what we have been programmed to believe we deserve.

Consider the fact that the church is the most powerful institution within the African American community. It is the only financially viable organization we own and operate. The church has been the base from which our civil rights movement evolved, our political leaders honed their thinking skills there and it has been the source of all of our music. If this institution means so much to our community, why would we allow a television program to make a mockery of it, its pastors, deacons and congregation. The program that I'm referring to is *Amen*. Even though this program had a brief network run, it will continue to be viewed for eternity in syndication reruns.

Negative images of Africans have been perpetuated worldwide. This 1938 cover of an exhibition guide entitled *Degenerate Music* was produced in Germany as part of an ongoing campaign, instituted by the Third Reich, to denigrate African people.

To those who feel television is simply a form of entertainment, consider this scenario: Due to the enormous popularity of *In Living Color*, Keenan Ivory Wayans is given the opportunity to create a television comedy of his own choosing. After great consideration, Mr. Wayans decides to produce a spin-off of *Amen* called *Shalom* and it will feature the hilarious escapades of a Rabbi's daughter who disguises herself as a male in order to fill the vacancy of a new Rabbi in the temple. This program could have all the makings of an Emmy winning smash, but I doubt seriously if it would ever make it out of production, let alone air on television, because of the expected protests from the Jewish community.

African-Centered Approaches to Children's Activities

In light of the extreme difficulties facing African Americans, it is important that new strategies be developed and implemented to ensure our survival. An important part of any plan must include the mental, physical and cultural nourishing of African American children. They are the ones who will be confronted with racist stereotypes in the media, classrooms and society. A constant diet of hopelessness will ultimately darken their mental skies and make them believe that their future is bleak and they will, therefore, develop the self-destructive behavior patterns so many of our youth currently exhibit.

Building self-esteem in any child is an arduous task, and building self-esteem in an African American child is even more difficult, but it can be accomplished. Several years ago the *Black Owned Communications Alliance* published an ad showing a young African American male child wearing a towel as a cape and pretending to be a super hero. As this child looked into the mirror he saw the image of a European man staring back at him. The caption accompanying this photograph asked the probing question, "What's wrong with this picture?"

What happens to children who grow up seeing everyone else portrayed as heroes, while they are given a steady diet of images portraying themselves as less than desirable? These children grow up falsely believing in the superiority of other groups while doubting themselves. All one has to do is look throughout any neighborhood in the country and you will find groups of unemployed and underachieving African American males with no real vision of themselves for the future. Images that are formed in early childhood generally stay with us for the rest of our lives. In the final analysis, television and radio are media that are too powerful to be left in the hands of children without proper supervision.

A recent survey conducted by the Center for Media and Public Affairs reported that cartoons represent the most violent programing of television today. Child experts agree that children between the ages of two and five may not be able to distinguish between the violence they witness in cartoons and the real thing. They, therefore, advise parents to monitor such programing. Studies also show an abundance of superhero-styled cartoons that feature more "human" characters than animal characters. These are believed to have an even stronger influence on children.

TV Guide
August 22-28, 1992

Jane Healy, educational psychologist and author of *Endangered Minds, Why Our Children Don't Think,* suggests that TV has the potential of reversing the evolution of the human brain. Healy feels that the electronic media, unstable family patterns, hectic life-styles and poor teaching methods all contribute to the changing of the brain structure within children. Scientific studies have shown that young minds are malleable. What children see and do on a daily basis changes their brain's function and structure. Any activity engaging a child's interest will stimulate the imagination and enrich the brain. The converse is also true. One Canadian researcher has documented a 20 percent creativity *decrease* in children and adults who have been exposed to television on a regular basis.

Everyday, parents are provided with opportunities where they can expose their children to new information while stimulating their young minds. When my daughter was in kindergarten she informed me that her class was having a Halloween party and that she wanted to go dressed as Cinderella. A question raced through my mind, "why Cinderella?" As I reflected on the question, I suddenly remembered that the movie had recently been re-released and advertisements were seen everywhere. This is obviously what influenced my daughter.

I told my child that I felt a Cinderella costume was inappropriate and we should look for a more acceptable alternative. While walking through the aisle of a local children's store, we saw costumes of Superman, Batman, Miss Piggy, Wonder Woman, witches and ghosts. I saw these costumes as figments of other people's imaginations, which could not reinforce within my child a healthy cultural self-image. As we left the store in disgust, I promised my daughter that I would make her a costume to wear to the party.

What's wrong with this picture?

A child dreams of being the latest superhero. What could be wrong with that?

Plenty, if the child is Black and can't even *imagine* a hero the same color he or she is.

It's like this: children learn by what they see. And if it weren't for Black media, a Black child wouldn't see the world as it really is...

with Black men and women doing positive things besides playing basketball and singing songs.

What can you do to make sure our kids have self pride? Decide which media shows them Blacks as Blacks *really* are.

And that's where BOCA comes in. BOCA, the Black Owned Communications

Alliance is an organization of Blacks working for Blacks.

We don't want your money. We want you to use the power you have to get what you deserve—a real picture of you. Your hopes. Your problems. Your needs.

We also want your opinion. So write us. We want to hear from you so we can set the picture straight.

BOCA The Black Owned Communications Alliance
P.O. Box 2757 Grand Central Station, New York, New York 10017

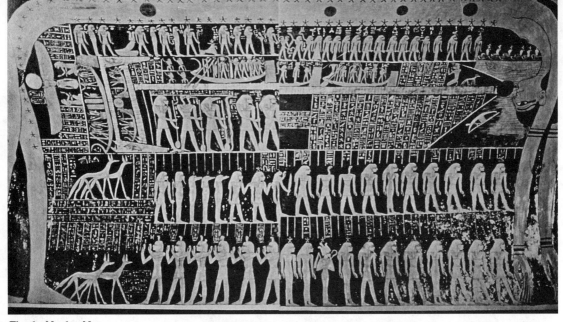

The sky Netcher Nut

I accepted the fact that Halloween costumes are designed based upon imaginary creatures and I decided to put my imagination to work. The costume I made for my daughter was patterned after an image I had seen in Egypt of the sky Netcher named Nut. This image can be found in the Temple of Dendera and several tombs in the Valley of the Kings where Nut's body can be seen stretching across the heavens while her feet and hands touch the earth. Scenes depicting Nut as the nighttime sky show her swallowing the red sun disc as it descends into the western horizon. The sun is then shown moving through the body of Nut and it emerges from her womb, in the eastern horizon, as a golden ball of light.

This image of Nut is profound because it reinforces the Nile Valley concept of women as being so significant that they are shown giving birth to the sun—an ageless symbol for God. If parents allow their children to dress as monsters, murderers or ghouls, they should not be too surprised if the children start acting like these characters. Conversely, if children are exposed to ageless images of wisdom and beauty there is a great likelihood that they will emulate those traits in their behavior

Atlantis (right) wears a black leotard which represents the evening sky and the three images of the sun show its movement through her body. The back of her costume is decorated with "strategically placed" stars and the word "Nut" written in English and Medu Netcher.

patterns. A creative approach to Halloween allows parents to turn a seemingly innocent event into an opportunity to teach cultural awareness. This same methodology can apply to holidays and other activities involving youth and adults. The only limitations to creating them exist in your mind.

Children are constantly bombarded with images that glorify underachievers such as "Bart Simpson," or violence-prone role models such as the "Teenage Mutant Ninja Turtles." There have been numerous accounts of small children seriously injuring their friends while imitating the martial arts aficionados known as the "Ninja Turtles." Recently, a London newspaper gave an account of a five-year-old child, dressed in a Batman costume, who found his father's gun and killed him while pretending that he was a bad guy. These types of stories have been reported for years, and while they are certainly nothing new, they have been increasing in frequency and the intensity of violence over the last decade.

In recent months a number of school principals have enacted regulations forbidding students from wearing the popular *Bart Simpson Underachiever T-shirt* for obvious reasons. The enormous success of *The Simpsons* has spawned a number of imitations including numerous characterizations of "Black Bart" and the entire Simpson family as African Americans. The irony of it all is that Matt Groening, the creator of *The Simpsons*, patterned them after black stereotypes.

Bart is portrayed as the typical underachieving black male child with a "serious attitude" and a fade hairstyle. Bart's sister Lisa plays saxophone in the school band and her mentor is a black blues musician. Homer is often referred to as "Homey" by his wife Madge and the name for the Simpson family is similar in spirit to the character of *Simple*, which was popularized by Langston Hughes in numerous newspaper columns. Many of Hughes's humorous sketches of black Life were collected in the 1961 publication *The Best of Simple.*

This mural of the "Black Simpsons" is painted on the side of an abandoned building located on the corner of 119th and Frederick Douglass Avenue in Harlem, New York. It features Bart, Maggie and Homer offering words of encouragement to the residents of Harlem.

Atlantis has discussed her travels to Egypt with audiences nationwide. She was congratulated by Dr. Clarke (above) following a presentation in Cleveland, Ohio.

My First Trip To Africa (below), which was co-authored by Atlantis and her father, is currently being used in classrooms and libraries throughout the country. Atlantis plans to write a series of books which will document her travels with her father. The proceeds from her book sales and speaking engagements will be used to finance Atlantis's college education.

As a part of my ongoing responsibility to educate my daughter Atlantis, I took her to Egypt in 1989 on one of my annual study tours. At the suggestion of a friend, my daughter and I co-authored a book entitled, *My First Trip To Africa,* which we published in 1991. This book chronicled the experiences of Atlantis's visit to Egypt, the cities and monuments she saw and the people she met. *My First Trip To Africa* highlighted the African origins of Kemet and its influence on world civilization, all from a child's perspective.

During the spring of 1991, a parent gave a copy of *My First Trip To Africa* to her ten-year-old son who later used it as the subject of a book report in class. His teacher reprimanded the child in front of the entire class and declared that his book report was unacceptable because it was entitled *"My First Trip To Africa,"* and the book report was about Egypt. The teacher then remarked, *"everyone knows that Egypt is not in Africa!"*

Needless to say, when news of this incident reached the child's mother, she immediately demanded a meeting with the school principal and her child's teacher. She then proceeded to give them both a lesson in history and geography. It is unfortunate that, in this day and time, and with the wealth of information available, so many people have remained ignorant of the history of Egypt and its location in northeast Africa. It just so happened that players in this unfortunate incident were of different ethnic persuasions; the child and parent were of African ancestry, while the teacher and principal were of European descent. But because most people have been victims of a systematic process of mis-education, the roles could have easily been reversed and yielded the same outcome.

There have been numerous attempts to represent traditional white mythological figures as black ones with some interesting, and revealing, results. During last year's Christmas season a shopping mall in suburban Washington, D.C., hired an African American to dress as Santa for photos with children. After numerous complaints from African American adults, the black Santa was replaced with a white one, because those parents insisted that their children be photographed with the "real Santa Claus."

Parents who are ignorant of their history and culture are incapable of properly directing the lives of their children. As youths we were all told about Santa Claus and believed in him. As we grew older we questioned his existence and asked our parents how it was possible for Santa to travel to every home in the world on the same night. The homes without chimneys posed an even more perplexing problem for parents who often met the inquiry with "creative" explanations. Participation in the Santa Claus myth deprives parents and children of an opportunity to explore their relationship and develop a deeper bond based on truth and responsibility. In light of the increasing popularity of Kwanzaa, other options are now readily available.

African-Centered Approaches to Life

> The purpose of education is to prepare young people to live and serve the society, and to transmit the knowledge, skills, values and attitudes of the society. Wherever education fails in any of these fields, there is social unrest as people find that their education has prepared them for a future which is not open to them.
>
> Mwalimu Julius Nyerere
> President of Tanzania

In the 1960's a young African Caribbean man coined a phrase which inspired African Americans and created a movement that inspired people of African descent throughout the world, while simultaneously intimidating people of European ancestry. The young man's name was Stokley Carmichael and the phrase that he added to the American lexicon was "Black Power."

Molefi Asante

In 1980, another young man, this one of African American descent, introduced a word that similarly mobilized one segment of society while alienating another. That man's name was Dr. Molefi Asante and his cultural contribution was the creation of the concept of "Afrocentricity." Since its introduction, there have been a number of discussions on the topic. Debates have focused on "what is Afrocentric" and "what is not." "Who is Afrocentric" and "who is not." However, the heart of the Afrocentric controversy has centered around education—African-centered education.

Afrocentricity (or African-centeredness) has been defined by Dr. Asante as:

> A frame of reference wherein phenomena are viewed from the perspective of the African person...it centers on placing people of African origin in control of their lives and attitudes about the world. This means that we examine every aspect of the dislocation of African people; culture, economics, psychology, health and religion....As an intellectual theory, Afrocentricity is the study of the ideas and events from the standpoint of Africans as the key players rather than victims. This theory becomes, by virtue of an authentic relationship to the centrality of our own reality, a fundamentally empirical project...it is Africa asserting itself intellectually and psychologically, breaking the bonds of Western domination in the mind as an analogue for breaking those bonds in every other field.

Afrocentricity is not a black version of Eurocentricity. Neither is it centered upon notions of racial exclusivity. Not every African person has the capacity to become African-centered, in fact, a number of advocates of African-centered issues are not of direct African ancestry. The primary objection that many people have regarding Afrocentricity is the fear that it is racist in its condemnation of European history. Another misconception is that any education that is centered on Africa could not possibly teach anything of value. Of course, both perspectives are seriously flawed and represent xenophobic views that have been ingrained in the minds of most people since childhood.

The reaction to African-centered education by the established leaders in American education has been quite harsh, as expected. It has been accused of being a fabrication of history designed "just to make black children feel good about themselves." Former Education Secretary William Bennett offered the following remarks in a speech before the Heritage Foundation in 1991:

> If I were grand kleagle of the Ku Klux Klan I could think of no better way to keep blacks out of the mainstream of American life than to give them a curriculum which is entirely divorced from the mainstream of American life. [Black children] need a bath in the culture of America and the west...they need an immersion in it for their sake, not for our sake...

These asinine remarks are quite similar to those made by the "defenders of traditional white supremacist curricula," during the 1960's when "Black Studies" was being advocated. They stated that it was a fabrication of lies and antiwhite rhetoric, which was being spewed forth by power crazed black nationalists. Predictions of the impending demise of Black Studies and its negative effect on academia have not materialized. Not only is Black Studies alive and well, but it has also played a major role in the emergence of the African-centered movement. A number of college students who majored in Black Studies 25 years ago are now among the most outspoken proponents of Afrocentricity. Many who are now tenured professors and presidents of colleges and universities are advocating their cultural viewpoints from within these institutions.

One of Newton's laws of physics stated that "for every action there was an equal and opposite reaction." One of the more acceptable reactions to Afrocentricity is multiculturalism. Just as in the 60's, when Black Studies led to the development of "Minority Studies," demands for an African-centered approach to education in the 90's has been met with an increasing cry of a need to teach the history and culture of "all people." A correct interpretation of multiculturalism is critical in order to avoid the failures of the existing educational system. Asante's views on the matter are as follows:

> Multiculturalism in education is a nonhierarchical approach that respects and celebrates a variety of cultural perspectives on world phenomena ....Multiculturalists assert that education, to have integrity, must begin with the proposition that all humans have contributed to world development and the flow of knowledge and information, and that most human achievements are the result of mutually interactive, international effort....The Afrocentric idea must be the stepping-stone from which the multicultural idea is launched. A truly authentic multicultural education, therefore, must be based upon the Afrocentric initiative. If this step is skipped, multicultural curricula, as they are increasingly being defined by white "resisters" will evolve without any substantive infusion of African American content, and the African American child will continue to be lost in the Eurocentric framework of education.

The development of Afrocentrism and multiculturalism was a natural response to a Eurocentric system which has defended and protected its involvement in the history of "slavery, colonialism, segregation, apartheid, racism and neoracism." There is no way a people can justify the enslavement and the enactment of genocidal policies against another human without the creation of religious and educational systems to legitimize their actions. The declaration of one's belief in a God and knowledge is antithetical to such actions. Yet, for the last 500 years, we have been exposed to lies such as "the white man's burden" as justification for the conquest of Africa, the Americas, Australia, Asia, and the islands of the Pacific. It would stand to reason that as the oppressed people of the world begin to assume positions of leadership, and define themselves and their history for themselves, their former oppressors would decry such acts as ludicrous.

As Dr. John Henrik Clarke has stated in numerous lectures:

> ...we have forgotten a recurring fact of history...that is, powerful people never have to prove anything to anyone. And by extension, powerful people never apologize to powerless people for the actions they take in order to remain in power....We will have taken one giant step forward when we face this reality: Powerful people never teach powerless people how to take their power away from them.

Members of the Amenta study group, in Washington, D.C., pose with Charles Finch (second from right) at a reception following a lecture.

One of the advantages of study groups sponsoring lecturers is that they often have the opportunity to engage in informal dialogue with the speakers following their engagements. This type of activity is greatly appreciated by the guest, who seldom has an opportunity to interact with a small group of interested and informed people in an informal setting.

The Importance of Study Groups

Within the past 15 years there has been a dramatic increase in the production and availability of material on African and African American history and culture. It is safe to say that there has been more information produced in recent years, in the form of books, tapes and lectures, than at any point in time within the past 500 years. At one point it was an accepted belief that "if you wanted to keep something hidden from black people, put it in a book." For increasing numbers of African Americans, fortunately, this is no longer the case. Information which once sat isolated on bookshelves in libraries and book- stores is now finding its way into conversations at the dinner table, in churches, private gatherings and the media. As a result, people are now beginning to re-evaluate their lives, the lives of their parents and antecedents, the lives of their chil- dren and those yet to be born.

People are coming together, in communities throughout the country, to discuss the secrets that they have uncovered in books. The development of study groups is one of the fastest growing phenomena in recent memory. They have had a profound impact on school systems in Washington, D.C., New York City, Atlanta, Detroit, Chicago, Los Angeles, Portland, Oregon and elsewhere. Study groups have also had a favorable influence on churches, businesses and the media. There are many types of study groups. Some focus primarily on African history, others devote their meeting to topics relating to spirituality, literature, economic empowerment and numer- ous other themes.

The following guidelines are to be considered for the devel- opment of a study group in your area. These guidelines are general in nature and will vary from group to group depend- ing on the size and the level of knowledge members bring to the gatherings.

Purpose and Objectives

1. The express purpose of a study group is to create an environment where people of like minds can meet with regularity to discuss various aspects of African history and culture. The purpose of these gatherings should not be for the selfish benefit of any individual or the group. Its objective should be for the attainment of accurate information about African people and the development of strategies for the practical application of that knowledge in the personal life, family life and community of each member.

2. Understanding that study groups may consist of people from various backgrounds (educational, economic, religious etc.), it should not be the purpose of the group to espouse a specific religious ideology unless that is agreed upon at the outset.

3. Members of the study group should agree to abide by specific guidelines for the benefit of the group. It is highly recommended that the *Ten Virtues* (as outlined in *Stolen Legacy*) be used, since they were originally created as "prerequisites for personal development." The first three virtues, *Control of thought, Control of action* and *Steadfastness* are of critical importance in developing one's personal behavior which will ultimately determine the success of the group.

Structure

1. The structure of a study group will vary depending on its size. It is recommended that a group consist of a minimum of five and a maximum of 25 persons. It is always best to start out with a smaller group of members, develop a strong base and then expand.

2. Meetings should be held no more than twice a month nor less than once a month. The length of each meeting should be one and a half to two hours per session. It is quite natural for new members to be excited about embarking on new fields of study and sharing information with people of like minds, but other responsibilities must not be overlooked in the process.

3. A regular meeting place must be established. It should not be in someone's home. Libraries, churches and schools all have facilities that are available to the public at little or no cost. They should be utilized. In many instances, your tax dollars help maintain them. Punctuality is a must; every meeting should start at the agreed upon time regardless of the number of people present. Care should also be taken to minimize distractions, and out of courtesy to others, children should not be in attendance.

"INFORMATION IS POWER"

WOL (1450-AM,) a local radio station in Washington, D.C., has been instrumental in the formation of more than a dozen study groups in the Washington metropolitan area. The station owner, Cathy Hughes, helps to promote the meetings and provides an opportunity for study group members to share their research on her radio program.

The above logo was developed for the WOL Study Group and symbolizes the profound love for African history and culture which the radio station and study group members share.

4. Each group should operate through a consensus of its membership. There should be no "leader" in the traditional sense. Direction should come from a three-person steering committee consisting of an *archivist, moderator* and *recorder.* The members of the steering committee should be elected by the membership, serve a six-month term and then be replaced by *three new members* at the completion of their term. The function of the committee is to administer the policies and procedures of the group and maintain a sense of direction. Each member of the steering committee has equal authority and the power of the committee as a whole should be determined by the collective membership. The steering committee's duties are:

<u>Archivist</u>-Maintains the historical records of the study group's activities and other relevant documents.

<u>Moderator</u>- Opens all sessions by leading or selecting someone to lead the group in an opening ritual.

States clearly the goals and objectives of each study session as determined by the group.

Maintains a balanced and focused flow during discussions by not allowing individuals to dominate the meetings/discussions.

Fifteen minutes prior to the closing of each session, makes certain that the agenda is set for the next meeting.

<u>Recorder</u>-Takes minutes during study group sessions and all steering committee meetings.

5. The selection of reading material to be discussed should be decided by the entire group. Careful consideration must be given to the first three books discussed. They should be books that focus on specific themes and can be easily read and discussed, as they will set the tone and direction of future meetings. Books for consideration should include:

Introduction To African Civilization by John G. Jackson
Africa At The Crossroads by John Henrik Clarke
Black Man Of The Nile And His Family
by Yosef ben-Jochannan
Introduction to Black Studies by Maulana Karenga
Destruction Of Black Civilization by Chancellor Williams
From The Browder File by Anthony T. Browder

It is strongly recommended that the group produce a summary of each book discussed as a record of its accomplishments. These summaries can be compiled and distributed at a future date.

Operation

1. Begin each session with 15 minutes of quiet time or meditation. This allows each person to put the thoughts of the day behind them and prepare for the activities at hand with a fresh mind.

2. It is recommended that a libation be poured and that the statement of purpose for the group be declared. Following these actions it is recommended that the objective for the meeting be stated.

3. The room should be set up in a manner to facilitate conversation and chairs should be arranged in a circle if at all possible. Televisions, radios and phones should be turned off and meetings should be conducted in a serious and orderly manner. If food or refreshments are served, it should be after the meeting.

4. The discussion of material should be led by the moderator, who is responsible for conducting the meeting in a timely manner and soliciting input from as many members as possible. Of course, the more members there are in a group, the more difficult this task will be, but great care must be taken to insure that one or two persons do not try to dominate the session.

5. The moderator is also responsible for summarizing the discussion and opening the floor for a brief discussion of new business.

6. The moderator, or other designated individual, should lead the group in a closing prayer or affirmation. The group should be standing in a circle while holding hands. It is important that these meetings be looked upon as a place of safe harbor where brothers and sisters come together to strengthen cultural bonds.

Other considerations for study groups

1. New members should be brought into the group at six-month intervals, until the maximum number is reached, then a new study group can be formed. It becomes very difficult to develop a bond within a group if membership is changing on a regular basis. Consistency is the key to the longevity of the group. If a new group is created, members from the original

group should serve as the first steering committee until the group has bonded, then new steering committee members should be selected from the new membership.

2. The invitation of guests to the study group meetings should be limited to invited speakers, and on occasion, prospective members. The group should avoid inviting guests for any reason, other than these.

Amenhotep, the son of Hapu, lived during the rule of Amenhotep III (ca. 1391 B.C.E.). Amenhotep, the son of Hapu, was a man of meager beginnings who rose to the rank of High Priest at Waset. He also distinguished himself by being designated "Chief Royal Scribe of Recruits" and he held positions as an administrative official and military leader.

Amenhotep, son of Hapu, was the "architect" responsible for designing the Ipet-Isut (Karnak Temple) which was described by Breasted as the "largest building of the Egyptian empire."

3. It is recommended that the group attend outside activities such as lectures, conferences, plays and movies, and discuss them in meetings as a change of pace from the regular book discussions. The sharing of audio or video tapes in the meetings will also provide interesting discussions.

4. Plan social activities for the group and their family members during the course of the year. Picnics or retreats during the summer months, Kwanzaa celebrations and the anniversary of the study group are excellent times to plan special events.

5. Members should select a topic of interest and endeavor to develop a level of expertise. Presentations may be given during the study group meetings in preparation for future community presentations. Churches, schools and organizations are always interested in speakers who are willing to share their research with others.

6. The study group should consider developing a lecture series and sponsor local and out-of-town presenters. These events will showcase the work of the study group while exposing the community to new information. This activity is also an excellent opportunity to recruit new members for the existing study group, or they can start new chapters.

The benefits of belonging to a study group are many. In addition to increasing one's understanding of history and culture, the opportunity to meet people who share your interests can prove to be a source of mental and spiritual relief. In many instances, study group members can purchase books in bulk and receive discounts ranging from ten to 40 percent, depending upon the merchant. A number of study groups and individuals throughout the country have developed data bases which can be easily accessed with the convenience of a PC and a modem.

Amenhotep
Son of Hapu

The struggle for the liberation of the minds of African people is a formidable one, for many will want to cling to the ideas and fears that have played a major role in their mis-education. It must be remembered that the creation of the Negro was a carefully calculated plan, which has been developed and implemented over the last 500 years. Any attempts to reverse this process will be a struggle costing time, money and lives. Frederick Douglass defined the parameters of a struggle more than 100 years ago when he declared:

> Those who profess to favor freedom and yet depreciate agitation are men who want crops without plowing up the ground. They want rain without thunder and lightening. They want the ocean without the awful roar of its mighty water. The struggle may be a moral one, or it may be a physical one, but it must be a struggle. Power concedes nothing without a demand. It never did and never will.

Frederick Douglass

Note:
This chapter concludes with a listing of resource persons and organizations that will be of valve in establishing cultural activities, study groups and lecture series.

Resource Persons
(Authors & Lecturers)

Na'im Akbar
Psychologist
PO Box 11221
Tallahassee, FL 32302
(904) 222-1764

Molefi Asante
Historian
Chair, Dept. African American Studies
Temple University
Philadelphia, PA 19122
(215) 787-4322

Yosef ben-Jochannan
Egyptologist
726 St Nicholas Ave
New York, NY 10031
(212) 281-7744

John Henrik Clarke
Historian
223 W 137th Street
New York, NY 10030
(212) 862-8187

Charles Finch
Physician, Historian
Morehouse School of Medicine
505 Fairburn Rd SW
Atlanta, GA 30331
(404) 752-1613

Asa G Hilliard, PhD
Educational Psychologist, Historian
PO Box 91123
East Point, GA 30364
(404) 651-1269

Linus Hoskins
Historian
Kent State University
Dept. of Pan-African Studies
Oscar Ritchie Hall
Kent, OH 44242-0001
(216) 672-2300

Leonard Jeffries
Historian
Department of Black Studies
City College of New York
137th & Convent Avenue
New York, NY 10031
(212) 690-8117

Jawanza Kunjufu
Educational Consultant
African American Images
1909 W. 95th Street
Chicago, IL 60643
(312) 445-0322

Ashra Kwesi
Historian
PO Box 41005
Dallas, TX 75241
(214) 371-0206

Patricia Newton
Psychiatrist
4100 N Charles Street #507
Baltimore, MD 21218-1024
(410) 752-2900

Edwin J Nichols
Industrial Psychologist
1523 Underwood St NW
Washington, DC 20012
(202) 723-2117

Wade Nobles
Psychologist
155 Filbert St #202
Oakland, CA 94607
(415) 836-3245

Runoko Rashidi
Historian
4140 Buckingham Road, Suite D
Los Angeles, CA 90008
(213) 293-5807

Dona Marimba Richards
Social Scientist
Dept. of Black & Puerto Rican Studies
Hunter College
695 Park Avenue
New York, NY 10021
(212) 772-5035

Ivan Van Sertima
Anthropologist
African Studies Department
Rutgers University
New Brunswick, NJ 08903
(908) 932-4023

James Small
Historian
470 W 148th Street
New York, NY 0031
(212) 281-7967

Alice Windom
Educator/Olmec & African Historian
PO Box 4846
St Louis, MO 63108
(314) 371-1248

Organizations

African Echoes
Lecturers
147 West End Avenue
Newark, NJ 07106
(201) 373-3826

Association For The Study of
Classical African Civilization
(ASCAC)
Conferences & Study Groups
ASCAC Foundation
3624 Country Club Drive
Los Angeles, CA 90019
(323) 734-1155

Black Unity and Spiritual Togetherness
(BUST)
Developer of Study Groups With a
Spiritual & Economic Direction
PO Box 1088
(318) 232-7672
Opelousas, LA 70570

DuSable Museum of African
American History
740 East 56th Place
Chicago, IL 60637
(312) 947-0600

1st World Alliance
Lectures
400 Convent Avenue #1
New York, NY 10031
(212) 368-7353

Institute for Independent Education
1313 North Capitol Street NE
Washington, DC 20015
(202) 745-0500

Kemetic Institute
Lectures/Study Groups
700 East Oakwood Blvd
Chicago, IL 60653
(312) 268-7500

National Conference of Artists
PO Box 73344
Washington, DC 20009
(202) 393-3116

Southern Education Foundation, Inc
Educational Conferences
153 Auburn Avenue
Atlanta, GA 30303
(404) 523-0001

The Third Eye
Sponsors Annual Conferences
PO Box 226064
Dallas, TX 75222
(214) 748-1736

Businesses

Afri Chart Products
Unique Charts & Maps
5868 East 71st #160
Indianapolis, IN 46220
(317) 545-8454

Black Classic Press
PO Box 13414
Baltimore, MD 21203
(410) 602-0980

The Clegg Series
Educational Publications
PO Box 324
Compton, CA 90223-324
(213) 631-2661

Cultural Circles
Original Art & Reproductions
1424 Belmont St NW
Washington, DC 20009
(202) 667-4324

Malcolm Aaron
Artist & Illustrator
204B Roberson Street
Chapel Hill, NC 27516
(919) 933-9091 or 933-6317

Cultural Projections Unlimited
Graphic Design
815 15th Street NW #532
Washington, DC 20005
(202) 393-1002

Egypt in Illustration
Educational Publications
PO Box 11163
Atlanta, GA 30310
(404) 344-7260

The Pyramid Complex
Cultural Novelty Items
1801 Clydesdale Pl NW #725
Washington, DC 20009
(202) 332-3908

Chapter Ten
Questions and Answers

I have been lecturing on various topics pertaining to African and African American history for more than 12 years. During that time I have received numerous inquiries from people desiring information on a variety of subjects including religion, philosophy, spirituality and the practicality of African History. This publication is concluded by sharing with you some of those most frequently asked questions and my responses to them.

Q   If the Nile Valley civilization was so great why did it fall? And if African people were responsible for creating the civilization of ancient Egypt, why are they suffering so?

A   One of the first lessons history teaches is that history is cyclical. Historical events follow specific patterns and cycles, which when studied, yield data that allow a person to understand the sequence of events which lead up to a specific activity and the consequences that follow. In this sense, *"All history is a current event"* because the activities which are transpiring today were set into motion by events that were initiated at some point in the past. If we understand this basic reality then we will realize that *"Nothing that comes stays, and nothing that goes is lost."*

Great civilizations have risen and fallen since the beginning of time. Contrary to what many theorists may wish to believe, civilization did not begin at a primitive level and rise steadily, producing cultures which were more sophisticated than the ones that preceded them. On the contrary, once a great civilization fell, it took hundreds of years before one of equal or greater significance evolved. Such is the case with Kemet, a civilization which lasted more than 3,000 years.

Many great civilizations of the ancient world have fallen. But none have endured as long as that of Kemet. The United States of America is only 216 years old and is currently recognized as the mightiest nation on Earth. But her power, economy and technological influence have waned significantly during the past 30 years. The Roman and Byzantine empires have fallen, the worldwide influence of the Spanish, British and French has diminished considerably. Many historians and political scientists suggest that a similar fate now confronts the United States of America. The demise of great civilizations is not unique to Kemet or Africa—it is a fact of life. But how one deals with these facts is another matter entirely. It determines your perception of reality and influences your ability to act.

With regard to the current status of African people, we must never forget the *Maafa*, or great disaster, which has befallen the African continent and African people worldwide. With the exception of the native Americans and the native Australians, no other people on Earth have had their continent snatched away by foreigners. Africans were the only people to have been enslaved and exported to other continents by the millions. These actions have depleted the human and natural resources of Africa, while simultaneously developing them in Europe and America. We are still experiencing the repercussions of that event.

Although the total number of Africans stolen from their homeland varies greatly from source to source, we can conservatively estimate that a minimum of 50 million people were displaced. When you consider the fact that one-third of the enslaved Africans never survived the trans-Atlantic journey, and of the number who did survive, approximately one-third died during the "seasoning" or breaking-in process; we are, therefore, talking about the deaths of more than 80 million people. These figures do not take into account the millions of Africans who died before they were loaded aboard the slave ships or the number of men, women and children who were raped, beaten to death or lynched once they arrived in the "new world."

H. G. Wells' classic novel, *War of the Worlds*, exemplifies the deep-seated fear Europeans have that aliens would do to them what they have done to others. Imagine an alien nation attacking the United States and enslaving its inhabitants. Imagine these beings taking the Washington Monument, the Golden Gate Bridge and the Statue of Liberty and putting them in *their* parks and public squares. Visualize alien scientists exhuming the bodies of dead presidents and putting them on display in *their* museums and art galleries. And then imagine alien children sitting in *their* classrooms discussing the lives of "primitive Americans." In many respects, truth is stranger than fiction.

One must also be aware of the impact that the Berlin Conference had on African people. Between 1884 and 1885, 14 European nations met in Berlin, Germany, and agreed to stop fighting among themselves for the possession of Africans. These "civilized" men decided to end the slave trade, not because it was the moral thing to do, but because they were

The only people not invited to the Berlin Conference were the Africans, whose lives would be irreparably altered by the decisions agreed upon by the European nations in attendance.

*The Berlin Conference
(1884-1885)*

making the Americans wealthy. They agreed to create a system of colonization and enslave the entire African continent.

Africa was subsequently divided by the representatives seated at the table in Berlin, and countries were given new names, such as the *Gold Coast, Ivory Coast, French Guinea* and the *Belgian Congo.* These new names reflected the imperialistic intent of the new colonial masters. It wasn't until 72 years later that Africans began to liberate themselves from the economic, political and social control of the Europeans. In 1957, The *Gold Coast* became the first African nation to gain its independence and it was renamed *Ghana* after an ancient African Kingdom. African Americans have been "free" for 127 years and the first independent African nation has had its freedom for only 35 years.

In reality, Africans are still struggling for their independence in South Africa, South America and South of the Canadian border. The extent to which African people see the relationship between all of these struggles is the degree to which they will be able to liberate themselves.

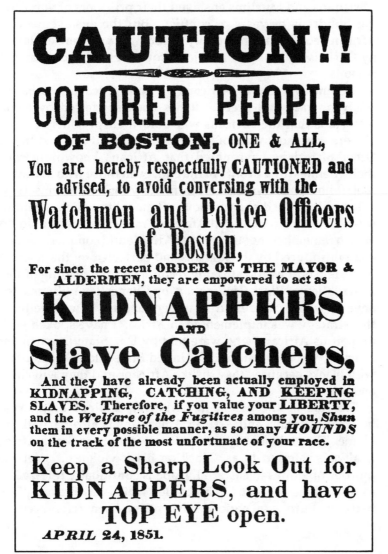

A warning posted for African American citizens of Boston, Massachusetts, in April, 1851.

John Ormond

John Ormond, a negro, known as "Mungo John" and "Mulatto Trader" was the principal slavetrader in West Africa in the late 1700's. Ormond, who had inherited vast territory from his African mother, a paramount chief, was educated in England. Arriving in Africa in 1758, he at once raised the price of slaves from $50 to $60 a head wholesale. Mungo, on the slightest pretext, would send his soldiers to raid native villages. One of his employees was Rezin Bowie a white Texan, and father of the celebrated Col. James Bowie, hero of the Alamo and inventor of the Bowie Knife.

J. A. Rogers
Your History

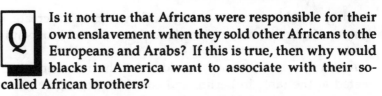

Q Is it not true that Africans were responsible for their own enslavement when they sold other Africans to the Europeans and Arabs? If this is true, then why would blacks in America want to associate with their so-called African brothers?

A There is not a race of people who have not had their Benedict Arnolds at some point in time, and Africans are no exception. Slavery is as old as mankind and in many instances most slaves were either prisoners of war, criminals or people who were unable to pay their debts. The word "slave" was coined in Europe and described the eastern Europeans who were enslaved by their western European cousins. Many African nations also enslaved their prisoners of war but they still respected the humanity of the enslaved individual and they were often allowed to marry and their spouses and offspring remained free.

Various religious conflicts have also played a major role in the history of slavery. The Hebrews were subjugated by the Egyptians, the Romans persecuted the Christians and both the Christians and Muslims enslaved their prisoners of war during hundreds of years of conflict. But the enslavement of African people was profoundly different. They were enslaved by Christians, Muslims and Jews for religious and financial reasons.

The enslavement of Africans by non-Africans was based solely on race and greed. It has been suggested by some historians that the Africans who sold their prisoners to foreigners were not aware of the horrific fate that awaited them. Other historians have noted that Africans knowingly sold their enemies for a profit. In the end, even those who betrayed their fellow countrymen were ultimately enslaved themselves.

Regarding the disharmonious relationship which is said to exist between Africans and African Americans, one would do well to remember the strategies of "divide and conquer," which were introduced by the Romans and perfected by the colonist imperialists. I would strongly recommend the reading of *The Destruction of Black Civilization*, by Chancellor Williams, for anyone who is interested in understanding how effectively this strategy was implemented in Africa. I have spoken with numerous Africans who were told by U.S. State Department officials, prior to visiting the United States, to avoid contact with blacks because "they dislike Africans and they will cheat and rob you."

The role of the media in harboring feelings of distrust between Africans and African Americans is also partially to blame. The violence between political factions in South Africa is always referred to as "black on black violence." Yet the murder of whites in eastern Europe is continually referred to as an "ethnic conflict." The battles which have taken place between European nations have never been referenced as "white on white violence," instead, they have been called "World War I" and "World War II."

Q As a Christian, how am I to respond to the information regarding the Nile Valley origins of Christianity? I have been told all of my life that the Bible is the word of God and that Jesus died for our sins. Now I am hearing that the Bible was derived from Egyptian texts and that the story of Jesus and Mary is patterned after Isis and Horus. There are even those who claim that the Ten Commandments have come from something called the Negative Confessions. What and whom am I to believe?

A This topic is always a sensitive one for people who have been raised in a Christian environment. Many have been taught to believe that it is sinful to question the Bible and they accept the entire book at face value. What must be remembered is that there are currently more than 140 different versions of the Holy Bible and the interpretation of specific texts varies greatly. If you are going to study the Bible, or any book for that matter, you must investigate the background and motives of the author.

Millions of people read the *King James Version* of the Bible but few, if any, know anything at all about King James. Who was he? What motivated him to undertake such an important task? One religious scholar has stated that "King James was a man who would make Adolph Hitler look like Santa Claus." If this is a fact, then what will happen to people who accept King James' version of the Bible as the truth? These questions must be asked because a person's concept of religion is too important to leave in the hands of just anybody.

It is a historical fact that the same people who have been responsible for interpreting and translating the Bible have also been involved in the enslavement and murder of millions of African and native Americans. Most of the images associated with biblical personalties have been portrayed as European when they were known to have been people of color. There is a very strong movement within black Catholic, Baptist and Methodist churches to reclaim the African origins of Christianity. This is the correct thing to do.

Every biblical scholar agrees with the fact that Jesus the Christ was a person of color. But most ministers refuse to acknowledge this reality for fear of the reaction from the congregation. Biblical scholars cannot agree on the date of the birth of Jesus the Christ, but they know he was not born on December 25. That date was agreed upon by the bishops who attended the Nicean Conference, in 332 A.C.E., because it commemorated the birth of the Sun and the Son of God thousands of years before the birth of Jesus the Christ. Very few people are aware of the fact that this conference took place and that it determined what doctrines would be incorporated

The King James Bible

The King James Version of the Bible was printed in 1611, 77 years after the Church of England broke away from the Vatican. This bible served as the "official translation" for most of the English-speaking protestants for more than 300 years. During the early years of its existence, women and the poor were forbidden from reading the Bible, under penalty of death.

When the ancient temples of Kemet were ordered closed by the Christian emperors Theodosius (in 391) and Justinian (in 527), many of the images of the Netcherw were chiseled out of the walls. On many occasions these temples were converted into churches and crosses were carved where ankhs and other images once stood.

into the Christian religion.

This is not to suggest that Christianity is a false religion, but one must be aware of the influence that African religious thought played in its development. There is a great deal of symbolism and allegory in the Bible. One must learn to distinguish between the information which should be taken literally and that which must be evaluated for greater understanding. The only viable solution to this quandary is to read and study all related information. It is impossible for a person to read one book and consider themselves all-knowledgeable on the subject matter.

One of the reasons African people continue to suffer today is because they still worship the God that was assigned to them by their former slave masters. Just as the African involvement in the historical development of world civilization has been ignored, the African spiritual concepts which have been incorporated into the world's major religious systems have also been forgotten. Human beings have used many names to identify the omnipresent force which has been referred to as God. Names such as Amen, Jehovah, Allah, Buddha, Shango and many others have been used by people to describe their special relationship to God. It is wrong to deny people the right to believe in their concept of the Creator and it is sinful to enslave them in the name of God. Any people who would engage in such activities are unworthy of the heavenly reward which they claim to seek.

Q My exposure to what I regard as the accurate history of African people has really turned my life around. For the first time in my life, I have come to value myself as a person, more specifically, a person of African descent. My problem lies in trying to share this knowledge and my enthusiasm with friends and family. They mock my decision to wear African clothing and they claim that I have become "too black" and that this "African stuff" is nothing but a lot of nonsense. How do I respond to them? I love them dearly but I know that what I am seeking is correct for me.

A The elation that you feel with regards to your new-found knowledge of self and the sadness and anxiety which it evokes among your family members is quite understandable. You are not alone. Those same feelings have been shared by thousands of brothers and sisters who have been confronted with similar challenges. History is important because everything that we do depends upon it. Doctors, lawyers and bankers all require background information on their clients. Adopted and orphaned individuals have a profound desire to know their true parents in order to know their true selves. Only people who have been successfully mis-educated have no desire to know their past and they resent those who do.

Several years ago Asa G. Hilliard, III, a well known, highly respected historian/educational psychologist, and I discussed some of the problems plaguing our communities. Dr. Hilliard described the ten most prevalent impediments to African unity in the introduction to my first book, *From The Browder File: 22 Essays On The African American Experience.* He stated:

> Consider these things carefully and realize that they account for our overall lack of a sense of unity and direction.
>
> **1. We let our names go.** The first step towards disorientation is to surrender your name.
> **2. We have surrendered our way of life (culture).** We have stopped speaking the language we knew and we have stopped behaving as African people behave. We have lost our way of doing things and we have adopted the ways of people unlike ourselves.
> **3. We have lost our appetite** because we have lost our names and our culture. Even when those among us recreate our culture and present it to us, we no longer have an appetite for it. We have a greater appetite for the culture of people other than ourselves.
> **4. We have a general loss of memory.** Few of us can tell the story of African people without beginning it with slavery. It is as if slavery were the only thing that happened to African people.
> **5. We have created false memories.** Not only have we lost the true memory of African people, we now have a host of other memories which are totally removed from the truth.
> **6. We lost our land.** Anytime you lose your mooring on the land, you lose your capacity to protect your possessions.
> **7. We have lost our independent production capacity.** We have become consumers, rather than producers.
> **8. We have lost independent control of ourselves.** We have little or no control of our educational process, our economic situation, our communications, or our politics.
> **9. We have lost our sensitivity.** We have lost the ability to perceive when people are doing things to us which are detrimental. We accept inaccurate perceptions without criticism.
> **10. As a cumulative result of all of things, we have lost our solidarity...our unity.** When we lost our unity, we lost our political advantage, economical advantage, and even our mental orientation. We lost a sense of self and a clear sense of belonging. We also lost a clear sense of wholeness, continuity and purpose.

STOLEN LEGACY

GEORGE G.M. JAMES

There is no amount of information alone which can correct all of the problems that I've just identified. A large part of what we must do is to get our memories back in tact and regain our orientation.

Identification with one's history and culture is truly the first step towards regaining a sense of consciousness. At the same time, however, you must be keenly aware that not all of your friends or family will embrace your move. A happy medium must be found because family is the central component in African culture. To lose your family while finding your culture is a paradoxical dilemma which still leaves you longing for a way to fill the same void which existed prior to your initial discovery. The challenges are many but they can be overcome with consistency, patience and devotion, to yourself and to those whom you love.

Q I am a young brother who is trying to make it in America. I can appreciate the fact that we were kings and queens in Africa, but how does that help me survive today? What good is it to seek knowledge if it can't help me get a job and put food on the table?

A We must remember that a tiny percentage of the population in Africa were kings and queens and members of the holy royal family. The vast majority of the populous in any kingdom (99.9 per cent) are common folk, farmers, carpenters, healers and the like. They developed their individual skills, formed trade associations and offered their services to the community. The king and queen served as models for the development of human potentiality and were often affiliated with the priesthood.

In the book *Stolen Legacy*, professor James described the prerequisites for personal development, which he referred to as the "Ten Virtues." This ancient tradition originated in the Nile Valley but has become an integral component in numerous African spiritual societies. The Ten Virtues are:

1. **Control of thought**
2. **Control of action**
3. **Steadfastness**

Every action that a person engages in is a direct result of that person's thought; *correct actions* denote *correct thought* and *steadfastness* is the ability to maintain correct thoughts which will continue to yield the desired results.

4. **Identity with higher ideals**
5. **Evidence of a mission**

The ability to maintain correct thoughts and actions allows a person to experience the *higher ideals* that life has to offer. Identification with these higher ideals allows individuals to realize their reason for being, thus to understand their *mission* in life.

6.   Evidence of a call to spiritual order
7.   Freedom from resentment (courage)

Once people have experienced their mission in life, they are empowered by a *call to spiritual order*, which equips them with the *courage* necessary to face the *resentment* they will meet from individuals who lack spiritual understanding.

8.   Confidence in the power of the master (teacher)
9.   Confidence in one's own abilities
10.   Preparedness for initiation

Every person who becomes properly motivated will encounter *mentors and role models* who will prepare them to assume positions of leadership. And when one gains authority, one must have *confidence in the ability* to exercise it correctly and prepare for the challenges waiting ahead. This cycle begins anew with the *initiation* into a new level of personal development.

Many people have undergone this type of personal transformation. One of the most striking examples which comes to mind is Malcolm X. As a young man Malcolm personified the incorrigible nature of a person gone astray. After his incarceration, Malcolm's personality was transformed through the acquisition and application of knowledge of self.

Despite the problems America has, this is still one of the best places in the world to live. There are numerous stories of foreigners who have immigrated to America with little or no money and an inability to speak the language, but they achieved a modicum of success despite numerous obstacles. While lacking an understanding of American culture, these people succeeded by relying on their own culture and values.

The key to success lies in knowing who you are, tapping into that ancestral and cultural reservoir and applying that knowledge. The history of the United States is replete with examples of immigrates who have achieved, in short duration, what millions of "black" Americans continue to dream of.

 I am a parent with a child in the public school system. What can I do to ensure that my child is properly educated?

Michael Jordan

Immediately after winning the 1991 NBA Championship, Michael Jordan appeared at a news conference wearing a Malcolm X cap. Within a week, more than 50,000 of these caps were sold nationwide, thus underscoring the power of the media to influence consumers.

Prior to the news conference, Jordan appeared in several TV commercials directed by Spike Lee. Jordan wore the Malcolm X cap as a favor to his friend Lee, who was then directing a movie on the life of Malcolm X.

The history, image and symbolism of Malcolm have been terribly manipulated over the last few years. In many respects, a superficial, reverence for Malcolm is often displayed by those wearing his image while engaged in criminal or inappropriate activity

When studying Malcolm (via books, recordings or films), particular emphasis should be focused on the value Malcolm placed on reading, self-respect, his love for African people and his spiritual evolution.

A Proper education begins in the home. Parents must take the time to instill within their children a respect for education and an understanding of the power associated with the attainment of knowledge. A teacher can only reinforce within children that which they bring to the classroom as a result of 'home training.' If a child lacks an appreciation for the process of education, the teacher will spend more time disciplining than teaching that child.

One of the major problems in most school systems is that the parents are so involved in making a living that they have abdicated their responsibility to their children and the educational process. It is a strong and active parental organization which helps to determine what goes on in the classroom. There is a dire need for volunteers in most classrooms. If a dozen adults in a community could adopt a school and spend one hour a week in the classroom, assisting the teacher or tutoring students, it would make a profound difference.

An education is an investment in the future of not only the child but the entire family. Elementary school students who lack proper motivation are more inclined to drop out of high school, which will have a deteriorative effect on their earning potential as adults, thus greatly hindering their ability to make a consistent financial contribution to their family. The equation is simple. Either you contribute to the education of your children today, or your grandchildren will suffer tomorrow and *you* will have to take care of them. How can one best begin this process?

1. Turn off the television
2. Sit down and read with your children and discuss what you've read in a family setting
3. Expose your children to new experiences regularly
4. Monitor the behavior of the adults in the household as well as the behavior of the youth. In most instances, children are a direct reflection of the attitudes of the adults in their immediate environment

Being a parent is a full-time job. But it is also one of the most rewarding experiences you will ever have in life if you perform your job successfully.

Q What is *karma?* I am vaguely familiar with the philosophy but I am confused as to the degree to which the events in ones life are predetermined. If life is predetermined, then what role does "free will" play?

A Karma is a concept which can be simply translated to mean "cause and effect." It is a belief that the events one experiences in this lifetime were determined by actions set in motion in previous lifetimes. It is closely

Maat

equated to the principles espoused in the "golden rule." In other words, what you do to others will be done unto you, or more specifically, what you do to yourself, will also be done unto you. Belief in karma encourages ethical behavior in order for one to receive their reward in the next life (heaven).

In recent years I have come to realize that there exists a great affinity between the principles of karma and the Nile Valley Netcher *Maat*. Maat represents the principles of righteousness, truth, justice, order, reciprocity, etc. The 42 Admonitions of Maat, also referred to as "Declarations of Innocence," were the determinatives against which the soul of the deceased was judged. It was this ancient belief in the judgement of the soul after death that motivated the living to behave righteously by applying the precepts of Maat in their daily lives.

The issues of predetermination become more clearly understood when one knows that the events which one experiences are the direct result of circumstances set in motion by one's thoughts and actions. The Ten Virtues, therefore, become the instrument through which karma or Maat operates. Granted, there are events which affect us that are outside our ability to control, but how often we are influenced by them is determined by our actions. Whether we are in the right place at the right time is determined by our desire to go some place.

There is no such thing as chance, coincidence or accident in a universe ruled by law and divine order. What has been commonly referred to as the "Egyptian's preoccupation with death" is, in fact, a profound preoccupation with life. Their writings were mistakenly referred to as "The Book of the Dead," but the people of Kemet originally called them "The Book of the Coming Forth by Day," which was in essence "The Book of Life." Their writing was called *Medu Netcher*—the word of the principles of creation, and they expressed a profound understanding of the reality that what one thinks, what one speaks, what one does, one becomes.

I have often been asked the question, "What happened to the people of Kemet?" The obvious answer is "They lost their history and they died." But the history and the spirit of Kemet and the Nile Valley is very much alive. It is being rediscovered by hundreds of people every day. It is my hope and desire for people to understand that it is only through the study and application of knowledge (history) that they will be given the tools with which to build for eternity.

Glossary

Abdullah Al Mamun
(d.833)

Caliph of Baghdad, son of Harun Al-Rashid. Responsible for the advancement of science and literature; created a number of universities and built an astronomical observatory near Baghdad; He is responsibile for breaking into the Great Pyramid in 820 in search of treasures.

Abu Simbel

Site of two temples created by Ramesses II about 1250 B.C.E.; located in northern Nubia near the Fifth Cataract.

Aigyptos

The Greek name for the northeast African nation now called "Egypt." Derived from the word "Hekaptah" (The Land of the Temple of Ptah.) Under Roman rule the name was Latinized into "Aegyptus." *See Kemet.*

Aha

First historic ruler of the First Dynasty of Kemet. He is recognized as having united the Upper and Lower Kingdoms into one nation and located the capitol in the city of Men-nefer (later called Memphis by the Greeks). He is also known as Narmer and was called Menes by the Greeks.

Akhenaton
(1388-1358 B.C.E.)

Revolutionary king of the Eighteenth Dynasty who changed his name from Amenhotep IV, and broke with the priests of Amon at Waset. He instituted the worship of a new Netcher called Aton who was symbolized by the sun disk. He was the son of Amenhotep III and Queen Tiye and the husband of Nefertiti.

Amon

Amon was considered the creator of other Netcheru, and to have had neither beginning or end. Also known as Amen.

Ancestor Worship

The deification and worship, or celebration of one's forebearers.

Ancient Empire

From the Third to Sixth Dynasties circa 2780 to 2280 B.C.E., a new form of building was introduced by King Zoser and his architect Imhotep. There is little historical data on this period. Many of the significant papyri have been destroyed.

Ankh

The tau cross, a symbol in Medu Netcher which means "life." It represents the union of the male and female principals. It is often viewed as the precurser to the Christian cross.

Anomalistic Year	365 days, 6 hours, 13 minutes, 48 seconds. The time it takes the earth to return in its elliptical orbit to the point nearest the sun -about 4 3/4 minutes longer than the sidereal year.
Architrave	Supporting structure of a temple which spans the tops of two or more columns.
Aset	Wife of Ausar and mother of Heru. She became one of the most popular Netcherw of Kemet. In the Late Period, she was worshipped as Isis by the Greeks in temples throughout Egypt. Festivals and temples dedicated to Isis (The Madonna) were quite popular throughout the Roman empire.
Atum	Name for the Sun, also known as Ra (Re).
Ausar	Husband of Aset and father of Heru. Was responsible for bringing agriculture to Nubia and Kemet. He was murdered by his brother Set and was later resurrected and became known as the "Lord of Judgement." He was worshipped as Osiris by the Greeks and Romans.
Ba	The divine and immortal essence of a person which is often referred to as the Soul. It is represented by a human head on the body of a bird.
The Book of the Dead	A collection of papyri from ancient Kemet which contained funerary and ritual texts. The writings were found in tombs and were incorrectly referred to as "The Book of the Dead." The correct translation is "The Books of the Coming Forth by Day" or "The Book of Life."
Books of Thoth	Forty-two books divided into six classes, according to Saint Clement of Alexandria (A.C.E. 150?-220?). The Books of Thoth concerned laws, gods, priestly education, worship, history, geography, astronomy and medicine among other topics.
Breasted, James Henry (1865-1935)	American Egyptologist; Professor of Egyptology at the University of Chicago from 1895, Oriental Institute from 1919; prolific author.
Budge, Sir Ernest Alfred Wallis (1857-1934)	British scholar, Director of Antiquities at British Museum; Translator of numerous Egyptian papyri.
Cataract	Fierce rapids formed by boulders in the Nile. Six cataracts are located in the Nile starting in the south near Khartoum, in the Sudan and extending north into Aswan. The cataracts referenced in this text are numbered in accordance with the northerly flow of the Nile River. Thus the first cataract is in the south and the sixth is in the north.

Celestial equator	A great circle produced by projecting the earth's equator outward to the celestial sphere.
Champollion, Jean-Francois	Champollion the Younger (1790-1832) has been called "The Founder of Egyptology" because of his decipherment of the hieroglyphics found on the Rosetta Stone.
Classical Greece	Greece in the fifth and fourth centuries B.C.E., the period which is generally held to have seen the greatest and 'purest' products of Greek genius.
Coffin Texts	Sacred writings painted on inside of coffins belonging to commoners.
Common Era	A term used to avoid the sectarianism of B.C. (Before Christ) and A.D. (Anno Domini - 'In The Year of our Lord'). May be written as B.C.E. (Before the Common Era) or A.C.E. (After the Common Era).
Coptic (Copt)	The language and culture of Christian Egypt. Spoken until the fifteenth or sixteenth century A.C.E., it remains the liturgical language of Egyptian Christians. Originally referred to native Egyptians of Graeco-Roman period onwards, eventually came to mean Christian Egyptians.
Crook	Hooked-staff or sceptre carried as symbol of authority by King of Egypt.
Dark Ages (Greek)	Name given to the period of Greek history after the fall of the Mycenaean palaces in the 12th century B.C.E. and before the rise of Archaic Greece in the eighth century B.C.E.
Dark Ages (Christian)	Name conventinally given to the period after the fall of the Western Roman Empire in the fifth century A.C.E. and before the Middle Ages, which are usually seen as beginning in the ninth or tenth century.
Decans	The Greek name for the ten-day periods marked by the passage of constellations by which the people of Kemet divided the year into thirty-six units which totaled 360 days. Astronomical tables were devised which allowed the astronomers of Kemet to tell the time at night based upon the position of a specific constellation. This division of the heavens into 360 degrees determined the "circumference" of a circle.
Demotic	Script used on business documents etc. from about 700 B.C.E. onwards. During the Graeco-Roman period it became the standard writing of everyday life. Word is derived from Greek "demoticos" which means popular.

Diodorus Siculus	Greek historian of the first century B.C.E. who came from Sicily and lived in Alexandria and Rome. Published *Bibliotheca Historica*, the first surviving book which deals with Egypt, to which he travelled about 60 B.C.E. In his geography he quotes various lost sources.
Diop, Cheikh Anta (1923-1986)	Senegalese born multi-disciplinarian who received degrees in Egyptology and nuclear physics. Vice president of the UNESCO Committee responsible for the General History of Africa and founder of the radio-carbon laboratory at the University of Dakar. The author of numerous works he, along with W.E.B. Dubois, was voted the most influential scholar of the twentieth century on the African world.
Djhuiti	The Netcher associated with divine articulation of speech, writing, science and medicine. A lunar deity with an ibis head and human body called Thoth by the Greeks. Was later associated with Hermes by the Greeks and Mercury by the Romans.
Dynasty	A period of rulership by one or more families. In the third century B.C.E., the history of Kemet was divided into dynasties by the scholar priest Manetho.
Egypt	*See Kemet and Aiguptos.*
Egyptian mysteries	Secret knowledge of the cosmos which was possessed by initiates and priestly scholars.
Ennead	Group of nine deities e.g. the Ennead of Heliopolis (from Greek for "nine.")
Epagomenal days	The five days added on to the Egyptian year of twelve months of thirty days to bring it up to 365 days (from Greek epagomenal or "added.")
Equinox	Time at which the sun crosses the equator in March and September (vernal and autumnal) when day and night are of equal length all over the earth.
Eratosthenes (275-195 B.C.E.)	Chief librarian of the great library at Alexandria. The first Greek to measure the circumference and tilt of the world.
Ethiopia	A Greek term adopted by both the Greeks and the Romans to designate the land of Kush and surrounding areas. Derived from the Greek *aethiop ("burnt-faced")*, it meant "Land of the Burnt Faces." The original name for the country was Abyssinia.

Fibonacci, Leonardo Bigollo (1179-1250) Italian mathematician, known as Leonardo da Pisa. His *Liber Abaci* (1202) was for years a standard work on algebra and arithmetic. He introduced Arabic numbers into Europe.

Flail Sometimes called flagellum. Symbol of royal authority used by the King and Queen in Kemet.

Funerary Boat Large boat designed for use by the souls of the pharaohs during their death journeys. Also referred to as a barque.

Geb A male Netcher who personified the earth. Geb was the husband of the sky Netcher Nut.

Geodetic gnomon A vertical pillar whose shadow can be used to determine time, distance and latitude.

Hapi The animating spirit of the Nile, self-engendered; represented by an androgynous Netcher.

Hathor *See Het-Heru.*

Hellacal rising Observation of a star as close as possible to the rising or setting of the sun.

Heliopolis (or On or Annu) The "City of the Sun," which was embellished by a series of kings from the Third Dynasty on. It was the seat of temple of priests who numbered as many as 12,000.

Hermes Son of Zeus and Maia in Greek mythology, depicted as a young, athletic god. Hermes was the messenger who heralded the other gods. The Romans identified Hermes with Mercury. He was derived from the Netcher Djhuiti who was later called Thoth by the Greeks.

Hermes Trismegistus Name meaning Hermes the thrice great. Hermes Trismegistus was the Greek name for the Egyptian god Thoth; identified with Hermes.

Hermetic Texts A collection of mystical, magical and philosophical teachings which were probably first written in Demotic in the second half of the 1st millennium B.C.E. and/or in Coptic between 200 and 400 A.C.E., attributed to the god Thoth/Hermes. They later became central to the science of Hermeticism.

Hermeticism Belief in the magical, mystical and philosophical power of the Hermetic Texts. The Hermeticist movement existed in Late Antiquity and again in the European Renaissance.

Herodotus (484-425 B.C.E.)	Earliest Greek historian from Halikarnassos in Asia Minor He visited Kemet towards the end of the first Persian domination and documented his travels in a book called *History*.
Her-em-akhet	One of the largest and oldest monuments created. It has the head of a man and the body of a reclining lion. The name means "Heru of the horizon" and was referred to as "Sphinx" by the Greeks.
Heru	Prehistoric Netcher from Nubia who became a central figure in the trinity of ancient Kemet. Son of Ausar and Aset who is often represented as a falcon. Referred to as the "Son of God" and called Horus by the Greeks. He was later identified with Apollo by the Greeks and Romans.
Het-Heru	The wife of Heru. She was often depicted as a sacred cow which symbolized her nurturing qualities. The Greeks called her Hathor and later identified her with Aphrodite. The Romans identified her with Venus, goddess of Love.
Hieratic	Cursive script derived from hieroglyphs. The word 'hieratic' is derived from the Greek 'hieratikos' which means priestly.
Hieroglyphs	Word derived from Greek "hieros" (*sacred*) "glupho" (*sculptures*) to describe Egyptian writing. *See Medu Netcher*.
Horus	*See Heru*.
Hyksos	Asiatic invaders of Kemet who formed the Thirteenth thru Seventeenth Dynasties (1783-1550 B.C.E.). They were chased out of Egypt by King Ahmose who founded the Eighteenth Dynasty.
Imhotep (ca. 2800 B.C.E.)	King Zoser's architect, who is accredited with the building of the stepped pyramid of Saqqara. He is reputed to have been an author, diplomat, architect and physician. He is recorded in history as the first "Christ." The Greeks identified him with Asclepius.
Inundation	The flood period of the annual overflowing of the Nile River.
Ipet-Isut	"The Most Select of Places," the greatest temple complex in Kemet. Located in the city of Waset now called Karnak, it covered an area of 30 acres.
Isis	*See Aset*.

Jupiter

God of Roman mythology prevailing over man and gods, identified by the Greeks with Zeus. Derived from The Netcher Amen.

Ka

The vital energy which both sustains and creates life, depicted as an etheric double of the physical body. Funerary rites were spoken to the ka of the deceased.

Karnak Temple

A temple complex which was dedicated to Amen-Ra. *See Ipet-Isut.*

Kekrops

Legendary founder and king of Athens. He was generally portrayed as autochthonous, but he is closely associated with the Pharoah Senwosret.

Kemet

The "Land of The Blacks." The indigenous name for the Northeast African nation now called Egypt.

Kerma

Powerful Nubian kingdom, located near the Third Cataract, that existed between 2000 and 1550 B.C.E.

Khepri

Re in the form of the scarab beetle. A symbol for the transformational power of the sun.

Khnum

Ram-headed Netcher who is said to have created man from clay on a potter's wheel.

Kush

Nubian name of a powerful kingdom. First mentioned in an inscription about 1900 B.C.; the name became standard for Nubia and was used by the Egyptians, Assyrians and biblical writers.

Leakey, Louis Seymour
Bazett (1903-1972)

British archeologist born in Kenya, the son of English missionaries; Curator of the Coryndon Memorial Museum, Nairobi, 1945-61; especially famous for his skeletal finds in Olduvai Gorge.

Lockyer, Sir Norman
(1836-1920)

English astronomer knighted for his work in spectroscopy and for identifying helium in the sun. The author of several books on the astronomy of ancient peoples, he was the first to provide evidence that Egyptian temples were used as solar and stellar observatories.

Lower Nubia

Northernmost part of Nubia, located between the Fifth and Sixth Cataracts.

Luxor Temple

Part of the ancient site of Waset. A huge temple dedicated to the Netcher Mut was built in the reign of Amenhotep III, and altered by succeeding Pharaohs, especially by Rameses II, who had many colossal statues of himself erected on the grounds. Also referred to as the "Southern Ipet."

Manetho of Sebennytos	A writer of the third century B.C.E. who chronicled the history of Egypt in Greek for Ptolemy I. His division of the kings of Egypt into thirty dynasties is still the basic structure underlying Egyptian history.
Mastaba	Private tomb of the Old Kingdom. An oblong, flat-roofed tomb with sloping sides reminiscent of the bench found outside village houses in Egypt and called in Arabic mastaba; hence the name of the tomb.
Medu Netcher	Picture-writing of Ancient Kemet which originated in the Upper Nile Valley. Derived from "Medu" *(writing)* "Netcher" *(God)* known as the "writing of God."
Menes	*See Aha.*
Meridian	A great circle passing through the poles of the celestial sphere and the zenith of a fixed point on earth.
Meroe	Royal residence of Kush during the Meroitic Period, about 270 B.C.E. to 350 A.C.E.
Middle Kingdom	Eleventh to Twelveth Dynasties, from 2150 to 2040 B.C.E. Follows first intermediate period of chaotic conditions. The capital was at Waset.
Mizrain	The name given Egypt by the early Haribu/Hebrew of the Hebrew Holy Torah.
Mizreer	Misr, the Arabic word for "Egypt" written in English characters.
Napata	Northern capital and chief religious center of the kingdom of Kush. The Napatan kings were buried in pyramid tombs nearby at el Kurru and Nuri.
Necropolis	Cemetery (from Greek *nekros*; corpse, *polis*; city.)
Neith	Self-created aspect of the Great Netcher of Wisdom and Crafts. Associated by the Greeks with Athena. The Romans identified her with Minerva.
Netcher	A personification of one of the divine principles of the Creator.
New Kingdom	Covers Eighteenth and Nineteenth Dynasties, 1550 to 1196 B.C.E. After the Hyksos invaders were crushed the military state embarked on wide conquest from as far as Kush to the south and Euphrates in Asia in order to secure its southern and northern borders.

Nome	Word first used by Greeks to describe the administrative districts or states of Kemet. There was a total of 42 nomes.
Nubia	Ancient region, originally called Kush, extending from the Nile Valley near Aswan southward to the modern Khartoum, east to the Red Sea and west to the Libyan desert. The culture of this land gave rise to civilization in Kemet in the north.
Nun	Personification of the watery abyss; the ground state of matter from which creation arises.
Nut	Netcher associated with the sky. She was the wife of Geb and mother of Ausar, Aset, Nebhet and Set. Nut was associated with the Greek Goddess Rhea.
Obelisk	*See Tekhen.*
Osiris	*See Ausar.*
Papyrus	Plant *(Cyperus papyrus L.)* which used to grow prolifically in Egypt, especially in Delta marshes. Used for making boats, ropes, baskets, sandals, etc. The pith of the papyrus plant was used to make paper and pages were stuck together to make scrolls (books.)
Pharoah	An Asian word for the king of Kemet. Was first used in a letter written to a 19th Dynasty Ruler.
Predynastic (4236-3200 B.C.E.)	Period of history that predates unification of Kemet into one state.
Ptah	Netcher of the city of Men-nefer, portrayed as a human figure in a tight mummy wrapping. Considered the creator of heaven and earth who produced visible phenomena through thought and the word. He was called Hephaistos by the Greeks.
Ptolemaic	Name given to Egyptian culture under the rule of the Greek Ptolemies.
Ptolemy	Name of a succession of descendants of Ptolemy I, a general of Alexander the Great who seized power in Egypt after Alexander's death. The last ruler of this dynasty was Cleopatra VII.
Pylon	A double tower with rectangular base pierced by a central door which led to the interior of a temple.

Pyramid	Royal tomb in use in Kemet from the Third Dynasty to the 17th Dynasty.
Pyramid Texts	The funerary literature of Kemet which was inscribed on interior walls and chambers of some pyramids during the Fifth and Sixth Dynasties.
Pyramidion	Pyramid-shaped tip of tekhen or capstone of pyramid.
Pythagoras (ca. 582-500 B.C.E.)	Greek philosopher and mathematician who studied in Kemet and brought back mathematical and religious principles to Greece and founded the Pythagorean brotherhood.
Pythagoreans	Followers of Pythagoras organized into a "brotherhood" which was similiar in structure to the priesthood of Kemet. The Pythagoreans played an important political, religious and scientific role in the Greek society of Sicily and Southern Italy in the fifth and fourth centuries B.C.E.
Ra	The Netcher associated with an aspect of the sun. Creator of the world, was said to be swallowed at night by Nut and was resurrected each morning.
Reisner, George Andrew (1867-1942)	American Egyptologist (Ph.D., Harvard Univ, 1893) and Professor of Egyptology at Harvard (1914-1942). Curator of the Museum of Fine Arts, Boston, and chief archaeologist for the Harvard University-Boston Museum of Fine Arts Expedition.
Rhind, Henry Alexander (1833-1963)	Scottish lawyer and traveler. Purchased a mathematical papyrus which he sold to the British Museum. This document is considered he oldest manuscript dealing with Egyptian mathematics.
Rosetta Stone	Ancient black basalt tablet bearing Medu Netcher, demotic and Greek characters. It was found at Rosetta, Egypt, in 1799 and it provided the key to deciphering ancient Kemetic writing.
Saqqara	A city 15 miles south of modern Cairo, just west of Memphis and south of Giza. Graves date from the First Dynasty. Site of the stepped pyramid built for King Zoser of the Third Dynasty by the architect Imhotep.
Scarab	Winged dung beetles, or their images, prepared with inscriptions on their underside and used as a seal or amulet. A symbol of transformation.

Set	Netcher of disorder, war and storms, brother and murderer of Ausar, defeated by Heru. Also called Seth.
Shu	Symbolic Netcher of atmosphere, space or void who separated Nut (sky) from Geb (earth). Shu was identified with Atlas in Greek mythology.
Solar year	The time between two succesive equinoxes: 365 days, 5 hours, 8 minutes, 49.7 seconds - 365 days, 5 hours, 48 minutes, 46 seconds.
Solstice	The two points - in summer and winter - when the sun is at its greatest declination north or south of the equator. From Greek meaning the "sun is still."
Sothic year	365 days, 6 hours - introduced in ancient Egypt to correct the civil calendar year of 365 days. A "Sothic cycle" began when civil and Sothic new year coincided.
Sphinx	Statue usually fashioned with the body of a lion and the head of a man, or sometimes that of a woman. See *Her-em-akhet.*
Stele/stela	A boulder or slab, rectangular in shape with curved top bearing inscriptions or designs, usually used as a marker.
Ta-Merry	One of the most ancient names used for the nation in Northeast Africa called "Egypt."
Ta Seti	Name given to Lower Nubia by the people of Kemet, meaning "Land of the Bow." The name referenced the famed archers of Nubia.
Takarka	Greatest of all Kushite rulers of the 25th Dynasty who is twice referenced as Tihirka in the Bible. His pyramid and rich grave goods, located in Nuri, were excavated by George Reisner for the Museum of Fine Arts in Boston.
Tekhen	A tapered four-sided pillar used for measuring shadow length, usually inscribed with hieroglyphs proclaiming the achievements of a King. Also called "obelisk" by the Greeks.
Thebes	*See Waset.*
Thoth	*See Djhuiti.*
The Two Lands	Egypt i.e. Upper Kemet (South) and Lower Kemet (North).

Upper Nubia	Area south of the Fifth Cataract, extending to modern-day Khartoum.
Uraeus/uraei	Most characteristic symbol of kingship, a rearing cobra worn on the forehead of Nubian and Egyptian pharaohs. The Nubian kings were known for wearing two uraei on their crowns.
Utchat	The sacred eye. Symbol of protection, health and happiness.
Valley of the Kings	The western bank of Waset where the New Kingdom kings from Thutmose I to Ramses XI were buried.
Volney, Count Constantin De (1757-1820)	French intellectual, member of the Estates-General, Constituent Assembly, French Academy and Society of Friends of the Blacks. His *Ruins of Empires* created a great interest in Egypt among Europeans in the eighteenth century.
Wa'set	The indigenous name for the city which was later called "Thebes" by the Greeks and "Luxor" by the Arabs. Its name in Medu Netcher means "the Septer." Ancient city in upper Kemet renowned in antiquity for its hundred gates. Became prominent with the Eleventh Dynasty (c. 2040 B.C.E.) for the worship of Amon. There is a nearby necropolis on the west bank of the Nile where kings, queens and nobles were entombed. The remains of the temples of Luxor and Karnak are located in this city.
Williams, Chancelor (1894-1992)	Renowned professor of African history at Howard University and research fellow at Oxford University. He is best known for his publications *The Rebirth of African Civilization* and *The Destruction of Black Civilization*.

Bibliography

Akbar, Na'im, *Visions for Black Men*, Winston-Derek, Nashville, TN, 1991.

Amen, Ra Un Nefer, *Metu Neter Vol. I*, Khamit Corp, Bronx, NY, 1990.

Ampim, Manu, *The Current Africentric Movement in the U.S.: The Centrality of Ancient Nile Valley Civilization*, 1990.

Anyike, James C, *African American Holidays*, Popular Truth, Inc, Chicago, IL, 1991.

Asante, Molefi Kete, *Afrocentricity*, Africa World Press, Trenton, NJ, 1988.
_____, *Kemet, Afrocentricity and Knowledge*, Africa World Press, 1990

Ausubel, Jesse H. and Langford, H. Dale, *Lasers Invention To Application*, National Academy Press, Washington, DC, 1987.

Baines, John and Malek, Jaromir, *Atlas of Ancient Egypt*, Phaidon Press Ltd, Oxford, England, 1986.

ben-Jochannan, Yosef, *African Origins of the Major "Western Religions,"* Alkebu-lan Books, New York, NY, 1970.
_____, *Black Man of the Nile and His Family*, Black Classic Press, Baltimore, MD, 1989.
_____, *Africa Mother Of Western Civilization*, Black Classic Press, 1988.
_____, *African Origins of The Major Western Religions*, Black Classic Press, 1991.
_____, *Abu Simbel to Ghizeh: A Guide Book & Manual*, Black Classic Press, 1987.
_____, and Clarke, John Henrik, *New Dimensions in African History*, Africa World Press, Trenton, NJ, 1991.

Bennett, Lerone, Jr., *Before the Mayflower: A History of Black America*, Johnson Publishing Co., Chicago, IL, 1962.
_____, *The Shaping of Black America*, Johnson Publishing Co., 1975.

Bernal, Martin, *Black Athena The Afroasiatic Roots of Classical Civilization*, Rutgers University Press, New Brunswick, N J, 1987.

Breasted, James Henry, *A History of Egypt*, Bantam Matrix Books, New York, NY, 1967.
_____, *Ancient Times*, Ginn & Company, Boston, MA, 1935

Browder, Anthony T., *From The Browder File: 22 Essays on the African American Experience*, The Institute of Karmic Guidance, Washington, DC, 1989.
_____, and Atlantis Tye, *My First Trip To Africa*, The Institute of Karmic Guidance, Washington, DC, 1991.

Brunson, James E., *Frat & Soror: The African Origin of Greek-Lettered Organizations*, A Cleage Group Publication, 1992.

Budge, E.A. Wallis, *The Gods of The Egyptians*, Dover Publications, New York, NY, 1969.
_____, *The Egyptian Book Of The Dead*, Dover Publications, 1967.

Busenbark, Ernest, *Symbols, Sex and the Stars*, Truth Seeker Company, Inc., New York, NY, 1949.

Campbell, Joseph with Moyers, Bill, *The Power of Myth*, Doubleday, New York, NY, 1988.

Clarke, John Henrik, *Notes For An African World Revolution: African at the Crossroads*, Africa World Press, Trenton, NJ, 1991.

Clegg, Legrand H. and Ahmed, Karima Y, *Egypt During The Golden Age,* The Clegg Series, Compton, CA, 1991.

Coe, Michael D, *America's First Civilization Discovering the Olmec*, American Heritage Publishing Co., New York, NY, 1968.

Conrad, Earl, *The Invention of the Negro*, Paul Eriksson, Inc., New York, NY, 1965.

Crosby, Edward W. and Hoskins, Linus A., *Africa for the Africans*, Institute for African American Affairs, Kent, OH, 1991.

Davidson, Basil, *Black Mother: The Years of Our African Slave Trade: Precolonial History, 1450-1850*, Atlantic-Little, Brown, Co., Boston, MA, 1961.
_____, *Discovering Our African Heritage*, Ginn and Co., Boston, MA, 1970.

Dennis, Denise, *Black History For Beginners*, Writers & Readers Publishing, New York, NY, 1984.

Diop, Cheikh Anta, *African Origins of Civilization: Myth or Reality*, Lawrence Hill & Co., New York, NY, 1974.
_____, *Civilization or Barbarism*, Lawrence Hill & Co., New York, NY, 1989.
_____, and Obenga Theophile, *The Origin of the Ancient Egyptians,* pp. 27-5, in *The Peopling of Ancient Egypt and the Deciphering of Meroitic Script*, UNESCO's *The General History of Africa Studies and Documents, I and II*.

Dollars & Sense, February/March 1983, National Publications Sales Agency, Chicago, IL, 1983.
_____, February/March 1982, National Publications Sales Agency, 1982.

Douglass, Frederick, *Life and Times of Frederick Douglass, the Complete Autobiography*, Collier Books, New York, NY, 1962.

Dubois, W.E.B., *The World and Africa*, International Publishers, New York, NY, 1965.

El-Amin, Mustafa, *Freemasonry Ancient Egypt And The Islamic Destiny*, New Mind Productions, Jersey City, NJ, 1990.

Fagan, Brian M., *The Rape of The Nile*, Charles Scribner's Sons, New York, NY, 1975.

Finch, Charles S., *The African Background to Medical Science Essays in African History, Science & Civilizations*, Karnak House, London, 1990.
_____, *Echoes of the Old Darkland*, Khenti, Inc., Decatur, GA., 1991.

Fix, William R., *Pyramid Odyssey*, Mayflower Books, New York, 1978.
_____, *Star Maps*, Octopus Books Limited, London, England, 1979.

Franklin, John Hope, *From Slavery to Freedom: A History of Negro Americans*, Alfred A. Knopf, New York, NY, 1980.

Gillispie, Charles Coulston and DeWachter, Michel, editors, *Monuments of Egypt The Napoleonic Edition*, Princeton Architectural Press, Princeton, NJ, 1987.

Gordon, Vivian Verdell, *Kemet and Other Ancient African Civilizations*, Third World Press, Chicago, IL, 1991.

Habachi, Labib, *The Obelisks Of Egypt Skyscrapers Of The Past*, The American University of Cairo Press, Cairo, Egypt, 1984.

Harding, Vincent, *There Is a River: The Black Struggle for Freedom in America*, Harcourt, Brace, Jovanovich, New York, NY, 1981.

Haynes, Joyce L, *Nubia Ancient Kingdoms of Africa*, Museum of Fine Arts, Boston, MA, 1992.

Herodotus, *The History of Herodotus*, translated by George Rawlinson, Tudor Publishing Co., New York, NY, 1939.

Hieronimus, Robert, *America's Secret Destiny Spriitual Vision & The Founding of a Nation*, Destiny Books, Rochester, VT, 1989.

Hilliard, Asa G. and Middleton, Listervelt, *Free Your Mind, Return to the Source: African Origins*, Waset Educational Productions, East Point, GA, 1988.
_____, *Master Keys*, Waset Educational Productions, 1991.
_____, and Payton-Stewart, Lucretia; Williams, Larry Obadele, *Infusion of African and African American Content in the School Curriculum*, Aaron Press, Morristown, NJ, 1990.
_____, and Williams, Larry; Damali, Nia (editors) *The Teachings of Ptahhotep The Oldest Book in the World*, Blackwood Press, Atlanta, GA, 1987.

Hoskins, Linus A, *Decoding European Geopolitics Afrocentric Perspectives*, Institute for African American Affairs, Kent, OH, 1990.

Houston, Drusilla Dunjee, *Wonderful Ethiopians of the Ancient Cushite Empire*, Black Classic Press, Baltimore, MD, 1985.

Jackson, John G., *Ethiopia and the Origin of Civilization*, Black Classic Press, Baltimore, MD, 1939.
_____, *Introduction to African Civilizations*, Citadel Press, Secaucus, NJ, 1970.
_____, *Man, God and Civilization*, Citadel Press, 1972.
_____, *Christianity Before Christ*, American Atheist Press, Austin, TX, 1985.
_____, *Ages Of Gold And Silver*, American Atheist Press, 1990.

Jalandris, *The Hall Of Records: Hidden Secrets of the Pyramid and Sphinx*, Holistic Life Travels, San Francisco, CA, 1980.

James, George G.M., *Stolen Legacy*, Julian Richardson Assoc, San Francisco, CA, 1954.

Jones, Del, *Culture Bandits Vol. 1*, Hikeka Press, Philadelphia, PA, 1990.

Jordan, Paul, *Egypt The Black Land*, E.P. Dutton & Co, New York, NY, 1976.

Kaiser, Ward L, *A New View Of The World*, Friendship Press, New York, NY, 1987.

Karenga, Maulana, *Introduction to Black Studies*, Kawaida Publication, Inglewood, CA.
_____, *The Book Of Coming Forth By Day*, University of Sankore Press, LA, CA, 1990.
_____, *Selections From The Husia*, University of Sankore Press, 1984.
_____, *Reconstructing Kemetic Culture*, University of Sankore Press, 1990.

King, Richard, *African Origin of Biological Psychiatry*, Seymour-Smith, Inc.,
      Germantown, TN, 1990.

Kush, Indus Khamit, *What They Never Told You In History Class*, Luxorr Publications,
      Bronx, NY, 1983.

Lamy, Lucie, *Egyptian Mysteries*, The Crossroad Publishing Co., New York, NY, 1981.

Madhubuti, Haki R., *Black Men: Obsolete, Single, Dangerous,?* Third World Press,
      Chicago, IL, 1990.

Massey, Gerald, *Ancient Egypt, The Light of the World*, Vols I and II, Black Classic
      Press, Baltimore, MD, 1992.

Mazrui, Ali A., *The Africans, A Triple Heritage*, Little, Brown & Co., Boston, MA, 1986.

Moore, Richard B., *The Name Negro - Its Origin and Evil Use*, Black Classic Press,
      Baltimore, MD, 1992.

Quarles, Benjamin, *The Negro and the Making of America*, Collier Books, New York, NY,
      1969.

Parker, George Wells, *The Children Of The Sun*, Black Classic Press, Baltimore, MD, 1981.

Raglan, Lord, *How Came Civilization*, Methuen & Company, London, England, 1939.

Richards, Dona Marimba, *Let The Circle Be Unbroken*, Red Sea Press, Trenton, NJ, 1989.

Robins, Gay and Shute, Charles, *The Rhind Mathematical Papyrus an Ancient Egyptian
      Text*, British Museum Publications Ltd, London WC1B 3QQ, 1987.

Rodney, Walter, *How Europe Underdeveloped Africa*, Howard University Press,
      Washington, DC, 1974.

Rogers, J.A., *World's Great Men of Color*, Vols. I & II, edited by John Henrik Clarke,
      Collier-MacMillan, New York, NY, 1972.
_____, *Sex and Race*, privately published by Rogers Publishing Co., c/o Mrs. J.A. Rogers
      St. Petersburg, FL.
_____, *Your History From The Beginning Of Time To The Present*, Black Classic Press,
      Baltimore, MD, 1983.

Sagan, Carl, *Cosmos*, Random House, New York, NY, 1980.

Schwaller de Lubicz, R.A., *The Temple in Man*, Inner Traditions International Ltd, New York, NY.
_____, *Sacred Science*, Inner Traditions International Ltd, 1982.

Smithsonian Magazine, *Unlocking the Secrets of the Giza Plateau* by Dora Jane Hamblin, Washington, DC, April 1986.

Snowden, Frank M., Jr., *Blacks in Antiquity: Ethiopians in the Greco-Roman Experience* The Belnap Press, Harvard Univ, Cambridge, MA, 1970.

Tompkins, Peter, *Secrets of The Great Pyramid*, Harper & Row, New York, NY, 1971.
_____, *The Magic Of Obelisks*, Harper & Row, 1981.

Van Sertima, Dr. Ivan, *They Came Before Columbus*, Random House, New York, 1976.
_____, editor, *The Journal of African Civilization*, Transactions Periodicals Consortium, Rutgers Univ, New Brunswick, NJ. See special issues, *The African Presence in Early Europe/Egypt Revisited/Nile Valley Civilizations/Black Women In Antiquity/Blacks In Science: Ancient & Modern/African Presence in Early America/Great Black Leaders: Ancient & Modern.*

Volney, C.F., *The Ruins of Empires*, Black Classics Press, Baltimore, MD 1990.

Von Wuthenau, Alexander, *Unexpected Faces In Ancient America*, Crown Publishers, New York, NY, 1982.

Welsing, Frances Cress, *The Isis Papers*, Third World Press, Chicago, IL, 1991.

West, John Anthony, *The Traveler's Key To Ancient Egypt*, Alfred A Knopf, New York, NY, 1985.
_____, *Serpent In The Sky The High Wisdom of Ancient Egypt*, Harper & Row, New York, NY, 1979.

Williams, Chancellor, *The Destruction of Black Civilization: Great Issues of a Race from 4500 B.C. to 2000 A.D.*, Third World Press, Chicago, IL, 1974.

Williams, Bruce, *The Lost Pharaohs of Nubia*, Archaeology Magazine, Vol. 33, No. 5, 1980.
_____, *The A-Group Royal Cemetery At Qustul: Cemetery L*, The Oriental Institute of the University of Chicago, Chicago, IL, 1986.

Woodson, Carter G., *African Heroes and Heroines*, Associated Publishers, Inc. Washington, DC, 1969.
_____, *Mis-Education Of The Negro*, Associated Publishers, 1969.
_____, *African Background Outlined*, Associated Publishers, 1936.

Index

Items in text are in regular print
Margin notes are in **boldface**
Illustrations and photos are in **(parenthesis)**

A

Aboul-Ela, 16
Abu-Hol, 113, **224**
Abu Simbel, 185, 206, **(207)**, 228, **(228)**
Adams, John, 201
Admonitions of Maat, **82**, 91, **92**, 267
Aeronautical Engineering, 132
Africa/African, 14, 27
    Accomplishments, 123, **129**, 131, 151, 155, 227
    Americans, 13, 26-28, 72, 74, 158-160, 221, 232, 245, 247, 248, 259, 260
    Civilization, 14, 17, **212**
    Geography, 27, 39, **40**, 46, 50, **50**, 149
    History, 13, 14, 31, 32, 36, 104, 105, 150, 191, 209, 211, 213, 259, 260
    People, 25-28, 30, 52, **52**, 69, 72, **142**, 143, 148, 149, 177, 253, 257, 258, 262
African American Summit, **28**
African Centered/Afro-Centric, 245, 247
Afrocentricity, 143, 245, 246
Afrocentrism, 41, 143, 156, 157, 247
Agriculture, 35, 45, 78, 80, 82
Aha (also see Narmer), 51, **(51)**, 143
Aker lions, **71, (71)**
Akhet, 112, 115, **(115)**
Akhenaton, 63, 93, 94, **94**, **(94)**, 126, **142**, **145**, **226**, **(226)**
Al Mamun, Abdullah, 104, 175, **(176)**
Alexander of Macedonia, **(64)**
    Conquest of Egypt, 64, 66, 143, 160-162, 180
    Death, 143, 162
    Early life, 143, 156, 157, 160, **160**, 161
    Son of Ammon, 161, **(161)**, 162, **162**, **(162)**
Alexandria, Egypt, **205**, 227
    Arab conquest, 173, 174, 177
    British conquest, 182
    French conquest, 179, 181
    Greek conquest, 66, 141, 143, 161, 162
    Roman conquest, 121, 191
    Library of, 62, 141, 153, 156, 162, 163, **163**, 164, **164**
    University of, 164
Ali, Mohammad, 121, 183, 184, **184**, **185**, **(185)**, **191**
Alpha Draconis, 109, **(109)**
Alphabet, 14, 169
    Greek, 169, **170**, **(170)**
    Kemetic/Egyptian, 165, 169, 183
    Roman, 169, **170**, **(170)**, **(171)**, 194

Alphi Centuri, 81
Amen, 85, **(85)**, **(96)**, 118, 195, 238, 239, 262
Amenemhet III, 63, **(233)**
Amenhotep, I 57
Amenhotep III, 63, **(64)**, **94**, 118, **142**, 185, **252**
Amenhotep IV, 63, **94**, **(94)**, **142**
Amon/Amon-Ra, **67**, 117
Ancient Times, 146, 147, **147**, **148**, 149
Ankh, **67**, 95, 125, **226**, **262**
Anpu (also see Anubis), 84, **(84)**, **89**, 90, **158**
Antony, Marc, 67, 141, 165
Anubis (also see Anpu), 84, 90
Aphrodite, 168
Apollo, **126**, **(126)**, 168
Archimedes, 130
Architecture, 66, 98, 151
    Cathedral design, 190, 195, 196
    Corinthian, 166
    Doric, 166
    Greco-Roman, 165, 166, **167**
    Ionic, 166
    Kemetic/Egyptian, 22, 45, 72, 74, 80-82, 99, **99**, 100, 105, 112, 120, 123, 129, 132, 165, 204, 206, 208
Aristotle, 129, 155, **(155)**, 156, 161, 162, 174, 175
Asante, Molefi, 245, **(245)**, 247
Asclepius (also see Imhotep), 102, **126**, **(126)**, 168
Aset (also see Isis), 68, **(68)**, 89, **(74)**, **(93)**, 95, 112, 118, **123**, 189
    Birth of Heru, 89, 95
    Impregnation by Ausar, 89
    Simularities with Mary, 95
Ass, 84
Astrology, 78, 81, 124
Astronomy, 74, 78, 81, 93, **106**, 107, 124, 151, 155, 157, 162, 164, 174, 175, 195
Aswan, 48, 56, 60, 108, **122**, **130**, **164**, 181, **229**
Aswan High Dam, 53, 56, **56**
Athena, **156**, **(156)**, **(158)**, 168
Aton, 63, 93, 94, **94**, 126, 155, **226**, **(226)**
Augustus, 65, **(65)**, 77, **(77)**, 144, **162**, **(162)**, 191
Ausar (also see Osiris), **(58)**, 68, **74**, **(74)**, 89, **89**, 95-97, **(97)**, 112, 118, **123**, **167**, 189, 193
    Death, of 89
    Lord of Judgement, 89, 90, 204
    Origin of Tekhen, 89, 121, 122, 191, 204
    Ressurection, 89

B

Ba, **90**, **91**, **(91)**, **226**
Babylon/Babylonians, 64, 80, 81, 162
Belzoni, Giovanni, 185, **(185)**
ben-Jochannan, Yosef, **(3)**, 48, **(48)**, 60, 94, 152
Benu Bird, **72**, 122
Berlin Bust of Nefertiti, **145**
Berlin Conference, 258, **258**, **(258)**
Bernal, Martin, 19, **145**, 161, **196**
Berry, Henry, 18
Bible, **27**, 93-96, **194**, 195, 197, 221, 261, 262
    Comparison with Book of the Dead,
    91, 92
        King James, 95, 261, **(261)**
        Ten Commandments, 92-94, **92**, 228
Big Mama Thornton, 160
Bird of Saqqara, 132, **(132)**, **(133)**
Black Athena, 19, 161
Black History Month, 72, 74
Black Madonna, 190
Blackwell, Otis, 160
Blumenbach, Johann, 19
Bonaparte, Napoleon, 37, 65, **(65)**, 68, 179-184,
(179), **180**, **(180)**, **196**, 222-224, 226, 236
Book of the Dead (also see Pert em hru), 66,
88, **(88)**, 91
        Anpu, 88, 90
        Ausar, 89, 90
        Definition, 66, 87, 267
        Djhuiti, 88, 90
        Maat, 88, 90
        Weighing of Soul, **(89)**, 90
Boston Museum of Fine Arts, 59, 149, 150
Boston Tea Party, 198
Breasted, James, 14, 87, **124**, 125, 146-150,
147, **148**, **252**
        Ancient Times, 146, 147, **147**, **148**, 149
        Oriental Institute, 53, 57, 146, 147, 149,
        150
Burges, John, 18
Burton, Richard, 18
Byzantine Empire, 65, 68, 145, 173, **173**,
(173), 174, 258

C

Caduceus, **168**, **(168)**, 229, **229**, **(229)**
Caesar, Julius, 67, 76, 77, 141, 165, **165**,
(165), 193
Cairo, Egypt, 13, **50**, 60, 74, 103, 104, 116,
131, 132, 174-177, 180, 182, **184**
Cairo Museum, 132, 133, 188, **223**
Cairo Symposium, 19, 20
Calendar, 72, 74, **75**, 217
        Georgian, 52, 77, 78
        Hebrew, 77, 78
        Islamic, 78
        Julian, 77
        Kemetic, 63, 75, **75**, 77, 81
        Lunar, 75, 78

        Roman, 76
        Sidereal, 76
        Solar, 75, 76
Campbell, Joseph, 203
Carnarvon, Lord, 188, **188**, **(188)**
Carter, Howard, 146, 185, 188, **188**, **(188)**
Cataract, 46, 48, 54-56, **54**
Champollion, Jean Francois, 183, **(183)**
Cheops (also see Khufu), 51
Chicago Tribune, 150
Christ, Jesus The, 52, **67**, 77, 84, 86, 118,
190, 191, **(191)**, 261
        Comparison with Heru, 96
Circumpolars, 109
Clarke, John Henrik, **(3)**, **(9)**, 22, 29, 30, 31,
36, 60, **(244)**, 247, 250
Clegg, Legrand, 15
Cleopatra VII, 64, **(64)**, 67, 76, 143, 144,
165, **165**, 232
Clepsydra, **75**, **124**, **(124)**
Clerestory window, 99, **99**
Coe, Michael, 217
Columbus, Christopher, 31, 34, 35, 40, 41,
(41), 143, 212
Conceptual incarceration, 21
Constantine, 65, 68, 145
Constellation, 78, 81, 109, 110, 163, 201, 202
Continuous screw, 130, **(130)**
Copher, Charles, 95
Critical thinking skills, 221, 222
Cyril, 164

D

Dallas Institute of Humanities and
Culture, 16
Decan, 78, **79**, 85, 110
Declaration of Independence, 199, **199**
Declarations of Innocence, 90
        Comparison with Ten
        Commandments, 92
        Definition, 91, 267
de Lubicz, R.A. Schwaller, 120
Demotic, 68, 182, **183**
Dendera, **(75)**, **79**, **(79)**, 145, 181, 242
Denon, Vivant, 183, 224
Description de L'Egypte, 68, **(172)**, 182, 183
Diop, Cheikh Anta, 19, 20, 23, **(23)**, 37, 81,
127, 149, 151, 190
Djhuiti (also see Thoth), 51, **(75)**, 83, **(83)**,
89, **89**, 90, 95, **126**, **127**, **(158)**, **168**, **(168)**,
193, 229
Druid, 193, **193**, 194
Du Bois, W. E. B., 60, 137, **137**, **(137)**

E

Ebers Papyrus, 125
Eduf Temple, 48, 81, 145
Edfu Text, 48, 49

Edwin Smith Papyrus, 125, **125**
Egypt, **52, 129, 142, 164, 165, (172), 178, 180, 182, 184, 193, 196, 226, (244)**
  Lower, 46, 166, 213
  Upper, 46, 53, 60, 68, **130**, 164, **164**, 166, 181
Eisenhower, Dwight David, **143**
Encyclopedia Britannica, 33
Ennead, **123**, 154, 168
Equinox, 107, **115**, 116, 122, **124**,
  Autumn, 81, 115, 215
  Spring, 77, 81, 115, 196, 204, 215
Erasthothenes, 146
Ethiopia, 45, 48-50, **50**, 61, 80, 81, 95, 131, 138, 139, **183, 212**
Euclid, 129, 163, 164, 174
Eye of Djhuiti, **127**, 229
Eye of Heru, **127**, 202, 229, 230, **(230)**

F

Falcon, 55, **55**, 83, **83, (96)**
Fibonacci, Leonardo, **129**
Finch, Charles, 49, 52, **(248)**
Founding Fathers, 197, 199, **202**, 203, 204
Franklin, Benjamin, 18, 201
Freemasonry, 22, 28, 196-204, 208
From The Browder File, 25, 232, 250, 263

G

Galen, 163, 164, 174, 229
Geb, **123**
Gehard, Kremer, 38
Geodesy, **106**
Giza, 63, 103, **(103)**, 109, 111, 112, 114-116, **(115)**, 131, **(131)**, 149, 180, 185, 205, 206, 208, 215, **224**
Glider of Saqqara, 133
Golden section, **128**
Goree Island, 32
Gossett, Louis, Jr., 61
Gottingen University, 19, 21
Great Northwest Quadrant, 147, 148
Great Pyramid, 63, 71, 87, 93, 103-112, 120, 131, 175, 180, 205, 206, 208, 215
Great Seal, 200, **(201)**, 202
  Design, 201
  Obverse, 201
  Reverse, 201, 202, 203

H

Habachi, Labib, 121
Haley, Alex, 34
Hansberry, William Leo, 11, 60

Hapi, 48, 49, **(49), 55**, 84, **(84)**
Hathor (also see Het-Heru), 95, 168
Hatshepsut, 63, **98**, 122, **122, (122)**, 143, 206
Hekaptah, 51
Hekat, 127, **127**
Heliopolis, **72**, 93, 102, 121
Her-em-akhet, 112, 114-116, **(115), (220), 222, (222), 231**
  Beard, 223, **(223)**
  Defacement, 222-226, **(224-225)**
  Meaning of, 112, 113
Hermes, 83, **(158)**, 168, **168, (168), 193**, 229
Hermes Trismegistus, **193, (193)**
Hermetic Sciences, **168, (168)**, 193, **193**
Herodotus, 16, 74, 110, 129, 138-140
Heron, 163
Hersetha, 124
Heru (also see Horus), 68, **(68), (74)**, 75, **75**, 76, **89**, 90, **(93)**, 95, **(96), 97, (97)**, 98, 112, **114**, 115, 118, **126**, 189, 190, 193, 203
  Battle with Set, 97
  Birth, 89, 95
  Comparison w/Jesus The Christ, 96, 190, 193
  Eye of, 203, 229, 230
  Symbolism of, 83, 97, 113, 168
Het-Heru (also see Hathor), 95, 168
Heyerdhal, Thor, 131, 213
Hieroglyphics (also see Medu Netcher), 54, 98, 120, 145
Hilliard, Asa, 21, 49, 124, **145**, 235, **(235)**, 263
Hippocrates, 102, **(126)**
Hippocratic Oath, **126**
Holy of Holies, 81, **98**, 99
Homer, 16, 114, 138, **(138), 168, 183**
Horoscope, 78
Horus (also see Heru), 48, 55, 68, 75, **75**, 76, 78, 89, 95-97, 115, 168, 175, 189-191, **190, (190)**, 261
House of Life, 125
Hume, David, 17
Hyksos, 63, 66, 151
Hypatia, 164, **(164)**

I

Ibis, 83
Illiad, 114, 168
Imhotep (also see Asclepius), 102, **(102), 125, 126, 168, 215, 221**
Inundation, 76, 80, 129
Ipet-Isut (also see Karnak Temple), **67, 99**, 114, 115, **116**, 118, 121, 122, **(122)**, 124, 228, **252**
Isis (also see Aset), 75, 89, 97, 121, 189-191, **190**, 261
  and Horus, 55, 56, 96, 97, 189, 190, **(190)**
Islam, 56, 58, 65, 78, **91**, 119, 173, 175, **196**

J

Jackal, **79**, 84
Jackson, John, **(3)**, 30, 48, **(48)**, 50, 60, 78, 86, 93, 94, 149, 206, 208, 250
Jackson, Michael, **(236)**, 237
Jairazbhoy, Rafique, 214
Jalapa Museum, **(211)**, 212, 217
James, George G. M., 22, 152-156, **(152)**, **(153)**, 264
Jefferson, Thomas, 18, 199, 201, 205
Jim Crow, 60, 143
Joint Center for Political Studies, 28
Justinian, 58, 65, 68, **(173)**, **262**

K

Ka, **90**, **91**, **(91)**
Ka-Kepra-Re-Sen-Wos-Ret I, 131
Kaaba, **91**
Kecrops, 131
Kemet, **51**, **52**, **67**, **71**, **72**, **75**, **92**, **94**, **126-128**, **(131)**, **145**, **167**, **262**
    Europeanization, 22, **(144)**
    French Invasion, 68, 179-183
    Greek Invasion, 62, 64, 66, 67, 141-145, 158, 160-164
    Historical Overview, 62-69
    Islamic Invasion, 69, 173-177
    Meaning of, 52
    Nubian Rule, 53-55, 57-61, 63, 64
    Persian Invasion, 64, 66, 140
    Roman Invasion, 62, 64, 67, 144, 145, 165
    KMT, 52, **52**
    Lower, **(49)**, 66, 81, 93, 100, 143, **168**, **(168)**, **229**
    Upper, **(49)**, 54, 55, 81, 100, 143, **168**, **(168)**, **229**
Kemiu, 52, **52**
Kendall Timothy, 59, 150
Kenya, **27**, **45**
Khartoum, 46, 48
Khufu (also see Cheops), 51, **(62)**, 104, **(104)**, 109, 115, **(115)**, 131, 206
Khunum, **90**
Kilimanjaro, 45, 46
Kom Ombo Temple, 145
Kush, 54, 57-59, 64

L

La Venta, 210, 214, 215
Lafayette, Marquis de, **197**, **(197)**, 199, **(199)**
Lake Nasser, 53, 55, 56, **56**
Lamy, Lucie, 109, 120
Leakey, Louis, 14
Leakey, Richard, **27**
Lefkowitz, Mary, 156, 157
Liberia, 27, 28

Lincoln, Abraham, 18, 205, 206, **(207)**
Lockyer, Norman, 117, 195, 196
Lotus, **89**, 99, **99**, 117, **167**
Louis IX, 30
Louis XIV, 30
Louis XVI, 199
Louis XVIII, 181
Louisiana, 30, 199
Louisville, KY, 199
Louvre Museum, **79**, 181, **182**, 189
Luther, Martin, **194**, **(194)**
Luxor (also see Thebes and Waset), 63, 64, **98**, 130, 205, 208
Luxor Temple, 66, 95, 114, 116-120, **(118)**, **120**, **(121)**, **167**, 183, 228

M

Maat, **82**, **89**, 90-92, 94, **(158)**, **189**, 191, **202**, 267, **(267)**
Mamelukes, 65, 179, 180, 182, 184, **184**, **(184)**
Manetho, 62, 64, 102
Mason/Masonry (also see Freemasonry), **193**, **196**, **(196)**, **197**, **198**, **(198)**, **(200)**, **202**, **203**, **205**
Massey, Gerald, 96
Mastaba, 100, 152, 214
Mathematics, 106, **106**, 108, **123**, 127-129, **129**, 151, 157, 162-164, 166, 174, 175, **193**
Mediterranean, 17, 36, 46-48, 66, **106**, 131, 141, 147, **148**, 157, 161, **164**, 169, **170**, **(170)**, 179, 180, 213
Medu Netcher, 52, 52, 54, 68, 85, 98, 120, 122, 141, 145, 169, 174, 182, 190, 267
Melanin dosage test, 20
Memphis, 50, 51, 57, 63, 115, 139, 162, 206
Memphis, TN, 204, 206
Men-Nefer, 51
Menes (also see Narmer), 50, 51, 63
Mentuhotep III, **(63)**
Mercator Projection Map, 38, **38**, **(38)**, **39**
Mercury, 75, 83, 168, **168**, **(168)**, 229
Mesoamerica, 22, 209, 213, 215, 217
Meyer, Edward, 87, 124
Mineralogy, 129-130
Minerva, **156**, **168**
Monrovia, Liberia, 28
Moses, **92**, **(92)**, 93, **(93)**, 94, 228
Mountain of the Moon, 46
Mubarak, Hosni, 65, **(65)**, **164**
Mummy, 177-178, **178**, 187
Museum of Man, 37
Mut, **67**
Mystery School, 124, 154, 193, 194

N

NAACP, 28, **137**
NASA, 133

Naguib, Muhammad, 60, 65
Narmer, 51, **(51)**, 63, **(63)**
Nasser, Gamal Abdel, 60, 65, **(65)**
National Council of Negro Women, 28
National Geographic Society, 209, 223, 228
Nature, **74**, 83, 86, 97, **106**, 113, 138, 193, 194
Nefertari, 64, **(228)**
Nefertiti, 63, **94, 144, 145, 22, (226)**
Negro, 26, 28, 60, 66, 72, 137, 138, 143, **143, 147**, 151, 159, 160, **184**, 209, 210, **212**, 221, **221**
    Creation of, 25, 31, 253
    Enslavement, 31, 137
    Negative interpretations, 17-19, 25, 27, 30-33, 147, 148
    Organizations, 28
Neith, **156**
Netcher, 52, **52, 72, 75, (75)**, 76, 83-85, 89-91, 95, 99, 118, 120, 122, **123, 126, (151)**, 154, **156, (158), 167, 168**, 191, 195, 204, 229, 242, **(242)**, 267
Netcherw, 75, **(75)**, 81, 83, 85, 86, 89-93, **90, 91**, 120, **123, 127**, 154, 155, 168, 174, 189, 227, 230, **262**
Netcherwy, 122, **123**
New Orleans, LA, 28, 30
New Republic, 156, **(157)**
New York Times, **53, 142, 160**
Newsweek, **143, (143), 157**
Newton, Isaac, 194, 246
Nicean Council, 190, 261
Nile, 48, 49, **54**, 55, 60, 63, **71, 74**, 85, 89, **90, 106**, 111, 121, **123, 124, 126, 127, 130**, 140, **141**, 150, 162, 204, 206, 208, **212**, 213, **231**
    Blue Nile, 45, 46, 48
    Delta, 103, 106, 139, 208
    Hapi, 48, 84
    Indunation, 76, 80, 84, 105, 110, 139
    White Nile, 45, 46, 48
Notre Dame, 117, 190
Nubia, 48, **54, 141**
    Civilization, 53-55, 63, 131, 213-214
    Contemporary, 60-61
    Expedition, 53-56, 149, 150
    People, 56-61, 64, 211
    Rulers of Kemet, 55, 57-58, 66, 211
Nut, 49, **123**, 242
Nyanza, 45

O

Obelisk (also see Tekhen), 89, 121, 185, 191, 195, 203, 204
Obenga Theophile, 19, 20
Odyssey, 168
Oedipus, 113, **113**
Olmec Civilization, **(209)**, 210, 211, **(211), 212**, 213, 214, 216, 217
Oracle of Amon, 138, 161, 162
Oriental Institute, 53, 57, 146, 147, 149, 150
Orion, 109, 110
Orleans, France, 30
Osiris (also see Ausar), 55, **(58)**, 68, **74**, 75, 89, 110, 121, 139, 144, 189, 204

P

Pa-di-Imen, 113
Papyrus, 68, 74, 87, 93, 99, **99**, 123, 131, 141, 162, **167**, 213
Papryus, Edwin Smith, 125, **125**
Papryus, Ebers, 125
Papyrus, Greenfield, **123**
Papyrus of Hunefer, 48
Papyrus of Moscow, 128
Papyrus, Rhine, 127-129, **129**
Paris Observatory, 105
Paris, France, 34, 37, 117, 121, 151, 180, 183, 190, **190**, 191, 199
People Magazine, 159
Per Ankh, 125
Persian Invasion, 64, 66, 104, 140, 144, 151, 160, 173, 189
Persians, 56, 63, 69, 104, 140, 161, 162
Pert Em Hru, 87
Peters Projection Map, 39, **(39), 40**
Peters, Arno, 39, 40
Petrie, Sir Flinders, 87
Pharaoh, 19, 51, 55, 60, 63, 64, 93, 109, 114, 124, 139, 193, 208, 213
Phi, 107, **128**
Philippe, Louis, 121, 183
Phillip II of Macedonia, 159, 160, 162
Phoenix, **72**, 122
Pi, 107
Piankhy, 57
Pindar, 161
Plato, 108, 155, 156, 174
Pope (misc), 31, 37, 193
    Celestine I, 194
    Eugenia IV, 32
    Gregory XIII, 77
    John Paul, II, 32, 190, 191
    Nicholas V, 32
Pope, John Russel, 206, **207**
Presley, Elvis, 159, **(159)**, 160, 208
Ptah, 50, 51, 120
Ptolemy, 62, 64, 67, 76, 144, 162, 163, 165, 174, 175, 182
Pyramid, 54, 63, 81, **(88)**, 98, 99, **(103), 115, (115)**, 116, 121, 127, 146, 147, 149, 152, 176, 180, 185, 201, 202, **202**, 203, 206, 208, 210, 213-215, **224**, 230
    Ascending Passage, 108
    Descending Passage, 108
    Grand Gallery, 108
    King's Chamber, 108, 109
    Nubian, 55, 59
    Queen's Chamber, 108
    Step, 100-102, **(100), (101)**, 215
    Text, 66, **88**, 168
    The Great, 71, 87, 93, 103-111, **(105)**, 112, 120, 131, **(131)**, 175, **(176)**, 180, **(180)**, 193, **196, 202**, 205, 206, 208, 215
Pythagorean Theorem, 127, **128**
Pythagorean Triangle, 108

Q

Qustul, 53-56, **(55)**

R

Ra (also see Re), 85, 131, 152, 213, 230
Races of Humanity, **61, (61)**
Raglan, Lord, 15
Rameses II, 64, **(64)**, 118, 120, **120, (146), 147**, 185, **(207), 228, (228)**
    Abu-Simbel, 206, **(207)**, 228, **(228)**
    Conference, 16, 17
    Distortions, 228
    Lincoln Memorial, 206
Re (also see Ra), 85, 121
Reisner, George, 59, 146, 149, 150
Religion, **82, 202**
    Bible, 93, 95, 195, 197, 221, 261, 262
    Christianity, 22, 23, 58, 65, 67, 68, 96, 102, 152, 189, 191, 193, 194, 261, 262
    Coptic, 58, 67, 118, 174
    Islam, 56, 58, 65, 78, 119, 175
    Koran, 174
    Nile Valley, 22, 74, 81, 82, 85, 86-97, 132, 140, 168, 169, 189, 191, 195-197, 215, 242, 261, 267
    Old Testament, 94, 95, 167
    Roman Catholic Church, 31, 173, 194
Revolutionary War, 198-200, 204
Rockefeller, John D., 146
Rockefeller, John D., Jr., 146, 149
Rogers, J. A., **143, 184, 260**
Rolling Stone Magazine, 160
Romulus and Remus, 165, **165, (165)**
Rosetta Stone, 145, 182-184, **182, (182)**
Rosicrucians, 194, 196
Ruins of Empires, 82, 137, 138
Ruwenzori, 46

S

Sadat, Anwar, 60, 61, 65, **(65)**
Saint George, **97, (97)**
Saint Patrick, 193, 194
San Lorenzo, 210, 214
Saqqara, 51, 63, 100, **(101)**, 102, 132, 133, **167**
Savants, 140, 179, 181, 182, 224, 226
Scarab beetle, 83, **(83)**, 185
Seal of Solomon, 203
Seele, Keith, 53
Seliguman, C. G., 17
Senwosret I, **(63)**, 139, 140
Serekh, 55, **55**
Sesostris, 139, 140
Set, 75, 84, **(84)**, 89, 97, **97**, **(97)**, 113, **123**
Seti I, **(56)**, 64, 185

Shabaka, 64
Shadow Clock, **75, 124, (124)**
Shemayit-Ipet, 114, 116, 118-120, **(118), (119), 120, (121)**
Shipbuilding, 131
Shu, **123, (123)**
Sirius, 76, 110
Slavery, 31, 32, 34-36, **35**, 137, 161, 235, 247, 260, 263
    Alex Haley, 34
    Goree Island, 32
    Pope John Paul II, 32, **41**
    The Portugese, 31, 32
Smithsonian Institution, 209
Smithsonian Magazine, 114, 115
Socrates, 155, **(155)**, 156
Solar year, 75-77
Sophocles, 113, 163
Sphinx (also see Her-em-akhet), 112-116, **114, 162, (162), 222, (222), 224**
    Reworked nose, 222-227, **227, (228)**
    Riddle of, 113, **(113)**, 222
St. Louis, MO, 30
Star of David, **203**
Stelle, 191, **191, (226), 231**
Stirling, Matthew, 209, **(209), 210**
Stolen Legacy, 22, 152, 154, 235, 249, 264
Stolen Legacy, 22, 114, 138, 152-160
Study Groups, 22, 248-253
Sudan, 45, 46, 48, 52, 53, 56, 59, 61, 81, **184**, 214
Sunday Times (London), 143

T

Ta-Seti, 53, 55, 62, 63, 66
Taharqa, 64, **(64)**
Tefnut, **123**
Tekhen (also see Obelisk), **75**, 120-122, **122, 124, (124)**, 155, 183, 191, 204, 206
    Origin of, 89, 121, **(121)**
    Unfinished, **(122)**
Temple in Man, 120, **120**
Ten Commandments, 92-94, **92**, 228
Ten Virtues, 249, 264, 267
Thebes (also see Waset and Luxor), 57, 58, 63, 64, 66, 80, 114, 138
    Greece, 113, 114, 116, 161
    United States, 208
Theodosius, 65, 141, 164, **262**
Third Eye (Dallas), 16
Thoth (also see Djhuiti), 51, 83, 89, 90, **(158)**, 168, **168, (168)**
Thutmose III, **67**, 121
Tiye, 63, **(63), 94, 142**, 143, **145**
Tompkins, Peter, 93, 193
Toynbee, Arnold, 17, 227, 230
Tres Zapotes, 209, 210, **212, (212), (217)**
Trinity, 55, 68, **(74), 95, 118**
Tutankhamun/Tutankhaton, 63, **94, 144**, 146, 185, 188, **(188), (233)**

U

UNESCO, 19, 20, 40
United States, 16, 22, 28, 30, 41, 45, 72, 74,
    120, **137**, 141, 143, **143**, 159, **160**, 197,
    199, **199**, **201**, **202**, 204, 207, 235, 257,
    258, 260, 265
    Constitution, 200
    Founding Fathers, 197-200, **202**
    Great Seal, 200-203, **(201)**
    Revolutionary War, 197-198
Uraeus, 193, **223**, **(223)**
Utchat Eye, 229, **(229)**

V

Van Sertima, Ivan, 211-213, **212**, **(213)**
Venus, 75, 168
Virgil, 168
Volney, Count Constantine de, 80, 82, 137,
(137), 138
Von Wuthenau, Alexander, **212**, 216, **(216)**, 217

W

Waset (also see Thebes and Luxor), 63, 64,
66, **98**, 114, 116-129, 138, 205, **252**
Washington, D.C., 22, **86**, 108, 204, 222,
232, 244, 248
    Lincoln Memorial, 206, **(207)**

Mall, 205, **(205)**, 206
Meridian, 204-205
Monument, 120, 204, **(204)**, **(206)**, 258
Potomac River, 205, **(205)**
Washington, George, **197**, **(197)**, 198, 199,
(200), 204, **205**
Washington Monument, 120, 204, **(204)**,
206, **(206)**, 258
Washington Post, **116**, **117**
Washington Times, 143
Weighing of the Soul, **(88)**, **89**, 90, **189**, **(189)**
West, John, 51, 68, 86, 105
Williams, Bruce, 53, 55, 150
Williams, Chancellor, 49, **49**, 52, 250, 260
Woodson, Carter G., 221, **221**, **(221)**, 222
World Book Encyclopedia, 17, 40, 59, 169

X

X, Malcolm, 30, **(30)**, 265, **265**

Z

Zeus, 116, 138, **139**, **(139)**, **156**, **158**, 161, 168
Zodiac, 78, 80
Zodiac of Dendera, 79, **(79)**, 181, **(181)**
Zoser, 63, **(63)**, 87, 100, **(100)**, 102

ANCIENT EGYPT LIGHT OF THE WORLD STUDY TOURS

Personally Escorted by Anthony T. Browder

All study tours include stops in Cairo, Giza, Memphis, Saqqara, Luxor, Aswan, Dendera, Abydos, Abu Simbel and several Nubian villages. On-site tours are scheduled during the mornings followed by lectures and group discussions which are conducted by Mr. Browder during the evenings.

For tour schedules call the **Institute of Karmic Guidance** at (301) 853-2465.

About the Author

Anthony T. Browder is a native of Chicago, Illinois and a graduate of Howard University's College of Fine Arts.

He is an author, publisher, cultural historian, artist and an educational consultant. He lectures extensively on topics pertaining to African and African American History and Culture.

He has lectured extensively throughout the United States and in Mexico, Africa, Japan and Europe.

Mr. Browder is the founder and director of the Institute of Karmic Guidance, a culturally oriented organization which is dedicated to the dissemination of "ancient Egyptian history and metaphysics." Mr. Browder holds fast to the belief that ancient Africans were the architects of civilization and that they developed the rudiments of what has become the scientific, religious and philosophical backbone of mankind. It is from this frameworks that IKG has concentrated its research and disseminated its findings.

Through the Institute, Mr. Browder sponsors lectures, seminars, African Centered tours of Washington, D.C., published his research and personally escorts study tours to Egypt and West Africa.

He is the author of *From The Browder File: 22 Essays on the African American Experience, Exploding the Myths, Volume I: Nile Valley Contributions to Civilization,* and *From The Browder File, Volume II: Survival Strategies for Africans in America.*

Mr. Browder is the co-author, along with his 24-year old daughter Atlantis Tye, of two publications, *My First Trip to Africa* and *africa on My Mind: Reflections of My Second Trip.*

My Browder's publications are currently being used in classrooms throughout the United States and in Ghana, Egypt, Japan and England.

"Tony" describes himself as a chronicler of facts and information relative to the positive portrayal of the worldwide African experience.

For information on
speaking engagements
and study tours to Africa,
call or write:
The Institute of Karmic Guidance
PO Box 73025
Washington, DC 20056
(301) 853-2465 Voice
(301) 853-6027 Fax
www.ikg-info.com

Atlantis and Anthony Browder

FROM THE BROWDER FILE:
22 Essays on the
African American Experience
by Anthony T. Browder

Paperback #100 / $15.00
Audio Tape #100A / $20.00
Book & Audio Cassette #100B / $30.00

"In his 22 Essays on the African American Experience, Tony Browder motivates us to establish the re-birth of our consciousness as a personal goal and a group goal. Experience *From The Browder File*, and incorporate Brother Browder's thought provoking information into your plan for moving from *disintegration* to *reintegration* for our people."

Dr. Asa G. Hilliard, III
From the Introduction

FROM THE BROWDER FILE
Volume II
Survival Strategies for
Africans in America-
13 Steps to Freedom
by Anthony T. Browder

Paperback #100J/$18.00

A compilation of essays which detail 13 steps necessary for Africans to achieve and maintain a state of freedom and stability within American society. Every step is divided into three components which provide practical guidelines for the application of the knowledge contained within. *Survival Strategies for Africans in America* retains the spirit of its predecessor *From The Browder File*, and was written to aid in the liberation of the African mind, body and soul.

MY FIRST TRIP TO AFRICA
by Atlantis Tye Browder
with Anthony T. Browder

Paperback #200/$8.95
Video #200/$30.00
Hardcover #201/$16.95

Chronicles the experience of 7-year-old Atlantis during a 13-day study tour to Egypt in November 1989. *My First Trip to Africa* provides youth and adults with a deeper understanding of ancient Egypt and its relationship to modern America, as seen through the eyes of a child. This publication contains 27 photos, 15 illustrations, 3 maps, a glossary, and a parent/teacher guide.

AFRICA ON MY MIND:
REFLECTIONS
OF MY SECOND TRIP
by Atlantis Tye Browder
with Anthony T. Browder

Paperback #202/$11.99
Hardcover #203/$24.99

Chronicles the experiences of 11-year-old Atlantis during a 15-day study tour to West Africa. Chapter 1 details her preparation for the journey and Chapters 2 thru 5 describe her adventures in the nations of Senegal, The Gambia, Ghana and Ivory Coast. Chapter 6 describes the return home and the final chapter consists of a conversation between Atlantis and her dad as they discuss the relevancy of her trip and the importance of preserving one's history and culture. This 104 page book contains 47 photographs, 18 illustrations, 9 maps, 2 charts, a glossary, an index, and a list of suggested readings.

EXPLODING THE MYTHS VOL. 1

NILE VALLEY
CONTRIBUTIONS TO
CIVILIZATION

ANTHONY T. BROWDER
AUTHOR OF FROM THE BROWDER FILE
INTRODUCTION BY DR. JOHN HENRIK CLARKE

EXPLODING THE MYTHS - Vol. 1:
NILE VALLEY CONTRIBUTIONS
TO CIVILIZATION
by Anthony T. Browder

Paperback #100C/$20.00
Hardcover #100D/$39.95
Full Color, 18x24 Poster #100E/$10.00
The Video #100F/$40.00
The Study Guide #100G/$10.00

The **Multi-Media Learning System** #100H/$65.00
(Consists of items #100 C, F & G. - A savings of $5.00)

The *Nile Valley Contributions To Civilization* text book, study guide, and video tape are all part of a new **Multi-Media Learning System** which is designed to enhance the reader's and viewer's understanding of African history and its relationship to world history.

The layout and design of the **Textbook**, including the margin notes, illustrations, maps, charts, and photographs are critical elements which help to tell the story of the rise and fall of Nile valley civilization and its impact upon succeeding civilizations.

The **Study Guide** was designed as a vehicle for an in-depth analysis and evaluation of the concepts explored in the parent text, *Nile Valley Contributions To Civilization*. It is intended for use in classrooms, study groups and home study.

The visually stimulating and informative **Video** captures the essence of *Nile Valley Contributions To Civilization* in vivid color and stunning computer graphic animation. It leaves a lasting impression and reinforces the most important passages in the textbook.

VIDEO AND AUDIO TAPE LIST
By Anthony T. Browder

•*Ancient Egypt: New Perspectives of an African Civilization:* A lecture and slide presentation which features a pictorial and historical overview of ancient Egyptian civilization. Emphasis is placed on the contemporary and historical application of Egyptian philosophy and symbolism.

VHS video tape: #101/$40   Audio tape: #101/$12   Time: 2 hours

•*Egyptian Origins of Science and Metaphysics:* An introduction to ancient knowledge of the human existence within the physical realm (Science) and the realm beyond the physical (Metaphysical). This lecture features demonstrations on light, color and levitation.

VHS video tape: #102/$40   Audio tape: #102/$12   Time: 2 hours

•*The African Origins of Christianity:* A revealing look at the African influence on religion and the history and symbolic meaning of the bible.

VHS video tape: #103/$40   Audio tape: #103/$12   Time: 2 hours

•**Spotlight Interviews:** A four part series produced by WHMM-TV at Howard University. Includes: An overview of Egyptian History and its impact on Civilization, Egyptian Orgins of Science and Metaphysics and an Afrocentric View of Washington, DC.

VHS video tape: #104/$40   Time: 2 hours

•*The Melanin Report:* A review of the "Third Annual Melanin Conference" and a candid discussion of the physical, mental and spiritual aspects of melanin.

Audio tape only: #105/$12   Time: 2 1/2 hrs

ELDERS SYMPOSIUM

In 1989, The Institute sponsored an historical symposium featuring John G. Jackson, John Henrik Clarke and Yosef ben Jochannan. The program featured individual presentations as well as a panel discussion.

Item	Description	Audio	Video
#22A Yosef ben Jochannan	"Nile Valley Contribution To Culture"	$ 6.00	$25.00
#22B. John G. Jackson	"Hubert Henry Harrison: The Black Socrates"		
John Henrik Clarke	"History Of The Search For African History"	$12.00	$40.00
#22C. ben Jochannan Clarke & Jackson	"Panel Discussion"	$12.00	$40.00

===

ORDER FORM

Item No.	Quantity	Description	Price Per Item	Total Price

Subtotal: $ ____

Shipping/Handling ($4.00) per 1st book, tape or poster; $2.00 per each additional item) $ ____

Total: $ ____

Name_____

Address_____City_____

State_____ Zip_____ Telephone (_____)_____

Send check or money order to: **The Institute of Karmic Guidance**
PO Box 73025 * Washington, DC 20056 * (301) 853-2465

Please call **The Institute** to place a credit card order on your Mastercard, Visa or American Express